COMMUNICATION FOR MANAGERS

A. VIELMA.

Paul Preston
University of Texas
at
San Antonio

PRENTICE-HALL, INC.
Englewood Cliffs, New Jersey 07632

Library of Congress Cataloging in Publication Data

Preston, Paul, (date)
  Communication for managers.

  Includes bibliographical references and index.
  1. Communication in management. I. Title.
HD30.3.P73   658.4'5   78-27092
ISBN 0-13-153957-4

Editorial/production supervision and interior
  design by Natalie Krivanek
Cover design by Saiki & Sprung Design
Manufacturing buyer: Harry Baisley

© 1979 by Prentice-Hall, Inc.
Englewood Cliffs, N.J. 07632

Printed in the United States of America
10 9 8 7 6 5 4

Prentice-Hall International, Inc., *London*
Prentice-Hall of Australia Pty. Limited, *Sydney*
Prentice-Hall of Canada, Ltd., *Toronto*
Prentice-Hall of India Private Limited, *New Delhi*
Prentice-Hall of Japan, Inc., *Tokyo*
Prentice-Hall of Southeast Asia Pte. Ltd., *Singapore*
Whitehall Books Limited, *Wellington, New Zealand*

To Kimberly Noël Preston

Credits

PHOTOGRAPHS

Photographs on pages 9, 49, 117, 156, 173, and 277 were provided through the courtesy of the Stockholder Relations Department, The Ford Motor Company, Dearborn, Michigan.

The illustrations on pages 25, 232, and 284 are copyright © 1975 by Preston Associates/Management Consultants, San Antonio, Texas. Used with permission.

CHAPTER OPENING QUOTES

Chapter 1   Frederick Herzberg, "The Dynamics of Caring," *Industry Week* (Aug. 7, 1978).

Chapter 2   Marshall McLuhan, *Understanding Media* (New York: New American Library, 1973).

Chapter 4   Robert Townsend, "The Will to Work," NATIONWIDE VIDEO CONFERENCE produced by *Industry Week* Magazine, Penton/IPC, Inc., 1975.

Chapter 5   Ralph Nichols, in R. G. Nichols and L. A. Stevens, *Are You Listening?* (New York: McGraw-Hill Book Co., 1957).

Chapter 6   Anthony Jay, "How to Run a Meeting," *Harvard Business Review* (March-April, 1976).

Chapter 7   Stephen Wallace, "A Cure for Toastmaster's Trembles," *MBS Magazine* (June, 1977).

Chapter 8   Douglas McGregor, *The Professional Manager* (New York: McGraw-Hill Book Co., 1967).

Chapter 9   Edward Hall, *The Silent Language* (New York: Doubleday & Co., 1959).

Chapter 11   Julius Fast, *Body Language* (New York: Simon & Schuster Pocket Books, 1971).

Chapter 13   Charles M. Schultz, *Peanuts Classics* (New York: Holt, Rinehart & Winston, 1970).

Chapter 14   Lawrence L. Steinmetz, *Managing the Marginal and Unsatisfactory Performer* (Reading, Mass.: Addison-Wesley, 1968).

Chapter 15   George Odiorne, *Management by Objectives* (New York: Pitman, 1965).

Chapter 16   Peter Drucker, *People and Performance* (New York: Harper & Row, 1977).

Chapter 17   Dean Inge, in J. M. Thomas and Warren Bennis, *Management of Change and Conflict* (Baltimore: Penguin Books, 1972).

Contents

III.   NONVERBAL COMMUNICATION

IV.   PROBLEM SOLVING COMMUNICATION

V.   SUMMING UP

Preface

There's nothing wrong with common sense in management. In fact, it is a virtual requirement if one is to succeed in any position with managerial responsibility. With common sense, we take academic theories and research study results and convert them into useful, practical management guides. With common sense, we regularly solve the thorniest of interpersonal problems. With common sense, we regulate our lives and perform our duties in a usually efficient way.

However, as Stuart Chase observed, common sense cannot always give us the best answer. It can also lead to one assuming that

> "... if it was good enough for grandpa (or whoever), it's good enough for me."

We resist beneficial change and new productive ideas. We keep old familiar methods and practices simply because they've served us adequately in the past. All this is done in the name of "common sense." Remember the young cook who cut the ends off a pot roast before serving it for dinner. When asked why, he replied that "My mother always does it that way. It's how pot roast is *supposed* to be served." When mother was asked for a reason, she replied that "My mother taught me. That's how it's supposed to be done." Finally Granny was asked for the reason. "It's simple," she replied. "If you don't cut off the ends, the pot roast won't fit in the pan." Two generations have passed, and they've already forgotten the reason for doing the things they do.

In this book, we're not disposing of common sense, nor are we trying to replace it with something better. We do intend to add some new insights and ideas to your existing knowledge and skill. We plan to make your common sense more reliable and more practical.

An honest communication book that purports to tell you *everything* there is to tell about communication cannot and likely will not ever be written. In this book, our objective is to give practical ideas and insights into the communication process. You already are aware of many topics and ideas we'll be discussing, so our purpose is to present these (and related) ideas in a new and different way. By helping you to see the familiar in unfamiliar ways, we can help you make significant improvements in your communications with your employees, colleagues, superiors, family and friends.

In a book on communication, Edward T. Hall* wrote that the one message he wished for his readers to get was that we must come to understand and appreciate the "out-of-awareness" aspects of communication. In the same book, Hall observed that those who intelligently keep their eyes open are constantly surprised by what they can learn from and about the world around them. We share Edward Hall's wish, and concur in his observation.

As you read and review this book, you'll find we've used many realistic examples taken from real-life experiences with interpersonal communication. In applying these experiences, we draw generalizations. We assume that what happens in a given situation is likely to recur in similar ways in other situations. We must be careful, however, when we generalize. It is reported that Supreme Court Justice Oliver Wendell Holmes once observed: "... no generalization is worth a darn, including *this* one." Despite this facetious commentary, we consider generalizations to be useful tools, and we've used them frequently throughout this book. To derive the most from your efforts at interpersonal communication you should take these ideas, examples, and generalizations and apply them to the people, problems, and situations that are most familiar *to you*. By doing this, you can make your interpersonal communications more effective and they can become the gateway to valuable shared experiences.

In writing this book, we've selected the ideas, examples and illustrations that best communicate what we want to convey. When we have presented a

*Edward T. Hall, *The Silent Language* (New York: Doubleday, 1959).

concept, we have tried to credit the individual or organization responsible for developing the concept, or for putting it in its present form. As you're aware by now, management is a shared experience. Good managers learn by swapping information and ideas with each other. When this occurs, it is sometimes difficult to know which person actually originated an idea. Rather than omit material because we did not know the source, we have decided to provide you and your colleagues with what we consider the most valuable information.

When we indicate that certain examples are "anonymous" or that the "source is unknown," it means that we've tried without success to find and give proper credit to the original author. If your work has been used without proper acknowledgment, we ask your forgiveness and hope you let us know so that we can credit you in future editions.

IS MANAGEMENT A PROFESSION?

We can't answer that question. Management has some of the hallmarks of a profession (for example, it involves a body of knowledge and standards for performance). Yet, perhaps it's more of an "art" (as in the art of dealing with people, or the art of communication). Some managers think that management is magic, or luck, or science.

It's not that important to resolve this question in a book about communication. What is important is that you develop your own unique view of the manager and his or her role in the management of organizations. If you take our ideas in the following chapters, combine them with your own ideas and those of your colleagues, your efforts will provide you with something more than an insight into supervisory communication. You'll become the proud owner of a personal theory of management. In the long run this will lead you to managing in a professional way.

THE ORGANIZATION OF THIS BOOK

We've divided the book into five sections. Within each section, topics with common elements appear one after the other. As you study the book, you may want to consider the topics in a different order. If you do, there is no reason not to alter the sequence. Each chapter will stand by itself, permitting you to "design your own book."

While the material has been organized into chapters, there are some topics that needed to be discussed in various chapters throughout the book. If you're interested in developing a complete view of our treatment of one topic (for example, "body language"), you should refer to the index. There we've listed all the pages on which you'll find information about that topic. As you will note, the presentation of this subject is not confined to Chapter 11 on "Making the Most of Body Language."

Chapter 18 is entitled "Cases in Communication." It contains some interesting and useful cases that illustrate some real management problems. At the end of each case, there are discussion questions. You may find it helpful to think about these questions, and about how the information in the earlier chapters applies to the problem that is presented in the case.

At the end of many chapters, we've listed some books to which you might want to refer for more information about the subject of a chapter. Many of these books are available in paperback. All are interesting and can give you some useful insights into the chapter topic. Many of these books were used as sources for the information in the chapter, so you'll be somewhat familiar with the area before you begin reading. If you want more information on particular topics, you might also look into some of the books and articles that we've cited at the end of the book in the "Notes" section.

OUR THANKS

Writing a book is not something one does in a vacuum. Many people contributed their efforts and ideas, and their writing and editing talents to the project. In particular, I'd like to thank the authors and editors who gave their permission for various materials that have been used in this book. Among them are Elaine Jorpeland, Dr. John Burns, Wilbur Martin, Kenneth Medley, Robert Gardner, Dr. Brian Hawkins, Ben Wolfenberger, Mike Welch, Jeanne Klemm, Allen J. Cox, Randy Kaebitzsch, Don North, and Gordon Gilkey, Jr.

Many other people contributed their talents to this book. In particular I wish to recognize the help of Rene G. Davila and MSgt. William C. Harwood, Jr. (USAF, Ret.). Dean E. D. Hodo and Dr. William D. Litzinger of the College of Business, University of Texas at San Antonio, contributed both their ideas and their support. Frances and Ellis M. Koontz gave considerable moral support, as did colleagues and friends from many corporations and trade and professional associations. Without attempting to thank each by name, some other friends include Richard Nowak of Friedrich Air Conditioning Co.; Sister Irene Krause of Providence Hospital, Washington, D.C.; Joe Floyd of the Aquatech Corporation, Brad Bruer and Bob Smith of Alamo National Bank, David Dillon and David Taylor of Citizens National Bank, and Jean Pittman of Frost National Bank, all in San Antonio; Thomas Irwin of the Farm Equipment Wholesalers Association; Jonna Lee Masters and Lynn Graham of the University of Texas Health Science Center; Ken Anderson, Jerry Kimbrough and Mike Nosil of La Quinta Motor Inns, Inc.; James Martin of the American College of Hospital Administrators; Robert Schnell of the Farm Equipment Manufacturers Association; R. J. Cunningham of the Alabama Association of Life Underwriters; Dr. Nelson Meckel of Southwest Research Institute; Michael Olson and David Williams of Olson, Williams Associates in Raleigh, N.C.; Russell Bond Jr. of the Wilson Lodge, Wheeling, W. Va.; Marilyn Monroe of the Texas Society of Association Executives; Charles and Kay Knapp of the Food Industry Association Executives; Paul J. Nicoletti, City Manager of North Palm Beach Village; Ned Wilford of the Halifax Hospital Medical Center in Dayton Beach, Florida; Carl Krepper of the Muskogee Iron Works, Inc.; Susan Novins of Codeco Inc.; Paul Hiznay of Union Carbide; John Dianis of the Monument Builders of North America; Jim Low, Buck Hoyle, LaRue Frye and Alan Rains of the American Society of Association Executives; Terry Townsend and Kellyn Murray of the Texas Motor Transportation Association; Jim Ritchie of the Alabama Trucking Association; Sandra Cook of the National Association of Banking Women; Duane Dekock of the Iowa Association of Life Underwriters; Robert B. Brittain of Standard Insurance Company; Gilbert Mobley of Associated Industries of Alabama; Robert LaRosa of Associated Industries of Massachusetts; Peggy McCollum of the Florida Society of Association Executives and Larry Munini and Peter Serenti of Wang Laboratories, Inc. There are of course countless others who have also contributed their ideas and their support to this text.

I would also like to thank Ted Jursek, Natalie Krivanek and Louis Baudean of Prentice-Hall Inc. for their help, and Franelle Preston, Jean Bolton and Bobbie Jean Roberts for their typing and editing assistance.

Finally, I would like to acknowledge my gratitude to the hundreds of men and women from all areas of business, government and associations who have taken part in management and communication seminars conducted by *Preston Associates Inc.* over the years. Their insights, observations, contributions and criticisms give the material in this book a more practical and realistic outlook. Without their involvement, this book would be merely about communication theory. Because of their help, you can learn more about how communication really works, and how to make it work *for you*.

Paul Preston
San Antonio, Texas

1

Introduction:
Do You Say What You Mean and Mean What You Say?

"We have to learn to communicate on the job with our boss, with our co-workers, and with our subordinates. At home we have to learn to communicate with our spouse, with our children."

Frederick Herzberg

Too often, we take interpersonal communication for granted. As managers supervisors, or salespeople, our jobs involve communicating with large numbers of people on a variety of often technical and/or emotional subjects. We do know how to make a telephone call, write a good letter, speak up at a meeting, give orders to employees, or present our ideas to a hostile or unsupportive audience. We engage in all sorts of communicative activities each day on the job and off. Yet, because of this, we tend to think of ourselves as communication experts. The only problem is that, although each of us may be an expert at *something*, usually an expert doesn't know any more about any given subject than anyone else—he or she is just better organized (and, of course, uses plenty of color slides). Remember, too, that Dr. David Reuben some years ago wrote an interesting book on another subject, a book in which he promised to tell us "*everything* we always wanted to know" about that subject, but were afraid to ask. Did he really tell us everything? Perhaps, perhaps not. Yet he was an "expert," just as many of us feel that we're "experts" in communicating with others.

1

There's a real danger in an attitude of being an "expert." Often, the really important messages that we send and receive happen without our being aware of them. In many excellent books, we're told that it is vital for each of us to understand and appreciate the "out-of-awareness" aspects of interpersonal communication. We should continuously ask "Do others understand what I want them to understand?" and "Am I really saying what I think I'm saying?"

SENDERS AND RECEIVERS

The communication process is quite simple. It consists of three basic elements: a sender, a receiver, and a message. (It also has a "villain" that we'll meet in a moment.) All three must be present for a communication to occur. Thus, simply standing in an empty room talking to yourself is not communicating because there is no receiver (unless you start answering yourself, of course). Although the concept of a SENDER—MESSAGE—RECEIVER model is quite simple, it's not enough to properly define communication. A good working definition of communication might be "sending a message to someone in a way that allows the receiver of the message to understand exactly what the sender means."

NOISE

Because the sender and the receiver don't always get the same meaning, something must go wrong between sender and receiver. The "something" is our communication villain—noise.

We usually think of noise as the physical interruption or distortion of a message. Loud music will interrupt or distort a conversation, just as a poor phone connection can distort your message to someone else. Although damaging to communication, physical noise is quite obvious, and, because it's so obvious, the sender or the receiver can work to avoid or eliminate it.

However, there is another kind of noise that causes many of the misunderstandings that occur in our communications with others. Each of us is the product of a completely unique set of experiences. These experiences shape our language, values, customs, attitudes, and behaviors. They "color" or alter the way in which each of us looks at reality. When a supervisor, an employee, and a "man on the street" look at the same situation, each will form a different opinion or evaluation of the situation by relating to his or her "frame of reference." Ask any police officer about "eyewitness" accounts of accidents. People viewing the same event often see entirely different things. The same thing happens all the time in communication. Messages are formed by a sender in a particular language, with specific meanings for words and expressions. These same words and expressions are then subject to *interpretation* by the receiver, and this interpretation can be quite different from what was intended.

Nonverbal "noise" can also occur because of conflicting messages sent by the sender. The doctor who tells you to stop smoking, while lighting up a cigarette, is giving you two distinct and contradictory messages. Significantly, the nonverbal message (lighting and smoking the cigarette) will have a much more powerful impact than the spoken warning to stop smoking. We often find ourselves in the position of giving contradictory signals or messages. Thus, when counseling our employees, we may stress with them the importance of promptness in getting to work in the morning. If we then develop or continue a pattern of personal tardiness with our own appointments, the messages to the employees become confused. In fact, what we *do* speaks louder than what we *say*.

BODY MESSAGES

In particular, we should constantly watch for ways that our physical attitude (more popularly called our "body language") conflicts or contradicts our verbal messages. According to those who study body language, more than half of all the messages that we send and receive in the course of a normal "transaction" or interaction with another person are "physical" messages that have no word content. When you consider the large number of spoken and written messages you produce, and the even larger numbers of word messages you see and hear in your normal day, you can begin to appreciate the impact of this nonword communication. These nonverbal messages can have a double impact, for they occur out of our awareness, making them difficult to hear, see, or evaluate. They can also have meanings that contradict our verbal messages, or the verbal messages of others. In such contradictions, the nonverbal message is usually the stronger. We've all become sophisticated enough today to realize that children learn more from watching and imitating the actions of their parents and playmates than they do from the written or spoken messages they are given. We all grow up, but we never stop learning and communicating nonverbally.

SPACE MESSAGES

An interesting way to study the effects of nonverbal communication is to look at space and spatial relationships. In North America, the size, distance, location, or relative position of persons, spaces, and objects is vitally important. Space arrangements give us clues about actions that are appropriate in certain circumstances. This is especially useful when we find ourselves in new and unusual situations or surroundings. Where we're asked to sit in a person's office for a meeting or the distance between ourselves, the other people at the meeting, and the office occupant can influence and control the messages that we send and receive. The physical surroundings, the style of clothes and the appearance of other individuals give us signals helping us adjust our own behavior. Without such signals (or where such signals conflict), we can become disjointed, confused, and nervous. In such situations, we are far less likely to communicate clearly and effectively.

COMFORTABLE IN A GROUP?

Think about the last time you rode in an elevator filled with strangers. Most of us in that kind of crowd become uncomfortable. We try to reduce our discomfort by engaging our fellow travelers in simple conversation. These attempts at reducing the potential threat posed by strangers standing "too close for comfort" usually result in comments about the speed of the elevator, the destination of the others, or the weather. The actual content of these simple messages is irrelevant. The real purpose of the communication is to reduce discomfort (and even threat) caused by the nonverbal messages of space. Because space, body messages, and nonverbal communication are so important in our interpersonal communications, you might consider reading one or two of the books listed at the end of this chapter.

SNIFFING

Next time you see two dogs sniffing each other, watch their reactions. Some encounters will end with the two merely drifting off in different directions; other times, the two will run and play, or snap back and snarl. Dogs, and most other animals, ask important questions by sniffing. They are trying to learn about this other animal, using a highly developed sense of smell to fill out the initial impression formed by visual inspection. The dog's behavior is an honest, open attempt to see if a communication link can be formed.

At cocktail parties with a lot of strangers, we often behave in a very similar way. We communicate by verbally and nonverbally "sniffing" to learn about others and establish communication links. With strangers, we seldom immediately venture into such subjects as sex, politics, religion, or football. Instead, we talk about the weather, or the hostess, or each other's jobs. The questions and the answers are usually unimportant. We are forming impressions from the postures, gestures, facial expressions, and voice tones of the other strangers. After a short time (four minutes or less), we will usually have

HOW'S THE WEATHER?

FIGURE 1-1

formed a fairly complete (although not necessarily accurate) image and impression of another individual. At this point, we can either precede into a deeper communication relationship or casually break off the contact and search again for other possible interactions.

In the first four minutes of an interpersonal contact, we develop an almost complete image of another person and his or her problems. This can be especially important in management and sales, because the "sizing up" process happens so quickly and yet is so important to later communication.

Let's not fool ourselves. First impressions are quite useful. If we didn't have some way of sorting out all of the information thrown at us in a normal day, we would quite literally go mad. They are the "tip" of the communication iceberg.

A COMMUNICATION "QUIZ"

Before we turn our attention to the many interesting aspects of managerial communication, let's test your knowledge about communication *and* management. The following ten statements deal with some basic issues in managerial communication. Take a moment to read each; then check whether you "agree" or "disagree" with each statement. In the last chapter, we'll review all ten and briefly summarize the "why" behind the "right answers."

	Agree	*Disagree*
1. Happy employees will always be productive employees.	✓	
2. A major danger to good communication is the illusion that we have effectively communicated.	✓	

		Agree	*Disagree*
3.	Managers should spend most of their time listening.	____	✓ ____
4.	In getting employees to listen, how you send a message is far more important than what you say.	✓ ____	____
5.	Managers short on time may have problems with delegation and communication.	____	✓ ____
6.	The best way to get feedback from employees or superiors is to ask, "Do you have any questions?"	✓ ____	____
7.	The use of a large vocabulary can hurt your communication effectiveness.	____	✓ ____
8.	If a message is written, it is almost certain to be more clear than if given orally.	____	✓ ____
9.	Groups of employees or managers will usually make better decisions than individual employees or managers.	✓ ____	____
10.	Groups of employees or managers tend to take more risks in decision making than do individual employees or managers.	✓ ____	____

SOME PEOPLE ARE LIKE KITES[1]

One of the most fascinating things about managing people is that it is an art, not a science. Rules exist, but they are so broad that they are seldom of much use. When rules are narrow enough to be effective, a good manager finds himself breaking them more often than abiding by them. This is, of course, particularly true about communication rules.

The trouble with trying to apply rules and formulas to communication with and management of people is that effective rules depend on fixed perceptions and values. Unfortunately, people are highly variable, and so are these perceptions and opinions about the world around them.

One rule does apply, however: You can get more out of people by treating them as individuals, each with his own peculiar and distinctive psychological machinery. To motivate them, you have to know them. A manager once put it this way: "Some people are like wheelbarrows—good if pushed. Some are like kites—they'll fly away if you don't keep a string on them. Others are like footballs—you never know which way they'll bounce. Some are like trailers—they must be pulled. Still others are like balloons—always ready to blow up ... ".

PURPOSE OF THIS BOOK

This book is dedicated to helping you and your fellow managers develop more skills in communication. These specific skills, such as writing, listening, speaking, and running meetings, are important for everyday managerial effectiveness.

However, managers who develop skills and fail to also develop an understanding and awareness of the basics of managerial communication are eventually doomed to failure. Thus, this book is also dedicated to improving supervisory ability by helping you to develop a greater sensitivity to the full range of communications facing you, as a sender and as a receiver.

HABITS

Often we don't "say what we mean" and we don't "mean what we say." By developing a habit of looking for *real* meaning behind the obvious message, we strengthen our managerial ability and make our relationships with others more profitable, and enjoyable. It's been said that the only real difference between the successful salesperson and the unsuccessful salesperson is that the successful seller has formed the *habit* of doing the things that the unsuccessful salesperson doesn't like to do. The point is that all salespeople know the basics of selling — they know how to sell. The successful salesperson is a success because he or she does those basic things out of a consciously developed habit. It's the same with better communication. We all know what must be done to communicate effectively. The successful communicator is conscious of the important steps in communication and performs those steps out of conscious, sensitive habits. Everything you've ever wanted to know about communication? You probably know it already. The key to successful communication is putting what you know into everyday practice.

Ways to Improve Your Communication Skills

1. Communication is a complex and challenging activity, one you can't avoid *or* master. Starting with yourself, begin to analyze how people behave and how communications become distorted. Keep your eyes, ears, and mind open and listen for what's there and for what's not there (or at least not obvious).
2. Look for summary points at the end of each chapter in this book. Some chapters will have only a few major summary points, others will have many. To check your understanding of a chapter, refer to the last section and see if you understand the summary points.

Further Readings

If you are interested in more study on the general subject of communication, here are three books you will find interesting:

EDWARD T. HALL, THE SILENT LANGUAGE (Doubleday)

> This book, written by an anthropologist, is somewhat academic and research based. It is, however, an excellent book in which the author suggests that many communication problems are caused by the speakers and listeners having different cultures and values. As a result, says Hall, we see the world from so many different points of view that it is possible to misunderstand the messages of the communications that others are sending us. In particular, Hall is concerned with the kinds of communication problems that occur as a result of different cultural viewpoints.

RUDOLPH VERDERBER, COMMUNICATE (Wadsworth)

> This book deals with the general area of communication. Although only a few of its examples relate to managerial communication, the author has a number of interesting and useful approaches to the subject.

LARRY L. BARKER, COMMUNICATION VIBRATIONS (Prentice-Hall)

> This book is a sort of "smorgasbord" of communication ideas and thoughts. Amid the cartoons and poetry on various aspects of communication are such articles as "How Words Change Our Lives," "Is Language Sexist?," "How to Cope with Social Disasters" (by Barbara Walters), "How Successful Men Make Decisions," and "The Fine Art of Complaining." It's a fascinating book.

I

MANAGERIAL COMMUNICATION

2

How Communication Works

"Each of us looks at life with his or her own set of idiosyncratic goggles ... each of us thinks that his or her goggles are the most wonderful goggles in all the world."

Marshall McLuhan

Communication is a simple idea that everyone understands.

Each of us has a different impression or definition of communication and how it works. For some people, communication is the telephone, or telegraph, or back fence gossip. Others connect communication with *media*, and media such as radio, television, films, and telephone are important parts of communication. We may also think of communication as the ability to speak and express our ideas to an employee, a boss, or a friend.[1]

Communication also includes reading, writing, sending and responding to signals. It seems so simple that most of us take it for granted. We assume that, because we understand some of the parts of the complicated communication process, we are experts. Having said this, we can then ignore any further study or consideration of the subject, and can become trapped. Unfortunately, there are few real "experts" in communication, so we will assume that, although we may know a lot about communication, there is still a lot we can learn.

11

THE SAFECRACKER

Reminisce for a moment. In the old crime movies, there was almost always a bank robbery. The safecracker in those films was usually a real professional, one who developed some unique skills and talents to do his job better. In the scene before the safe was cracked, the safecracker could usually be found sitting by himself in a corner. Most likely, he would be sandpapering his fingertips. When it came time to "do his thing," the nerve endings in his fingertips were irritated and closer to the surface of the skin. He was supersensitive, because doing his job professionally required sensitivity. He could almost "feel" the tumblers in the lock falling into place.

In some respects, the purpose of this book is to sandpaper your mental fingertips, to help you become more sensitive to the messages and communications around you.

In a large insurance company work area, we recently saw a sign that said

"I know that you believe you understand what you think I said, but I am not sure you realize that what you heard is not what I meant."

Confusing? Of course, but it makes more sense the more you think about it. Communication, especially on the job, is often affected by misunderstandings, even about things that everyone "ought" to understand. Perhaps we could say the same thing in a little different way by asking the question, DO YOU SAY WHAT YOU MEAN AND MEAN WHAT YOU SAY? Often, what you *want* to say is not what others *understand* you to say. The result is confusion, misunderstanding, missing signals — miscommunication.

There is no one "best way" to communicate. In the days of Merlin the magician, alchemists searched for what they called the "philosopher's stone." This magic potion was supposed to turn lead into gold. They never found that secret, and today we often go on searching for our own magic formula that will do the same for us. There is no philosopher's stone that will convert ordinary communications into more successful communications. But do not stop looking. By sensitizing ourselves, we can overcome many of the problems that we will otherwise shrug off as "impossible" to solve.

SATISFIED WITH THINGS AS THEY ARE .

ARE YOU A "CONTENTED" COMMUNICATOR?

Many managers find themselves in communication difficulty because they become complacent. Contented. Unwilling to change their habits, their activities, or their methods of management.

SELF SATISFACTION

12

The Carnation Milk Company used to advertise that "our milk comes from contented cows." Perhaps because they had better grass or more sunshine (or friendlier bulls), they were supposed to be more contented than the Sealtest cows or the Borden cows. This, in turn, was supposed to mean better milk. Perhaps contentment improves a cow's performance, but it seldom works for managers. Contented managers often develop attitudes of complacency, and communication dangers are just around the corner. Be sensitive, be willing to change. It's the first rule for better communication, and for better management.

SENDERS AND RECEIVERS

The basic process of communication can be both simple and complex. No matter where or when it takes place, any communication involves three elements—a *sender*, a *receiver*, and a *message* (see Figure 2-1). Simple enough. The sender can be an individual, a group, or a mass of people. Same with the receiver. All that is required for effective communication is that the sender and receiver take a message to mean the same thing, whatever is sent is received the same way.

FIGURE 2-1

THE SENDER

The sender is the transmitter or starter of a communication. Without some sender, communication would never take place. The sender can be a single individual, a group, or a large mass of persons who have no direct contact.

You are constantly sending messages. You do so when you write a letter, complete an order form, or speak out at a meeting. You are also a message sender when you tell someone by the expression on your face, or your tone of voice, that you are upset with their message. Sender communication does not have to be verbal, and it does not have to be conscious. You may be the friendliest manager in the organization, but the message you may be sending to your employees (or your boss) may be that you don't really care about their feelings or ideas.

The sender has an important responsibility in communication, because it is the sender who starts the entire process, and it is the sender who must bear the burden of framing a message so it will be received in the same spirit as it is sent.

The sender can also be a group or a large mass of persons. When you vote on election day, your vote and those of thousands of other people combine to form a message. Past political slogans such as "Send 'em a message" or "Tell Springfield what you want" are indications of a group sending a message as a single unit.

The sender in a communication system fails when the message sent is garbled, transmitted too fast, or uses words and meanings that can be confused or misunderstood. For example, if you were to stand up in a group meeting and ask that an item be "tabled," most of your colleagues would understand that you wanted the item held over for the next meeting. However, in some parts of the country, to "table" an item is to "bring it on the table" or "lay it on the table" — just the opposite of what you might think. Thus, out of carelessness, ignorance, or misunderstanding, the sender fails to do his or her job properly. The result is a possibility for miscommunication.

MESSAGES

A message contains information. Usually, we confine our thinking about messages to spoken and written signals between people, with a few of the more obvious nonverbal signals thrown in. No one disagrees with the notion that a hand gesture, a wink, a smile, or a frown are signals, messages. The girl and boy on a park bench looking into each other's eyes are exchanging a message. One old comedian correctly observed that you can communicate even when lying flat out on the sidewalk, not moving a muscle. The message? Dead. You don't even have to be conscious to communicate.

For centuries, a favorite topic of philosophers has been the question, "If a tree falls in the forest and no one is there to hear, has a sound been made?" Technically, there can be no communication without a receiver. Still, the debate goes on.

Garbling

Some years back, a group of navy reservists were on a training cruise aboard an aircraft carrier in the Pacific. The reservists were doing many of the jobs normally done by regular navy personnel. One such operation involved the job of deck officer during the launching of aircraft. A reservist was in charge of giving the signal to release the aircraft from the catapult on the flight deck. When the plane was ready to take off, one reservist yelled out the order to FIRE. The reservist operating the catapult understood the order to "fire the plane" and activated the catapult. However, the pilot of the aircraft (a regular navy pilot) understood the word "fire" to mean something quite different. To him, fire means that there was a blaze on board and that the aircraft's engines should be immediately shut down. The conflict over the meaning of the message resulted in the plane's being pushed off the flight deck with only the catapult power, and the pilot was killed. The correct word to launch the aircraft with the catapult was the word "release." A simple word like "fire" can have far different meanings. One message does not carry the same meaning to all persons who hear it.

Goggles

Marshall McLuhan's notion of "goggles" suggests that what you see in a situation is not necessarily what someone else will see when looking at the same situation. A group of men on a street engaged in a heated conversation could simply be that, a conversation. However, with the goggles of another passerby, the same scene could be labeled as a fight, a racial incident, or a confrontation. The message in a scene or problem is whatever your goggles tells you is there.

McLuhan's goggles are also called our *fields of experience*. No two people (even identical twins) have done or seen the same things, solved the same problems, or been to the same places. Each of us is unique, an individual, a one of a kind. Just as no two snowflakes are ever alike, so it is with people. Your goggles do not necessarily show you what is right. They give you only one viewpoint. We can all be fooled, and we are all subject to distortions in a message. Think about the conflicts you've had recently with employees—who was right? Chances are that you both *thought* you were right. No one is immune to distortion.

THE RECEIVER

There can be many senders of a message, and there can be many receivers of a message. When you sit down in front of the television to watch the evening news or the weekend ball game, you are but one of millions of other receivers of the commercial or broadcast message. Receivers can also be singular. When you write a confidential letter to your boss, you assume that the boss is the only one who will read it. A single receiver. However, if you have the letter typed, the typist will have some idea of what is going on. If that typist does not have all the facts about the situation in the letter, he or she will probably "fill in the blanks." A different message from what was intended. Receivers, like senders, have goggles or fields of experience that distort or block parts of a message.

NOISE

Every good story has a villain. The villain in our communication story is *noise* (Figure 2-2). If someone is making loud noises when you are trying to talk to an employee, some distortion of the message is likely to occur. Physical noise usually does no serious damage to the message because we are aware that it exists. We can soundproof our offices, workrooms, and homes, cover our ears, shade our eyes, and remove some of the distortions caused by sound and sight noise.

But noise can also be cultural. Noise can occur between the sender and receiver with neither being aware of what is happening. Cultural noise can result from the differences in language and customs that we develop as we grow up. It can be the result of differences in fields of experience. Communication problems with employees from different cultural or ethnic groups is

FIGURE 2-2

often caused by cultural noise. What seems to be a simple message is not so simple when conflicting viewpoints interpret it.

In a manufacturing plant in Arizona, a supervisor on her daily "rounds" was talking to a group of employees about a particular job that was overdue. The supervisor pointed in the general direction of the job and said, "We better get that stuff outta here." One employee, not familiar with the supervisor's simple expression, decided to help out. The next day, panic set in. No one could find the materials for the overdue job. Explained the employee who had the material shipped to storage, "She said to get it out, and I did. What's the problem?"

One middle manager found himself confronted with employees who disregarded or refused to believe any of the policy statements that he made at his biweekly staff meetings. Through an awareness of cultural noise, he realized that the facial expressions he used in making policy statements gave his people the impression the message was to be disregarded—and they did so. Body language messages are far more intense than oral or written messages because they occur out of our conscious awareness. The cure is quite simple—we have to develop a greater awareness of the cultural noise at work in our communications. Remember, too, that each of us is unique, one of a kind. When we interpret what we see, the result can be distortion that is as damaging as the distortion caused by physical noise.

How does your field of experience develop? It is the result of everything that you see, hear, do, and think. It is an extension of your personality. The images you form in your mind when you hear a word, smell a smell (like bread being baked), see a scene, or read a line of poetry come from your field of experience. Farm-raised people would find images of summer, good times, and family when they smell fresh-cut hay. City-raised people are not likely to conjure up any images from the same smell, but they might be reminded of the "good old days" by the smell of diesel fumes or the sound of taxi horns.

"Cultural," or goggles, noise happened to a woman when she was driving through the hill country of Texas. She was going down a straight stretch of road toward a small hill behind which the road curved. As she drove along, a car came from around the hill, heading straight for her. The driver of the other car was driving down the center of the road, honking his horn and madly waving his arm out the window. Just before he ran her off the road, he swerved to his own side. As he passed, he yelled "P-I-G" at her.

Naturally, she was furious. She regained her control and continued driving down the road toward the hill. It was bad enough to run her off the road, but to insult her as well! As she rounded the curve behind the hill, she ran smack into a huge pig standing in the middle of the road.

She had heard the man's signal. She thought she heard him call her a pig. What she missed was the message "Lady, there's a pig in the middle of the road." Who was right? Who was at fault?

OUT OF AWARENESS

The real danger of the noise we have labeled cultural is that it happens without being aware that it exists. Knowing about a problem can lead to a solution. Not knowing that anything is wrong is doubly dangerous.

Have you ever said to yourself after meeting a stranger, "There's something about that guy I don't like?" You might also have the feeling that you like someone without really knowing why. Often, we get messages from people who are unaware that they are sending and we are equally unaware of receiving. These messages may be in the form of gestures, facial expressions, postures, or other forms of body language. The message may also be in the tone of voice used to transmit a spoken message. Without being aware, we also send messages when we don't speak. Often, the unstated message or the omitted fact is the most important part of an otherwise simple or straightforward message.

The out-of-awareness messages that we send and receive often reveal more about our true feelings than do our conscious messages. In later chapters, we will explore some of the out-of-awareness messages involved in body language as well as the noise that develops between people when confronted with differences in culture and social or ethnic background.

DIMENSIONS OF COMMUNICATION

By now, we have no doubt convinced you that communication is not as simple, or direct, as we might be led to believe. The purpose of this book is to explore as many areas or dimensions of managerial communication as we can. Some are obvious—writing, speaking, listening. Others are understandable but shrouded in mystery and mystique—symbols, kinesics (body language), perception. Some communication dimensions are not in our everyday vocabulary and do not have any meaning for us—general semantics, territorality, temporality.

The job of a manager carries with it many different responsibilities. Before becoming a manager, most people have some knowledge about the major responsibilities of supervision. However, it is only after one becomes a manager that the many hidden responsibilities and activities of the job comes into view. Every President of the United States has had the same feeling after taking office. Without exception, our recent presidents have remarked about how much more the job involved once they entered office. It is exactly the same with communication in management. On the surface, communication looks simple to understand and to do. Once you start exploring communication, your view of it changes.

The many dimensions of communications are a little bit like a patchwork quilt. They overlap, duplicate each other, come in different shapes and sizes, are seen in some situations and not in others. In our brief look at some of these dimensions, we will examine them one at a time. Remember, however, that in real life these dimensions are all jumbled up. Making sense out of them leads to a better ability to communicate effectively as a supervisor (Figure 2-3).

The best place to start our review of the dimensions of communication is with F-I-T, or formal, informal, and technical communication. They describe the three ways in which we communicate. Let us examine each one in turn.

FIGURE 2-3 Dimensions of Communication

Formal Communication

Formal communication is "two-way" communication. When you and a friend engage in a conversation, you have entered into a two-way communication. Two-way communication involves a sender's sending a message to a receiver and the receiver's returning a message to the initial sender. It's not really as complicated as it might seem. For example, suppose that you are explaining a job to a fellow employee. You might start the conversation by telling the individual the first thing to be done. While you're talking, you are also watching the facial expressions, the eyes, and the motions of the other person.

After you have spoken, the other person will speak. He or she may ask a question to clarify what you said. The person may agree and ask what the second step is to be. He or she may not "say" anything, at least not in words. No doubt you have noticed that when an individual is unsure of a message, his face will take on a questioning expression. A trained and sensitive communicator will immediately recognize when an individual is not sure of an order. It is far easier to make a correction at this stage than it is to wait until something totally wrong happens.

Formal communication is simple to perform and usually results in few miscommunications. When you and your friend have a chance to learn if you understand each other's messages, you reduce the chances of a misunderstanding taking place.

If formal communication involves a two-way face-to-face exchange of information and ideas, is it also formal communication when you address a meeting or large group. THIS IS AN OFTEN OVERLOOKED PART OF FORMAL COMMUNICATIONS. Even though the speaker in a meeting is not getting any words in response to the statements he is making, the audience is still sending messages. Imagine how you would feel if you were talking in a meeting, and, when you looked around, you saw half the people asleep. It is hoped that you would change the way you were talking or at least throw in a story or a joke to get your listeners back with you. The reactions of people to things being said is as much a part of two-way or formal communication as is the direct response spoken in a conversation or dialogue. The reactions of people to the things being said, which is as much a part of two-way or formal communications as the direct response, spoken in a conversation expressed when you are communicating, is called *feedback*. Without feedback, we would not be able to determine if a message is "getting through."

The effective manager is one who makes other people comfortable when they do provide feedback. We will discuss this idea in a later chapter, when we discuss phoney feedback. The feedback you receive from your communication with employees can provide you with a valuable check on your own communication ability. Encourage and use feedback. It can be a great friend.

Technical Communication

We usually associate "technical communication" with technology. However, technical communication is merely the "one-way" transmission of information. Unlike formal or two-way communication, technical communication does not have a feedback element built in. In technical communications, the message that the sender sends is received by the receiver, but the receiver has no way of responding to the message. There is no direct means for the sender to get information about the meanings that the receiver has received.

Perhaps the best example of technical communication occurs when we write something. In writing, the reader (or receiver) has the message from the sender, but there is often no way for the receiver to ask questions of the sender. The Constitution of the United States was written 200 years ago by wise and thoughtful men who knew that they could not write a document that would stand up under all the changes that would take place. Because of this, they wrote the constitution in a way that permitted it to be *interpreted*. They also provided that the Supreme Court and the other courts in the land would be given the responsibility for doing the interpretation. Now, whenever a controversy about a law arises, the court reviews the law and interprets the constitutional questions involved. Each time a constitutional question is decided, the judges go back to the papers of the founding fathers to see if they can learn what the intent was in a particular part of the Constitution. The same process takes place everyday in courts across the country. When judges look for the "legislative intent" in a law, they are trying to learn what the legislators intended when they wrote the law.

If something as precise as the law is subject to interpretation, so are the messages that *we* write day after day. This is the major problem of technical communication. When you write memos, orders, plans, or directives to be read and acted upon by others, your written words are subject to interpretation. Ask yourself, "Can I afford to have my employees interpreting, and maybe misunderstanding, the things that I write?" Obviously, the answer is no, yet it is amazing how many people look at their writing and say confidently, "There is no way anyone can goof this up."

Technical communication, especially writing for people who will act without having any direct contact with the sender of the message, requires a special sensitivity that managers should develop. When you write, remember that you must think for both the sender and the receiver too. You must not only put your ideas into writing, you must then analyze your words to see if there are ways that others might misunderstand. In this book, we have given great attention to doing just that. Often, in making a point that we believe is especially important, we will repeat ourselves, or use an example. In doing so, we are trying to get our technical communication (the written message) as "misunderstanding free" as our formal conversations.

Although technical communication is one-way, with the receiver of the message having little chance to question the sender, technical messages do work in two directions. As a manager, you are continuously faced with a need to read and interpret written messages. These messages may be job specifications, blueprints and technical drawings, or management memos on company policies. All require that you understand what the writer was trying to say; often, you don't have the opportunity to ask questions if you don't understand. Your boss may expect that your ability and expertise enables you to follow the written instructions with no difficulty. When we face the problems of technical communiction from the receiver's point of view, we must try to put ourselves in the place of the sender. Ask as you read, "What did the sender expect to accomplish from this message?" Or, "What are the other possible meanings in this message?" "Which of them is closest to what the writer intended?" The American Indians have a saying from which we can all profit: "Grant that I not criticize my brother until I have walked a mile in his moccasins." Putting yourself in the other person's shoes is an effective way to overcome many communication difficulties, especially when faced with technical communication.

Informal Communication

Formal communication is a two-way information exchange. Technical communication is a one-way information transfer. Informal communication is the transmission of messages by example. If you have ever told your children, "Do as I say, not as I do," you are giving heed to the importance of the informal dimension of communication. Often people will respond not to the message the sender is speaking or writing but to the way the speaker behaves when giving the message.

Think about how you learned your first language, the one you spoke in your home as a child. That language was learned by informal communication. Our parents may have prodded us to say certain favorite words (such as Daddy or Mommy), but most of our language was learned simply by imitating the example set by the adults and older children in the home. This accounts for the fact that people in different parts of the country speak with different accents. No one directly tells a southern child to say "y'all." It is communicated by example. We learn our personal standards of morality, justice, and rightness not so much from formal or technical communication as we do from the examples set by parents and others that we respect.

Informal communication continues to affect our behavior long after childhood. The supervisor who tells his or her employees the value of arriving for work promptly and then makes it a habit of coming into work late is showing an ignorance of the power of informal communication. People will respond far more to the example message than they will to the spoken or written message. If you want to have your employees (or your superiors) trust you and have confidence in you, you must demonstrate to them (by informal communication, your example) that you are worthy of that trust and confidence. Walking around with a shirt saying "TRUST ME—TRUST ME" won't go very far.

Putting on Airs? Watch when one of your friends returns from a trip to an English-speaking country abroad (England, for example), or even from some other part of the United States. He or she will probably speak a little differently. Without realizing it, each of us is affected by the examples and the informal messages around us. Watch a small boy walking down the street with his father, or a little girl with her mother. The child will walk like the parent. But the real reason for the unconscious imitation is that the child has been told, by example, that that is the way boys, or girls, walk.

Implied Messages. A supervisor in a General Motors assembly plant found himself in a strange but revealing situation involving informal communication. He was hired by the company and trained at their Technical Institute in Flint, Michigan. During his training, he worked as a "co-op" employee in the assembly plant, as a sort of supervisor-trainee. One day, while walking through the work area, he went by an old, gruff (and very big) worker. Without stopping to look up, the worker hit Al (the supervisor-trainee) with enough cuss words to make a stevedore blush. Al was astounded. He hardly knew the man's name, and he had had no direct involvement in supervising the man's work. The verbal attack seemed totally unprovoked.

When he recovered his composure, Al asked the employee why the abuse. Again without looking up (and with the same string of obscenities), the worker simply explained "Some day, you no-good _____, you'll be a real supervisor around here. I hate supervisors, but, if I tell 'em what I really think of them, I'd get booted out. But with you, I won't have to say anything. Whenever I look at you, you'll know exactly what I think about you — and you won't be able to do anything about it."

The employee was conditioning his supervisor even before the fellow had a chance on the job. From then on, a simple stare would carry an implied message — unmistakable and as real as writing or speaking.

Out-of-Awareness Messages. In formal and technical communication, we are usually aware of the messages being sent. They are in writing, or they are in spoken words. However, this is not usually the case with informal communication. Often, the informal (or nonverbal) messages that we send are done with neither the sender's nor the receiver's being conscious that a message has been sent. The doctor who tells you that "Smoking is bad," while lighting up a cigarette, may not even realize that his or her messages conflict. You as the patient may not really understand the message you are getting, but the message is there nonetheless. You will probably not take that doctor's advice.

Suppose that you are talking to a group of your employees, explaining to them the company's new sick leave policy. At one point, you state that the policy of the company is that sick leave days should be used only when there is a need for them. However, when you are saying this, you give a wink to the people listening. Even if you did not intend to wink, and even if most of the employees listening did not "see" the wink, it still has an effect. The example you set by your out-of-awareness message will be far more powerful than the words you spoke.

Communicating informally can be a double-edged sword. Properly and consciously done, informally sent messages have a great impact on people, be they your employees, your superiors, or your family and friends. However, if you fail to recognize your informal messages (sent *and* received), you are ignoring a major source of communication difficulty for managers.

Informal communication is powerful. It can help you to communicate better by reinforcing the spoken and written messages you send. It can also destroy your ability to develop "commonness" with others without your even being aware of it. One way to develop more awareness of these informal forces and communications is to change our attitudes about communication.

CHANGING ATTITUDES

Most of us think about communication as a variety of activities. We speak, write, listen, frown, gesture, and read. We associate communication with media. Communication is "doing" things. There's really no doubt that active communication is important. Without some activity, there would be little communication. However, we often make a serious error that upsets our ability to communicate. We simply confuse *activity* with *accomplishment*.

Caterpillars

Jean Fabré, the French naturalist, was one day observing processionary caterpillars. These are little fellows, about an inch long, that form up into long strings and move over trees eating leaves and insects. Fabré was able to get them onto the rim of an old red flower pot and had them close up their circle. As they moved around the rim in an unbroken circle, he figured that they would soon realize that they were going in circles and would stop. Yet they starved to death within reach of food. They confused activity with accomplishment. They were active as could be, moving along staying busy. They just weren't getting anywhere.

Attitudes Versus Accomplishments

Too many of us find ourselves in the same situation as the caterpillars'. We are always on the go, moving from one activity to the next, always busy, obviously communicating. Yet, the activity we are showing may be hiding the fact that we're not really communicating at all. It takes practice and sensitivity to ask yourself, "Did Sally really understand me?" "What did that attempt at communication *really* accomplish?" Instead of worrying as much about *how* we should communicate with others, let's concentrate on *what* we're going to communicate, and what we're going to accomplish with the communication.

Perception

When we communicate, the "what," or content, of our messages is important. Yet, as we have already seen, no two people will get the same meanings from a situation or a message. Our ability to communicate is based on our perceptions. When you tell someone about something you saw, or heard, or read, you are not really telling facts. Rather, you are telling your perception of those facts. Look at a blot of ink, or a smear of paint, or clouds going by in the sky. Images you see in those abstract shapes are not the same as the images others form. Ask any police officer about eyewitness accounts of a crime, or a simple traffic accident. So-called eyewitnesses usually can't agree on even the basic facts of the event, much less on the more elusive details.

The Impossible Box

Look closely at the box in the photograph in Figure 2-4. The more you look at it, the more unreal it becomes. Obviously, it is a trick. The man seems real, yet the box defies our logical sense of what can be or ought to be. The photograph was not retouched, it is just an illusion.

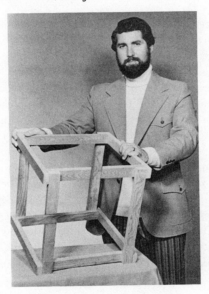

FIGURE 2-4 The "Impossible" Box

The author and the photographers worked for hours just to get a well-constructed wood cube into the right angle, the right distance from the camera, to create the illusion. At any other angle, the illusion wouldn't work. At a distance closer to the camera, or further from the camera, the illusion wouldn't work. Yet, at one specific point, something that logically is impossible becomes quite possible, quite real.

We worked very hard to create an illusion, one that would fool your eye and confuse your logic. Yet, around us every day are countless hundreds of situations in which illusion and appearance conflict with logic.

Look at some optical illusions. They're fun to see, and they should remind us that what we see is not always what is there. Reality is in the "eye of the beholder."

Self-Image

Experts tell us that one of the most important forces forming our perceptions of the world is our self-image. Each of us has a view — an image — of ourselves. We "see" ourselves in a certain way, usually a good or positive way. However, the way we see ourselves is not always the way others see us. And this difference in perception between our self-image and the perception others have of us represents a potential for a breakdown in communication. To overcome the images that others have and to put ourselves in a better light when communicating, we often wear masks.

Masks?

Not the Halloween kind, but behavioral masks. When you are communicating as a parent to your child, you are wearing a mask. Your expressions, tone of voice, words and examples, and possibly even your clothes become a mask, an image that helps you to communicate.

Sales people are always putting on masks. Before going in to call on a customer, a salesman will "set" his tie, smooth his jacket lapels, "shoot" his shirt cuffs out, run his hand over his hair. A saleswoman will smooth her blouse, run her hand over the front of her skirt, touch her lips, and "bounce" the bottom of her hair. These motions, usually performed unconsciously, are a form of mask donning. These sales people are saying to the customer "Mister, you better watch yourself, because I'm the BEST seller in the world. You're going to buy everything I'm selling." This is often called positive thinking. Telling yourself that you can do it is a large part of being successful.

The teacher in front of a class, the manager working with employees, the television personality, doctor, lawyer, accountant, and lover all wear masks. We judge others, and they judge us, by their perceptions of the masks we put on.

Dogs and Cocktail Parties

Watch two dogs meeting for the first time. They sniff. This behavior may embarrass some people, but the dogs are just asking questions. "Are you a dog?" (With long hair and today's unusual wearing apparel, it could be a funky looking skunk). Notice that, after the two dogs have sniffed for a while, their reactions run in one of three patterns. They might go off together, they may simply wander off apart, or they may growl and try to fight. Their actions are based on the signals they get from sniffing. These first impressions determine their subsequent behavior.

Have you ever said to yourself after meeting a stranger "There's something about that guy I just don't like?" These feelings are the result of signals that we get from others, signals that are probably sent and received in total un-awareness.

People at cocktail parties behave in much the way that dogs do when meeting strangers, just not directly in the sense of physical sniffing. People at cocktail parties, or other gatherings of strangers, are sniffing. They are talking small talk (which experts call "phatic" communication). When first visiting with a stranger, or a group of strangers, it is unlikely anyone will bring up any controversial topics. Such subjects as religion, sex, and politics (and in some parts of the country, football) are sensitive to many of us. In a group of strangers, expressing an opinion on one of these subjects is likely to get you a punch in the nose. So, unless we're brave, foolish, or both, we confine our talk to "small" talk. "How's the weather?"

We spend much of our time trying to get behind the masks that other people wear, while trying to keep our own masks intact. In the following chapters, we will explore some of the masks and goggles that we wear and that others around us wear.

Communication is a subject that demands involvement. You can communicate while being passive, but you cannot understand communication and improve your ability to communicate unless you get "active."

Ways to Improve Your Communication Skills

1. There is no one "best" way to communicate. Mix up your media, and experiment with your communications.
2. Commonness is the goal of communication. Don't confuse activity with accomplishment.
3. The out-of-awareness aspects of communication, the informal message, and the masks we wear are the most powerful. Writing, speaking, and listening are important, but real understanding of others will develop best when the out-of-awareness communications are emphasized.
4. Examine your goggles and your masks. Let's not try to reduce every one to the same thing. Better communication will result when we sensitize ourselves to the differences in people and take pleasure in those differences.

3

Know Thyself:
First Step Into
the Management Minefield

"To lead or attempt to lead without first a knowledge of self is foolhardy, and sure to bring disaster and defeat."

Machiavelli, The Prince

Since ancient times, philosophers have advised those seeking power and influence to first "know thyself." In Chapter 2, we discussed the problem of different people having different goggles and seeing different messages in the same things. With all the barriers and dimensions of communication we've now discussed, management begins to take on the appearance of a huge minefield, with dangers and challenges at every turn. This is only a small exaggeration, because the untrained, unsuspecting, and insensitive manager can quickly become ensnared in problems and situations that could have been foreseen and avoided. Taking Machiavelli's advice, it is difficult to make real progress in any activity until you've learned something about your own strengths and weaknesses.[1]

Hitchhiking on the "pop psychology" view that "... if you're not part of the solution, you're part of the problem," it's important to know when you're supposed to be looking for answers and when you're standing in the way of an answer. A little occasional self-analysis from time to time should give you the information you need to make this distinction clear. As a manager in an organization, it is quite possible that the best solution to a thorny problem is inside you and not necessarily buried deep in the minds of your fellow employees, your boss, your customers and clients, or your family.

For some time managers have been aware of the important link between good management and good communication. Good communication, in turn, hinges on being able to put yourself in the other person's shoes — to see things from his or her point of view. Because no two people are alike, it is easy to assume (incorrectly) that other people see things exactly as you see them. Thus, a new product or service that looks great to you will be enthusiastically received by your customers, clients and employees as well — right?

We'd like to say ALWAYS!, but we know it's not so. Each person has a point of view that gives that individual a unique message or attitude about any situation or event. Even an image as clear and uncomplicated as you — a manager or employee in an organization — can be taken many ways by many people. Most management people have a fairly positive self-image. They feel themselves to be intelligent, competent, decisive, upward mobile, experienced, firm but fair, farsighted, and yet concerned about detail. In short, a practically perfect person. This "true view" is fortunately shared by most of our mothers, some of our children, a few of our spouses, and practically no one else.

Suppose you asked some people who deal with or work in your organization to draw a verbal picture of you (and, for simplicity, let's assume that you are the top administrator in your organization). How would they "draw" you? Would the portraits sound something like this?

THE MANAGER AS SEEN BY:	
THE BOARD OF DIRECTORS	Asleep at the wheel, gofer (as in go for that report, etc.), a perfect example of the Peter principle (managers rise to their level of incompetence)
YOUR EMPLOYEES	Curmudgeon, whips and claws, perpetual snarl, ivory tower
THE FINANCIAL COMMITTEE	Las Vegas dealer, Mexican laundry truck, high roller, river boats, risk
YOUR BARBER OR HAIRDRESSER	Expects too much, resurrection is far more difficult than birth
YOUR CUSTOMER OR CLIENT	Gofer (see board of directors), financial wizard (small minority), ole what'sizname (vast majority), overpaid, who cares? (almost everyone)

Don't be upset by these caricatures. After all, they're not really what others think of a typical manager. Don't we wish! As we've already seen, the plain truth is that perception is a funny business. What people see in other people, in situations, experiences, and in themselves is true — to them. The validity of one's perceptions is not affected by any absolute standard of accuracy or inaccuracy.

If people can be wrong about perceptions of everyday events, it should be reasonable that our perceptions of ourselves can be just as distorted. Thus, the advice to "get into someone else's head" to improve communication should be just as relevant for getting inside our own heads. In short, know thyself.

EASY TO SAY—HARD TO DO

Self-analysis is difficult and useful only if it's done honestly. Telling yourself what you want to hear bears about as much relationship to the truth as the mirror owned by Snow White's stepmother. Honest, careful, and periodic self-analysis will give you a big headstart in improving your communications with others and your ability to manage in your organization.

Instead of studying a long questionnaire filled with trick (or tricky to answer) questions, let's begin by considering several important self-analysis issues. Then we'll use a questionnaire, but one that contains some common-sense ideas about communication and leadership.

Can You Objectively Evaluate Yourself?

This may seem somewhat superfluous, since we're already knee-deep in a chapter on self-analysis, but it's a very relevant question.

Strange as it may seem, the same managers who are capable and self-assured when evaluating the performance of their employees or the needs of their clients and customers are often unable to turn the mirror on themselves. In particular, they are able to identify their own weakness, but they come up short when forced to list or identify their strengths. Although managers usually have good, positive self-images, they often have difficulty being objective. Just because others may not see you in the same light that you shine on yourself is no reason to shrink from making an objective assessment.

How Do You Take Bad News? (see how close to home self-analysis can come)

Do you react poorly when a member of your staff brings you information that's bad? Does your response to bad news ever take the form of accusing the bad-news bearer of being the cause of the bad news? Does your facial expression suggest (even if your voice doesn't) that you are holding the news-bearer personally responsible?

Managers who are good at handling bad news are fully aware of the impact nonverbal (or body) messages can have, especially in pressure or anxiety-producing situations. They know, too, that the surest way to eliminate bad news is to make people feel that you don't want any bad news. Of course, this doesn't make the bad news go away. It's still there waiting in the weeds to jump out at you when you're not expecting it. As a manager in an organization, you like to receive good news. You like to hear that savings account deposits are up, that the Dow Jones industrials is strong, that sales are booming, that production is up, that employees are contented and productive, and that the conditions in the market are the best that they've been in years. Although good news is nice to get, you realize that it's the bad news you need to do the job your bosses, customers, and clients pay you to do. Without bad news to handle, there would be little reason for your job in the organization. Cutting off your sources of vital information is foolhardy. If you're guilty, consider the following ideas.

Good bad-news takers learn to delay their reactions to information, whether delivered orally or in writing. Because first reactions are usually impulsive, they don't really reflect your true feeling anyway. They can usually cause only harm. Also, reinforce people who bring you bad news by showing in some way that you appreciated their prompt report. Of course, if the person who brings you bad news is the one responsible for the bad news, delayed reaction *is* still good advice. Assuming that people learn from their errors, a delayed reaction can help maintain an open line of communication for the next time that the culprit brings you his tale of woe.

Do You Learn From Your Mistakes, or Do You Constantly Reinvent the Wheel?

Practically perfect people rarely make mistakes, but few organizational managers are PPPs. Therefore, when mistakes happen, you have two choices. You can admit nothing, blame it on "poor staff work" and risk the same thing happening again.

Or, you can admit error, take realistic stock of causes and implications, and make changes to avoid a recurrence. Managerial effectiveness is judged on one's rate of good-to-bad decisions, not on some absolute standard of perfection. You can improve your "win-lose" record when you plan ahead and foresee potential errors and problems. Failure to honestly appraise errors (especially your own) also deprives you of information that can make the next similar error easier to handle. Without this "experimental information," each new outcropping of an old problem becomes a novel situation. In effect, you must reinvent the wheel for each trip instead of building on the performance and experience of the past.

Can You Listen to Others and Learn From Them?

Listening is a skill that we often take for granted. We confuse listening with hearing, which is a physical process. In contrast, listening involves understanding and evaluating what others say, making their inputs a part of your frame of reference. If you find your attention wandering as you listen to others, or if you are thinking about your next comment instead of concentrating on what the other person is saying, you may have a listening handicap.

Overcoming listening problems requires a change in your personal way of communicating with people. Become person oriented. Try to understand not just what a person says but also why he says it. Assume when you're listening that you are responsible for both ends of the message (sender and receiver), not just your part. You'll develop what experts call "active listening skills."

Can You Filter Out Unnecessary Information?

Although listening skills are essential to good management, too much information can be dangerous. Individuals who are unable to decide between the relevant and irrelevant information coming at them from all directions run the risk of "information overload." In its extreme form, it can result in an inability to function as a manager. There is simply too much data for a person to find the *necessary* data. The end result is almost the same as a complete absence of information.

For most managers, information overload is not quite so serious. Its usual symptoms are a feeling there's never enough time to get everything done. The manager feels pressured. He seems to be searching for more data, even though perhaps too much data is available already.

There is a simple cure for information overload. You can begin to develop "mental filters" capable of sorting out the "wheat from the chaf." This can be done by assigning priorities to various kinds of inputs and then staying with your priorities. It can be done by attaching a time frame to everything you hear. For example, if you're told that the scheduling committee has prepared a policy statement, evaluate whether this information should be handled immediately or whether it can be temporarily ignored. If it fits the latter category, put it aside and keep it from cluttering up your "handle immediately" information.

A manager in Nebraska suggests that his "filter" is to preface every piece of data he receives with the question "Will it be important six months from now?" If the answer is no, he ignores the information, putting it aside until he has otherwise free time. Perhaps your time horizon is one year, or one week. Nevertheless, such devices can help you avoid overload problems.

Can You Delegate, or Must You Take Personal Charge of All Activities?

Failure to delegate can often be a manager's sign of lack of trust in his or her subordinates. It can also indicate a personal insecurity that is both counter-productive and time consuming. The result of failure to delegate can often be the information overload to which we referred above.

Improving your delegation skill might involve better training for the people on your staff. It may mean breaking what Rensis Likert called the "low-trust, low-performance" cycle.[2] In Likert's view, low management trust (such as failure to delegate) leads to employees' performance slipping. This, in turn, leads to further erosion of your trust in them. To break the cycle, Likert suggests that managers take a crucial first step and give employees responsibility in situations where perhaps they haven't earned such responsibility. This step won't always work, but it does work often enough to suggest that it is possible to improve one's delegation.

Can You Make a Firm Decision After Reasonable Deliberation?

Do you jump at the first impulse, to get the decision making over with quickly. Or do you search and search for more and more information, hoping the decision will be made for you?

Decisions made too quickly or after too much deliberation may reflect your insecurity with the information you have. By your actions, you are suggesting that you have too much, too little or inaccurate information. You resolve your dilemma by either getting the decision over with quickly or by putting it off. This may make you feel better, but it also creates information problems for others. Information is either swept away and ignored, or allowed to "jam" while you deliberate.

In either case, practice following the seven simple steps to effective decision making.

1. Determine your objective and how it's to be measured
2. Define the conditions and limits
3. Gather information
4. Identify feasible alternatives
5. Weigh or evaluate alternatives
6. Select the best alternatives
7. Implement the chosen alternatives and follow through

These steps aren't foolproof, but they are the "professional" way in which to make decisions.

Can You Leave Your Work at Work?

Managing a part of an organization (or the whole show for that matter) is not an 8-to-5 job. It requires enthusiasm, dedication, involvement, personal commitment, and much more. If you're effective at your job, you work long hours, take work home after hours, and spend at least part of your vacation on the phone "checking on things in the shop." Although all this dedication is admirable, it also holds the potential for some serious problems.

See how much of this true story fits you. A vice president of a large West Coast bank was faced with a dilemma. His annual vacation was approaching, and he was too busy to get away for even a week, yet like all bank employees, he was required to take a minimum one-week vacation every year. During that time, vacationing employees were not permitted inside the bank, even on personal business and in "civilian" clothes. This policy is meant to keep employees from covering up illegal or "shady" activities. They would not be able to "cover their tracks" when away from their normal work station. To be effective, the policy included everyone in the bank, from janitor to president.

Our vice president in this example wasn't engaged in "creative banking." He was simply avoiding a vacation because he was too busy, too involved in important ongoing projects. His solution?

For the full week of his enforced vacation, he set himself up in the back booth of a restaurant across the street from the bank. Every day he would arrive at 10:00 A.M. and leave at 2:00 P.M., dressed as always in a three-piece suit. Every day he would visit with his colleagues over lunch. Every day between 10:00 A.M. and 2:00 P.M. his employees, one by one, would troop across the street, files and printouts in hand, to confer with their exiled leader. He was running his division as though he'd never left. Naturally, such behavior is very untypical of managers in most organizations. Or is it?

Aside from the ethical issues involved in short circuiting a company policy, this man's behavior was a classic example of a "workaholic." He was physically incapable of leaving his work at work, even for a short period. He will bend and break rules rather than admit that no one (including himself) is indispensable. Apparently, he is convinced that, without him on the job every day of the week, his bank would fold.

Time away from the job, mentally and physically, is important for giving a person a sense of perspective. Without it, there's a danger of being too close to the trees to see the shape of the forest. Perhaps with this thought and the publicity of previous administrations in mind, Jimmy Carter early in his presidency addressed this very issue. He suggested that, although he would demand much of his staff, he also knew the value of time away from work spent with family and friends. He demanded that his staff follow his example and from time to time leave work at work in favor of other pursuits. It's good advice for management people just as it's good advice for cabinet officers and the White House staff.

HOW'S YOUR "LEADERSHIP" QUOTIENT?

Leadership and communication are directly related. Good leaders are invariably good at communicating with others. This does not mean that all leaders are expert public speakers or that to be a good leader one must be able to write like Hemingway or Drucker. However, good leadership begins with an ability to communicate ideas and information to people in a way that helps them to understand what is expected of them. Therefore, an important part of self-analysis includes a brief look at your leadership skills. Try your hand with Arthur Pell's "Leadership Quotient Test."[3] Answer "agree" or "disagree" for each of the following 25 statements. When you've finished, read through the "correct" answers and add up the number you answered correct.

THE LEADERSHIP QUOTIENT TEST

	Agree	*Disagree*
1. In correcting an employee's errors, the leader should point out the employee's good points, then lead into a discussion of the mistakes.		X
2. It is not necessary for a leader to discuss long-range goals with his or her people. So long as they are aware of the immediate objective, they can do their work effectively.		X
3. The best way to make a reprimand effective is to dress down the offender in front of his or her fellow workers.		X
4. Grievances and morale problems should be handled by the immediate supervisor rather than by a person especially assigned to this work.	X	
5. In setting goals for your staff, it is always best to give them more work than it is possible for them to complete.		X
6. A leader's main job is the enforcement of rules and regulations.	X	
7. The person who is most popular with his or her colleagues is the natural choice for leadership.		X

8. A leader will lose the respect of subordinates if he or she admits mistakes to them.
    Agree: ___   Disagree: X

9. A leader shows ignorance and risks possible loss of face among his or her people if he or she answers a question, "I don't know, but I'll find out and let you know."
    Agree: ___   Disagree: X

10. A leader technically qualified to do a job is qualified to teach others to do it.
    Agree: ___   Disagree: X

11. Leaders are born, not made.
    Agree: ___   Disagree: X

12. It pays for the leader to spend a lot of time with a new employee to see that he is well trained for his job.
    Agree: X   Disagree: ___

13. A good way to put a loudmouth in his or her place is by a sarcastic remark.
    Agree: ___   Disagree: ___

14. The best way to make sure that rules are obeyed is to put plenty of teeth in them.
    Agree: ___   Disagree: X

15. Leaders should ask their subordinates for their ideas on work methods.
    Agree: X   Disagree: ___

16. A good executive should, wherever possible, delegate both authority and responsibility for some of his or her work to subordinate staff.
    Agree: X   Disagree: ___

17. To be absolutely fair, a leader must handle all persons in exactly the same way regardless of differences between individuals.
    Agree: ___   Disagree: X

18. A manager should not keep reminding a subordinate of past mistakes. Once corrected, mistakes should be forgotten.
    Agree: X   Disagree: ___

19. A good bawling out now and then will keep the average employee on his or her toes.
    Agree: ___   Disagree: X

20. When disciplining a subordinate, one should be careful to avoid saying or doing anything that might make that employee resent you.
    Agree: X   Disagree: ___

21. An employee will work best for a tough, demanding leader.
    Agree: ___   Disagree: X

22. If a new employee has not learned his or her job well, he or she has not been properly taught.
    Agree: X   Disagree: ___

23. It is more important for a leader to like his or her job than it is to be efficient.
    Agree: ___   Disagree: X

24. The work will be done most efficiently if the leader lays it out in great detail.
    Agree: X   Disagree: ___

25. For a leader to do a job effectively, he or she must always have access to the feelings, attitudes, and ideas of subordinates.
    Agree: X   Disagree: ___

Now that you've committed yourself on these statements, see how you scored. Each "right" answer represents the viewpoint of the experts in communication and human relations.

1. *Agree.* People are more receptive to criticism and correction if you tell them their good points. They become less defensive and will accept the criticism with less resentment.

2. *Disagree.* Persons who know where they are going—who can visualize the long-range picture—are more committed to reaching those objectives and will work harder to attain them.

3. *Disagree.* Dressing a person down does not solve problems, it only makes the person feel small in front of his or her fellows. A good reprimand should correct a problem without humiliating the person. It is best to reprimand in private—never in front of others.

4. *Agree.* It is a prime function of line leaders to take care of grievances. The "chaplain" or special grievance officer is not necessary where good leadership exists.

5. *Disagree.* Setting too high a goal discourages a person. He or she feels that he will never make it and therefore won't try. Best goals are just a little higher than previous experience, so it is possible to achieve. This encourages a person really to try to reach the goals.

6. *Disagree.* The main job of a leader is to inspire, lead, train, and direct his or her people. Enforcement of rules and regulations will become secondary if he or she is a good leader.

7. *Disagree.* Popularity is neither an indication of good or bad leadership. Some popular people make excellent leaders; others may be more concerned with their popularity than their ability to lead.

8. *Disagree.* It is better to admit an error rather than to try to bluff it out. It will be discovered anyway, so admit it and people will have more respect for you.

9. *Disagree.* Same reason as for 8.

10. *Disagree.* Technical competence is important. But, to teach others, one must know how to communicate this knowledge effectively.

11. *Disagree.* Experience has shown that, by proper training and encouragement, almost every person can be developed into a leader.

12. *Agree.* The most important step in developing the full capabilities of employees is good training by their leaders. If they spend the time in the beginning, leaders can lay the foundation for developing each newcomer into a valuable asset for the organization.

13. *Disagree.* Sarcasm rarely puts anyone in their place. It usually only causes resentment. A loudmouth can be best controlled by finding out what motivates him or her and channeling it into constructive uses.

14. *Disagree.* The best way to enforce rules is to make sure that everyone understands what they are and why they have been made.

15. *Agree.* Persons directly involved with the job often can contribute good ideas toward the solution of problems that they are close to.

16. *Agree.* No job can be done effectively if an executive fails to delegate authority to his or her subordinates. Train them and be confident of their capability and then let them carry the ball.

17. *Disagree.* Fairness does not mean treating everyone equally. It means understanding the strengths and weaknesses of everyone and expecting the best from each according to his or her ability. It means not playing favorites—but it does not mean that you can expect everyone to be able to perform equally well.

18. *Agree.* Nagging never works. Once a person has been corrected, forget it unless the problem recurs.

19. *Disagree.* Nonsense. A bawling out lowers a person's self-esteem and does not encourage him or her to grow. Constructive criticism, yes; bawling out, no.

20. *Agree.* Resentment creates low morale and often leads to conscious or subconscious sabotage.

21. *Disagree.* Tough and demanding is not as important as fair and inspiring.

22. *Agree.* A good teacher gets feedback on whether or not the student has learned a lesson. Poor students need extra coaching.

23. *Disagree.* Happiness on the job is important but is secondary to getting the job done.

24. *Disagree.* Psychologists have shown that people work better when they are given broad guidelines and can work out details themselves.

25. *Agree.* Communication is a two-way street. Unless the leader has a means of reading his or her subordinates' minds, he or she cannot anticipate problems or properly motivate his or her people.

To score yourself on this test of leadership and communication skill, multiply your correct answers by four. A total score (your leadership quotient) of 90 or more indicates excellent leadership and communication skills, 80–90 is good, 70–80 is average, and below 70 is poor. Of course, you may not agree with all of the "right" answers suggested by the experts, and in the following chapters we will consider many of these concepts and ideas and help you develop a better understanding of the reasons for the "correct" answers being correct.

SUMMARY

Self-analysis need not be difficult or threatening. If you look at yourself and your skills honestly and with an eye toward improving those areas in which you've spotted some weaknesses, you will find that the entire experience can be a very pleasant and profitable one. When you find real or potential problems, take some common-sense steps to correct them before they get too far out of hand and become major problems.

In the next few chapters, we will take a further look into self-analysis. We'll also begin to develop the important relationship between communication, motivation, and persuasion, and we'll base that relationship on the notion that, to effectively motivate, an individual must first have a firm grasp of his or her strengths and weaknesses. If you've done your self-analysis, you're ready for a look at the many elements in managerial communication.

Ways to Improve Your Communication Skills

1. Keep in mind that others do not see you in quite the way that you see yourself. This difference in perceptions is a common problem in communication, yet too often we forget that it applies to the most important person in our lives—ourselves. Once you remember that others have different viewpoints about you, you're on the way to self-analysis and to better communication.
2. Do some serious self-analysis regularly.
3. Your leadership style and your communication style are directly related. If you have found serious discrepancies between your answers and the "expert" point of view, it doesn't necessarily mean that you're lousy at either. It should, however, give you some clues to possible improvements.
4. By this point, you've read and considered some of the self-analysis ideas. You're ready for some of the substantive aspects of communication. As you read each chapter, examine yourself to see if you've been using the various techniques to the best advantage.

Further Reading

To follow up on the material in this chapter, you may also want to read:

DESMOND MORRIS, THE NAKED APE (McGraw-Hill)

This book is a zoologist's view of man and his behavior and provides an interesting insight into the way people use space, time, gestures, and other forms of nonverbal communication and how these various messages and techniques came into being.

4

Building Motivation and Morale

"The 'Mickey-Mouse' in management may help the boss feel more important, but it also says to the employees, 'you're unimportant around here!' Removing some of these barriers can be a real boost to morale and one can really improve the will to work."

Robert Townsend

In many of the communication strategies we discuss in this book, the concept of a "communicative atmosphere" or "motivating climate" keeps popping up. The idea is that, if we are to be successful as managers *and* communicators, we must do more than simply handle problems and develop and apply specific skills. We must also pay close attention to the overall environment in which our managerial talents are applied. Later chapters address some of the skills and problems involved in effective managerial communication, so let's first look at some of the environmental factors in communication.

PEOPLE POWER

In a famous Pogo cartoon strip, cartoonist Walt Kelly's hero suggests "we have met the enemy, and they are us!" We often forget that the central focus of any aspect of management has to be people. This may seem to be an enormous overstatement, but there is a surprising number of managers who fail to develop a people-centered approach to management. They are also the managers who'll likely cite "communication problems" as the cause for their failures, when in fact the cause lies in their unwillingness to develop an appreciation for the human factors in motivation and management.

The key to people-centered communication and management is *trust*. When employees are told that they must trust their bosses, or that the organization has their best interests at heart, but they see easy evidence all around them that this is not the case, there will be a gradual distrust of the organization and it's representatives, including their immediate superior. This is an important point that must be made before we venture too far into studying the various personal skills and strategies for better managerial communication, because, without a climate of trust between employees, their boss, and the overall organization, the communication techniques will be useless.

Many signals and symbols show management's feeling about employees. Some of these signals are well meant and are simply misunderstood or misperceived by the employees. Others seem to be calculated precisely because they give employees a sense of "their place" in the organization. For example, in many companies, there is a separate parking lot for management above a certain level, and in some cases, the senior managers park inside, where their cars are washed while they work. There are, of course, some good reasons for preferred parking, including the fact that the managers often have to leave during the day and would waste time walking through a huge parking lot looking for their cars. However, when employees must trudge in through the snow and rain on a cold winter day, past the large management cars snuggled up against the building, they have "proof" that the organization has a low opinion of them. The same goes for management dining rooms, private offices, or the "right" to be addressed as Mr. or Ms. instead of "Harvey," or "Lynne," or "Carlos."

Many of these status signals are matters that have been decided on at the highest levels in your organization, and you as an individual manager have little or no control over them. Yet, they create social distance, and they also create seeds of mistrust in the minds of employees.

As we discussed earlier, each of our perceptions is different. Each of us sees the world from a different point of view, through different goggles. Thus, what you or the top management take for granted, employees may question. What you or the top management realize is a necessary part of doing your job (as many so-called status symbols really are), employees may feel are unnecessary discriminations against them.

This feeling of distance and the mistrust that it breeds can even be seen in the way that information is handled. For example, a company was having one of its best years. Sales were booming, and the production facilities were becoming overcrowded. Management felt that this was the start of a long uptrend and began to actively search for locations for a new and larger plant. To keep unnecessary rumors from interfering with their negotiations (and hiking up the price they'd have to pay for land), management decided to keep all word of their plans secret until the "right time."

An important element in the plan was the fact that the company was going to shift most of the routine subassembly work over to the new plant and upgrade the work in their present plant. This would mean new job assignments and higher pay for all of their employees. The present plant, when reoutfitted, would be the most modern in the industry, years ahead of the competition. Management also planned to experiment with some of the newer "job enrichment" concepts, including work teams and "participative management" when the old plant was reoutfitted. During the two weeks the old plant was shut down for renovation, all employees were to be given a vacation with pay. In short, management's plans for the work force were clearly beneficial to the employees and reflected management's high regard for the employees and the work they had done in the past.

The only problem with all these plans is that the employees weren't told what was going to happen. Or, rather, the employees didn't know all the information, although they *did* know what was going to happen to them. They knew, for instance, that they would most likely not be invited to move to the new plant when their present plant was shut down. Also, they knew that those few employees who did move to the new plant 30 miles away would have to compete for jobs with others from the area who were applying for jobs. Finally, they knew that with the massive layoffs from their present plant, they would have a tough time getting a new job in their present city unless they started as soon as possible applying at other companies in the area. As a result of this information, many employees, including some of the best and most experienced employees and lower-level supervisors and managers began actively looking for other jobs in the area. Several found jobs with firms competing with their present employer. This was, of course, a coup for the competitor, because these employees were experienced and they know some of the front-runner's trade secrets. Realizing management's apparent unconcern for their welfare, the employees had acted on their own to protect their interests.

Does It Sound Like You've Been Reading Two Different Stories? It should. Yet, both are true, and both stories refer to the same company at the same point in time. The difference is that the first viewpoint is management's. The second viewpoint is the employees'. Remember, management chose (for some very good reasons) to keep secret their plans for the new plant and the reoutfitting and upgrading of the old plant. However, whereas they could keep secret their *intentions*, they could not conceal all of their actions. Thus, employees saw some equipment from their old plant being shipped out (to make way for the new equipment that would arrive later). They overheard top managers walking through the shop discussing hiring problems in the new location. They heard engineers discussing plans for "stripping everything out of this area as soon as we shut down the plant" (remember that two-week paid layoff?). They saw some new managers, hired for the new plant, advertising for employees to do the jobs that they were now doing (remember that the present employees were going to be given upgraded, participative work assignments?).

What management failed to recognize was that it is impossible to *not* communicate. Good intentions and a willingness to "tell all when the time is right" are not enough. When faced with doubt and uncertainty, we all try to reduce the feelings of threat by filling in the missing spaces. These employees knew that something was going on, and they knew that they had a stake in the action. However, when their management indicated its distrust by not sharing vitally important (to them) information, the employees simply made up their own information. This information was true, *to the employees*. It was their perception of the situation, and it was as true as the intentions of the management were *to the management*.

FIGURE 4-1

The problem in this case was resolved before irreparable damage was done. The issue came to top management's attention when one of the best assembly supervisors (himself in line for the old plant superintendent's job), announced that he was leaving for a job with the company's major competitor across town. In questioning why he was moving, top management learned the details of the story as the employees had it and realized that it was to blame for the unrest, confusion, and miscommunication that was taking place. A general meeting of all employees was held, and management carefully laid out all its plans in detail, responded to employee questions for several hours, and apparently convinced the majority of the employees of the sincerity of their intentions. It did lose several key employees and supervisors, but in general management resolved the situation. A simple matter like confidential information can easily become a major problem, simply because trust and open communication was lacking. Morale, which we as managers often take for granted, contributed to a major disaster that could have been devastating to the company and its plans for the future.

MORALE AND COMMUNICATION

When the morale of your employees is high, as it should be, your department is on a sound footing. No one needs to tell you when the morale of your staff is high. You see signs of it everywhere. Your people are cheerful, pleasant, easy to get along with, enthusiastic about their work — and ready to pitch in and do whatever is necessary to get the job done.[1]

When the morale of your people is high, the only thing you have to do is to make sure you keep it that way. In other words, don't do anything to destroy the good morale you have. It's an asset you have to use.

If the morale of your people is low — or tending in that direction — no one needs to call that fact to your attention. Low morale makes itself known very plainly and very painfully. Your people are grumpy. They complain. They find reason for being absent from work. They resent being asked to do something that they consider outside their regular duties. The spirit of cooperation is absent. Work output is neglected. Things get misplaced and can't be found when needed. The turnover of your staff is greater than it should be. And you find key people quitting to take jobs elsewhere.

If you should see signs like this in your organization, don't just sit there hoping the situation will get better. It won't. It will merely get worse. At any rate, the idea of how to lift the morale of your staff to a higher level, and to keep it there, is something worth thinking about and worth devoting some effort to achieving.

Some Practical Ways to Build Morale

Here are some practical suggestions on how to build good morale on the part of the people who work under your direction:

1. Work on yourself first. Get yourself straightened out.
2. Give a great deal of attention to discovering emotions, feelings, and highly colored personal attitudes that block highest efficiency. Study your employees—use their personalities to work for the program, not against it. Discuss undesirable attitudes as they begin to develop. Anticipate them; prevent them.
3. Consider causes for dissatisfaction fairly and promptly and try to do something about them. Point out at once what is being done.
4. Always give credit when credit is due.
5. When you have to criticize someone, do it immediately—and in private.
6. Tell your workers why. Give them the reasons.
7. Take a conscientious interest in improving each worker's working conditions.
8. Don't make promises you cannot keep, and keep the promises you do make.
9. Place your people where their training and experience can be used best.
10. Take the employee into your confidence. Tell him or her about things. Make him a part of the organization. Develop that "we" attitude.
11. Remember that the reasons first given for the employee's complaints are usually not the real reasons for low morale or disinterest.
12. Build up the job. Show its importance. Just because you think that the job is important isn't enough. You have to *communicate* your views in a way that employees can understand and appreciate.

The purpose behind each suggestion—with the exception of the first one—is to motivate the individual, to make him or her *want* to be more productive.

Salary Is Important

In motivating an employee, remember that salary is important. Each person will weigh his or her contribution to the organization in terms of the salary that he or she receives.

Salary has become a universal measuring stick. Salary, however, is not everything. Salary is most important when it is too low. At best, it is an elusive yardstick—and it is not the prime motivator to productivity and personal satisfaction that it was at one time thought to be.

A person will compare his or her salary with the salaries received by fellow workers and with the salary paid by another firm for similar work. If salary compares favorably, the person will not be overly concerned about his or her income, provided that there are other incentives connected with the job.

Make Sure That Incentives Exist

Your problem, then, is to make certain that the incentives exist and that they are real and worthwhile to each employee. Over and beyond that, your problem is to encourage each person to do a better job than anyone else. Factors involving motivation are varied and complex. They are not as simple as the manager who permits an organization to drift along might believe them to be.

The desire on the part of each individual to be a success must be high on the priority list. Every person has the desire to be a success to some extent, yet he or she must follow the rules: work around the clock, beat the competitor, establish a goal in life, decide on a course of action, and then follow through.

To be somebody, to build a name, to be accepted as a constructive and important person is a strong motive that anyone can use to encourage employees to be more productive.

Some organizations seem reluctant to give proper credit to their people. For some reason, the boss seems to feel threatened when a staff member becomes popular with other employees or managers.

If you want to motivate your employees to higher productivity, it is absolutely necessary for you to fight to give them credit for what they have done. Do this, and you will be a motivator; the morale in your organization will be positive, and your communications will be more effective.

Building a name is a highly interesting game, and this motive is all important to the staff member. The game can be played in such a way that the motivational force in building a personality is so great that the income of the individual becomes a simple byproduct of the process. When this happens, the individual is on his way. He will be a high producer, and his income will rise. One takes care of the other.

There is a peculiar aspect of success. The person who likes the easy road cannot lead the austere, disciplined life necessary to build success. A person who is of a caliber to drive forward toward his goal in the face of obstacles and deprivations is not unduly attracted toward luxury.

It is anything but easy to be successful, and this message must be conveyed to your staff.

Staff development is a two-way street. A person has to make an irrevocable decision to want to grow. It is rare to find a person who has made himself a success by working part time. Successful staff members are intensely competitive in all things. They are willing to give, in order to get, but the chief characteristic of a good staff member is the willingness to work and to sacrifice to arrive at the end result — recognition.

Remember, credit is almost impossible to give away; some of it always sticks to you. It is quite easy to usurp credit, and, if you do frequently, you'll likely find yourself in a position where you neither have credit to give, nor to receive, outside of that which you can produce yourself.

Ways to Improve Your Communication Skills

1. Use the job description as a basis for setting performance standards rather than trying to evaluate the employee's personal traits.
2. Evaluate total performance over a period of time. Don't be overly impressed by recent incidents or happenings.
3. Observe performance continually and discuss it with the individual employee whenever the situation warrants it. If a problem exists, don't wait for a predetermined review period to correct the situation.
4. Let employees know what is expected of them.
5. Discuss the establishment of performance standards with employees. Don't surprise a person with standards that suit you but make no sense to him or her.
6. Listen to employee ideas and suggestions for performance requirements.
7. Check performance for total results rather than fussing over the little details and overlooking the total aspects of the job.
8. Set standards for average performance rather than standards that are too high or too low.
9. If necessary, put performance requirements in writing.
10. Keep records of performance-review discussions.

II

VERBAL COMMUNICATION

5

Listening Habits
and Listening Skills

"The improvement of listening, or simply an effort to make people aware of how important their listening is, can be of great value in today's business."

Ralph Nichols

In this chapter, we turn our attention to receiver communications, or listening. Some of our earlier study dealt with special forms of listening. When we watch someone's eyes for signs of inner expression or watch for actions that follow instructions, we are "listening." However, most of us think of listening as an activity related directly to hearing.[1]

HEARING IS NOT LISTENING

In fact, that's the problem with listening. We often confuse listening with hearing. Listening is such a common activity that we often take it for granted.

Watch children playing "sense" games. By closing their eyes, their seeing is stopped. But there is no way to stop their hearing, even by putting their fingers in their ears. The result is an adult view that hearing requires no conscious activity and that hearing and listening are the same thing—they are not.

Hearing words as they are spoken is a mechanical process. It involves the hammer, anvil, the stirrup, and the eardrum of the inner ear. When a person's hearing is impaired, mechanical devices can often restore some of the lost hearing ability.

Because hearing is mechanical and because it happens with no outward activity on our part, we assume that, when a communication failure occurs, it is someone else's fault.

FAULT OF THE SENDER

When listening is interrupted, or when a miscommunication occurs, most of us are quick to blame the sender. His voice was not loud enough. Her ideas were poorly presented. They spoke too fast, or too slow, or too long, or not long enough. Hearing the words spoken, even making sense of the words being said, is not listening.

ACTIVE LISTENING

Listening is an active process. It involves understanding the meanings of words, expressions, and ideas. It is evaluating the content of the message. It requires the listener to assimilate, or make a part of himself, the message or the thought being sent. Each of these processes—understanding, evaluating, and assimilating—requires the conscious action of the listener.

Human relations experts have frequently suggested that the greatest barrier to people's understanding people is our basic inability to actively listen to others. In the words of another manager "everyone has learned to talk, but no one has learned to listen."

LISTENING HABITS

Habits are actions that are performed without thinking. When you brush your teeth, or say "thank you," or even breathe, you do it out of habit. Habits are developed by consciously doing something over and over again, until your mind no longer needs a conscious signal to perform. Some of our habits are good—they cause us to take beneficial or profitable action. Other habits are not so good, leading us to unthinkingly do things that are harmful, or unproductive, or stupid.

Good listening results from careful cultivation of positive listening activities. Although listening is an active process, it need not be a completely conscious one. The secret to better listening is to develop good listening habits.

FIGURE 5-1

A Conversation or a Speech?

Most of the important aspects of good listening apply to a formal speech as well as a quiet conversation between a manager and an employee. Some listening problems happen more often in a large group while one person is talking, whereas other problems are more commonly found when two or three individuals communicate face to face. By developing good listening habits, you can overcome many communication difficulties that plague management. These same "good habits of listening" can add measurably to the quantity *and* quality of information available to you as you work to meet your managerial responsibilities.

Earlier we suggested that the habits we form have a powerful and long-lasting effect on our communicative behavior. Some of these habits are productive and help us communicate better. Other habits are "bad" and keep us from fully developing our communication skills. In listening, bad habits are developed from years of experience, and they can cause us to distort and miss messages that we ought to get.[2] Because we assume that some listeners have some bad listening habits, let's look at how these bad habits can be "reversed" to produce some "good listening habits" or practices.

53

Concentrate on the Speaker's Strength

Few people are blessed with the winning combination of a good delivery and an interesting, stimulating subject. When either the subject or the speaker is dull, we often find it easy to "tune out" and then blame the speaker for our listening failure. Some of the blame for listening failure is, of course, the fault of the speaker. However, this should not bother the good listener. The good listener has developed the habit of focusing his or her attention on the key aspects of a presentation, either in a two-person conversation or a large audience lecture.

If the speaker is dull, repetitive, or lacking vocal color, the good listener doesn't "tune out." Instead, he or she works harder to focus more attention on the subject being discussed. No matter what the subject, there is at least one or two facts (or at least some inferences) that can be extracted and used. The active listener works at finding and evaluating those facts and inferences.

If the subject is really dull, boring, totally irrelevant, and beyond salvation, the good listener focuses on the speaker's delivery. How does she pronounce words? What does her voice accent say about where she grew up? By observing people, the good listener is able to turn an otherwise wasted time into some beneficial outcome.

But what if both speaker *and* subject are dull, boring, repetitive, colorless? As a last resort, the good listener may turn his attention to the reactions of the audience. What body postures or facial expressions indicate how they feel about the experience?

Perhaps we are carrying our point a bit too far. Still, active listening implies a conscious strategy to understand, evaluate and assimilate, and profit personally from any listening situation. Assuming that you have no choice *but* to stay and endure, why not make the best of it? With this attitude, no situation, however bleak, is a total listening "loss." Positive listening habits can be a good defense against boredom and fatigue.

Stay Cool

Often, while we're listening, a word or a phrase or an expression can trigger an emotional reaction. We get overstimulated and immediately block out whatever else is said. Good listeners develop the habit of staying cool when an emotional situation develops. No one is immune to emotion, but the good listener has a habit of recognizing the emotional trigger and can neutralize it *before* it blocks the rest of the message. This requires concentration and the ability to move your attention quickly.

Often, emotional words come into a conversation (although rarely in a speech) from some racial or ethnic prejudice. A Polish-American sales manager would "see red" everytime a certain ethnic slur slipped into a conversation, either by mistake or on purpose. Knowing his hatred for such a slur, two of his employees delighted in upsetting their boss whenever his discomfort would help them reach their goals. The "lack of cool" became a major barrier to listening. The sales manager missed many important ideas and bits of information in meetings, simply because he was unable to overcome his listening defect.

No one likes to be insulted, and such insults are usually a display of a speaker's ignorance. Managers who habitually use such expressions run a great risk of blocking the listening of others around them (not to mention their alienation and distrust). And managers who fail to recognize the effects of such emotional words on their own listening ability are likely to encounter more problems as they go.

Many police experts realize the damaging effects of emotional words on the behavior of officers. Police reaction to demonstrators of the 1960s were often linked to an involuntary reaction to taunts and insults. Racial slurs, shouts of "pig" and other obscenities, caused a temporary blocking of rational thought processes. To combat such reactions, police departments instituted "sensitivity" training, which many experts credit with helping police under verbal fire to retain their "cool" and to perform their jobs in the usual, professional manner.

Sensitivity training is not universally accepted as a means of overcoming listening blocks. It can, however, give you an insight into your own "pattern of biases." Next time you're listening to a speech or engaged in conversation with an employee, watch for words or expressions that raise your pulse or breathing, or cause you to lose track of your thoughts. Knowing what "turns you off" can be important in keeping your listening ability "turned on."

Overstimulation

Another bad habit of listening is closely related to emotional words, because it causes a similar reaction. In a meeting or discussion, a controversial or provocative idea may pop into your head. Whether the idea is good or bad, your reaction will usually be the same. If you are not a good listener, you will immediately start making mental or written notes about the idea and ignore what the speaker says next. This isn't as much of a problem if you're tape recording the conversation. You can let your mind wander and get the speaker's other points later. However, the taped speech lacks the speaker's body communication, which can be a major portion of his or her total message. Even taping may not overcome all the problems, but, without such a "back up," you risk losing important information.

Ellen Sanchez is an experienced manager working for a large textile company. She frequently found herself in management meetings jumping up to make a point that the speaker had already covered. She was guilty of overstimulation. She allowed a provocative idea to block her listening of the speakers following points. By the time she finished taking her written or mental notes about the details she wanted to retain, the speaker or the discussion was several points further into the topic, and Ellen was missing some potentially important information. In her rush to make notes of important information, she frequently found herself behind in the conversation, bringing up points that had already been covered while she was writing or thinking about a previous point.

Ellen found a two-pronged solution. She bought a small recorder to tape meetings and thus avoid losing key ideas she would need later. She also trained herself to make quick notes about her personal reactions to things that were being said. In this way, she was able to reduce the harmful effects of over-stimulation by taking away the self-imposed need to take detailed notes and was able to keep her concentration on the information currently being presented. By focusing one's attention on the *current* remarks of a speaker, you are better able to respond intelligently. With the taped back-up, Ellen could relax and devote her full attention to the points as they appeared in the speaker's presentation or remarks.

Don't Think About Elephants!

Suppose you were told, "Whatever you do, don't think about elephants!"

What do you think would be on your mind? Either you would be thinking about elephants, or you'd be trying very hard to *not* think about elephants. Either way, you've been distracted from what you wanted to do.

Causing a distraction is rude. There is little excuse for doing so. But, too often, tolerating a distraction can be just as damaging to your powers of listening as the actual distraction itself. Because many people can't control where or when a conversation with an employee will take place, they're at the mercy of all sorts of distractions—loud noise, others present within earshot, or phones ringing, for example. Trying to overcome these distractions by tolerating them can lead to some unfortunate consequences.

One operating group at General Motors had many opportunities to participate in staff meetings. The boss was a hard-working, capable manager, whose philosophy of management included a minimum number of meetings. When he did call a meeting, everyone of his employees knew that what he said would be important. There was plenty of motivation for good, active listening.

The boss had one disturbing habit. Every time he'd get up to talk, his hand would rattle the coins in his pocket. This was a distraction, and everyone in the meetings knew it. To compensate, everyone in the meeting worked very hard to overlook the obvious distraction. In fact, they tried too hard. Instead of being distracted by the jingling coins, they were distracted by the act of *tolerating the distraction*.

Good listeners who face distraction must walk a delicate balance. They must overlook the distraction itself, while not getting too wrapped up in tolerating it. When distractions do occur, try concentrating in a positive way on the ideas the other person is giving you. In this way, the distraction is minimized without the need for toleration.

Just the Facts, Nothing but the Facts

Everyone takes justifiable pride in being able to "size up" people and potential in a factual, objective way. Too much subjectivity, we've been told, leads to ill feelings, poor communications, and inefficiency in management.

Yet, listening only for facts is a filtering process that can be a source of noise or distortion. To learn more about a person or a situation, we must become more sensitive to the *context* as well as to the actual facts. Much can be learned from attitudes, feelings, and inferences. Blocking or filtering them out is a bad listening habit.

A good listener overcomes the "inference-observation" confusion by correctly labeling and using both kinds of information. Obviously, feelings and inferences alone are usually a poor guide to action. But so are facts alone.

Good, active listeners make lists, either on paper or in their heads. One list is titled "fact," a second "feelings/attitudes of the speaker," and perhaps a third labeled "how *I* feel about what the speaker said." Doing so accomplishes a number of good results. It helps a listener to avoid getting trapped with incomplete information. It correctly labels information for future use. It also helps to make sense out of a speaker whose remarks are not presented according to some outline.

Outline Everything

In school, we're taught to make an outline before writing or speaking. An outline helps us to organize thoughts in a logical manner and prevents confusion and rambling. There's no question about the importance of an outline to a sender.

However, most conversations and many formal presentations have no outline. Instead, the speaker simply says whatever pops into his or her mind. The words spoken may or may not be related to the subject being discussed. Trying to put those kinds of remarks into a neat, academic outline simply won't work.

Good listeners know this and avoid consciously trying to "shoehorn" everything into an outline. Instead, they use the three-column method for mental or written notes. On your note pad, draw two vertical lines down the page. Label one column "facts," another "opinions," and the third "my feelings." If a speaker in a formal presentation is speaking from an outline, the three-column notes you take will look like an outline. If not, your notes will still be well organized. You will have the best chance for coming away from the presentation or conversation with usable, meaningful information.

Suppose a production run was ruined because of incorrect material specifications, and the problem is discussed in a production meeting. Your meeting notes should show that your lead worker was suspicious of the specifications in the first place. Opinions *plus* facts can prevent a similar error in the future. If you try to outline the facts alone, you may "reinvent" the wheel and make the same error again.

The Listening Posture

Most of us can remember adults telling us to "sit up and pay attention when I'm talking to you!" A listening posture is important to the talker as well as the listener. If you slouch in your chair or let your eyes wander while someone is talking to you, you may give them the impression that you don't care for their ideas or their needs. You'll give negative body signals that may seriously damage communication. Using body language to encourage the speaker is a good strategy for improving communication, especially in small group conversations and discussions. (In Chapter 11, we discuss in detail how you can use your body language as a positive management tool.)

There is also a negative side to taking a listening "posture." Too often, we prepare to listen by sitting erect, eyes forward, arms folded on the chest or resting on the table, and chin up. Once this posture is assumed, we are then "absolved" from any blame if a communication failure does occur. Having taken a listening posture, the poor listener *assumes* that there is no way to keep from listening.

This attitude reflects the confusion between hearing and listening. As we've said, hearing is a physical activity. Taking a listening posture can help your ability to hear better. But hearing is not listening, and listening is mental activity. It requires conscious and continuous activity.

Test yourself. The next time you are in a meeting ask yourself if you are assuming too much by simply sitting in a listening position. Chances are, you find your mind wandering even though you feel mentally comfortable because you *think* you're listening.

Teachers and managers know that students and employees seem to be able to sleep with their eyes open. Don't fall into the bad habit of assuming that your physical posture *automatically* keeps you actively listening.

Reading the Funnies

Often, managers find themselves in a listening "rut" because they listen to the same kinds of people with the same problems day after day. They don't take (or make) opportunities to challenge and improve their listening skills. If you never read anything more challenging than the Sunday funnies, your ability to read will never grow beyond the funnies. The same is true of listening.

A common bad habit of listening is to listen only to familiar ideas and familiar people in familiar surroundings. This sameness quickly results in a severely limited ability to listen to (and understand) more complex and complicated ideas.

Good listeners challenge themselves regularly. A Texas supervisor in an airport maintenance shop regularly sits in on public lectures at a local community college. He admits that many of the speakers and their presentations are "way over his head," but he believes that this challenge helps keep his listening ability sharp, and prevents what he calls "mental rusting." You're no further away from listening challenges than your home television. All networks (especially the public television network) regularly present speakers and topics that challenge your listening ability. You don't have to agree with the speaker or share his viewpoint. You gain as an active listener by simply exposing yourself to a listening challenge and by working to take even one new idea from a difficult presentation. Managers who work in bilingual or multilingual environments can use television for another listening exercise. English-speaking managers report much improved communication with their French- or Spanish-speaking employees when they (the managers) develop the habit of watching some television programs broadcast in the "foreign" language. Try it. You may not actually learn a new language, but you will gain a better understanding of your non-English-speaking employees. By "tuning in" to Spanish- or French-accented speaking, your listening skills will be profitably improved.

Why Do We Daydream?

Have you ever found yourself in a listening situation in which your mind began to wander? For each of us, daydreaming is a common feeling. Listening experts tell us that part of the reason we daydream or wander while we're supposed to be listening is that our mind works faster than most talkers can talk. Most people speak about 125 words per minute in normal conversation. Yet, the average mind is able to listen to and comprehend as many as 400 words per minute. The wide difference between speaking and listening rates gives us plenty of time for daydreams.

Bad listeners have a habit of wasting this additional listening power. In contrast, good listeners use the speed differential to review what the speaker has already said and to anticipate where the speaker is going.

CORRECTING OUR "BAD" HABITS

We've examined several habits that can contribute to poor listening. For each bad habit, there is a corrective, a good habit to help make you a better listener. Let's summarize by looking at three positive strategies for becoming an active listener.

1. Anticipate the next point and how you'll respond to it.
2. Break down a conversation into its main and supporting elements.
3. Make periodic mental summaries and assure yourself that you're on the same tract as the speaker.

Listening and Counseling

Counseling is an important responsibility for all managers. To motivate, managers today must be prepared to go beyond simply watching the results. Motivation means communicating with employees as individuals. Their needs, problems and perceptions are directly related to their willingness to perform on the job.

Many managers feel that the problems of their employees have no place on the job. For these managers, counseling employees and listening to their problems is treated as a minor annoyance. Yet, as management becomes more and more tied to human behavior psychology, management people will be expected to operate comfortably on this level.

Even if you assume that counseling employees is not your responsibility, you cannot overlook the importance of actively listening to them. From years of psychoanalytical and psychological study of human behavior, experts have learned much that can be helpful in improving our listening skills.

Patience

When you're listening, let the other person finish what he or she is trying to say. Many people have great difficulty putting their thoughts and ideas into words. They pause, stammer, and repeat while trying to find the right words. If you try to rush them or finish the thought before the sentence is complete, you'll only succeed in causing more hesitation, more uncertainty. Even if you believe what you're being told is wrong (or irrelevant), give the speaker a chance at self-expression. You can help overcome reluctance or insecurity by giving simple signs of acceptance. These signs do not have to mean that you agree with the speaker, only that you are listening with interest and understanding.

Give Encouraging Gestures

Be mindful of the powerful impact of your nonverbal messages. Your posture, facial expression, hand gestures and voice cues all transmit messages to the person speaking. You can communicate disinterest or hostility by avoiding eye contact or by keeping your arms tightly crossed over your chest and your body turned away from the other person. Gestures can also be approving or encouraging. They can help put the prospect at ease and promote more open and honest communication. Try to maintain frequent eye contact without staring or looking "through" your speaker. Lean forward and keep your facial expression open and direct. Watch for opportunities to nod or murmur "I see" or "um-hm." None of these gestures need signify agreement, only interest and concern.

Listen for Feelings

Often, the most important things to listen for are the feelings and attitudes of the speaker. Even if a person is good at reporting facts or describing events, he or she may be unable to adequately express his or her needs, desires, and feelings. Careful attention to such detail is essential. As you listen, restate the other person's idea thought or feeling. With a brief but accurate restatement, you act as a mirror. You encourage your speaker to continue talking while you demonstrate your interest in his or her thoughts. Such comments as, "You say Joe seems to be the cause?" or "You feel that you're ready to be reconsidered?" don't have to imply anything on your part. Such statements simply help maintain a neutral listening environment.

You can use the same device to get more facts. Simply add a question mark to your voice as you restate the other person's thought. For example, if the speaker feels that your project is in trouble, you can respond by saying, "The project is in trouble?" With this encouragement, the speaker will likely amplify the statement and bring up some new facts, objections, or opinions. You can then make a more intelligent and informed response to those facts, objections, or opinions.

Because feelings are delicate and easily turned off, try to avoid direct or threatening statements at least until you have a firm grasp of the situation *as the speaker sees it*. Comments such as "You're wrong," "Hold on a minute, look at the facts," or "I don't believe you" can quickly put the speaker into a defensive (and less communicative) mood. Even if you know the speaker is wrong (or worse, lying), try to keep your verbal responses and body expressions neutral for as long as possible. Later, you may want to take the offensive and probe areas where contradictions appear. However, as long as the speaker volunteers information and that information is relevant to solving a problem, challenging the speaker can be unproductive.

What You Don't Say

Listen for what the speaker is saying and listen also for what the speaker is not saying. Omission of particular parts of a subject or problem even after some encouragement from you may indicate that the subject is delicate. It may be the clue to solving a problem. Many of us cover up our reluctance to discuss certain facts by using too many cliches or by repeating facts already mentioned. Develop a sensitivity to cliches and contents and to obvious evasions or omissions. They may be important clues.

A polygraph (lie detector) is designed to measure very small changes in heartbeat, skin temperature, and dryness. The machines work on the assumption that there is a direct relationship between these changes and a person's conscious attempts to avoid the truth. As an active listener, you can use this concept to your advantage. Watch for hand gestures (gripping tightly, sweaty palms), excessive eye contact, or squirming in the chair. These and other signals may tip you off to a lie, or an evasion of important facts. Naturally, you can't be as sensitive or accurate as a polygraph, but you can measurably improve your ability to read signals.

Watch the Great "I"

Beware of too much direct personal involvement, especially in the early stages of a conversation. If the speaker really wants to hear your thoughts or opinion, give an honest reply. Too much evasion on your part can be damaging. There is, of course, no rule that applies in all cases. Wherever possible during a listening encounter, reflect the speaker's views and try to avoid direct statement of personal views. Often, managers find that employees ask for their opinion to know what things are appropriate to discuss. "Reading the boss" may be useful to employees, but it can seriously hamper identification of problems.

It is a common human emotion to like being told what we want to hear. However, when people play "guess what you're thinking," good communication suffers. By keeping your opinions and ideas out of a conversation, you encourage free and more open communication.

Along with holding back your personal views (or those of your organization), good listeners also avoid getting themselves emotionally involved. Too much emotion is bad because it can quickly pull the listening encounter away from where it ought to be.

Allow Time

Nothing subverts good managerial communication more than interruptions. When you are talking or listening to an employee, try to find a time and place where your conversation can continue uninterrupted. Even when the subject under discussion is impersonal or unimportant, an employee will quickly lose track of his or her thoughts when other people pop in unexpectedly or when the telephone rings. A good listening setting is one where people communicating are free from unnecessary interruption.

Listening can also be improved when there is enough time to allow a thorough airing of all sides of an issue or problem. A thought left hanging because time ran out is likely to be distorted or forgotten when the discussion resumes. Cutting short an employee before the central problem has been resolved can lead to employee feelings of frustration and anger. Although permitting the conversation to continue its natural course may take time, the investment is probably well worth the cost.

Allowing time to listen also means picking a *good time* to communicate. Late in the afternoon (especially Friday afternoon), employees and their managers are usually tired or are thinking about the upcoming weekend. Listening becomes tedious, and conflicts are more likely to get out of hand. Early in the week and in the morning are usually better times to schedule conferences, especially to solve problems. However, don't overlook the fact that people operate with different body "clocks." Some of us are early risers, at our best in the morning. Others, given the chance, would sleep late and stay up late at night. These people are usually at their "peak" in the after-noon. As a manager, you will likely prefer to schedule meetings and counsel-ing sessions when you're at your best, during your "peak" part of the day. This way, you can put your best efforts into solving problems.

If the person you're working with operates on a different body cycle, you may want to reschedule the meeting to a time better suited to the employee. Better yet, see if you can agree on a mutually beneficial time for your meeting.

This means that you must do some subjective research on your employees. Discover from their actions and conversations what their "peak" and "valley" times are during the day. A sales manager in Illinois teaches each of his sales-people to keep detailed records about each customer. Those records include the salesperson's estimate of each customer's body clock cycle and the best time to call on the customer to make a sale. Many managers do the same with each of their employees. Having this information helps them plan general staff meetings as well as personal and small group conferences.

The place of the listening "encounter" is just as important as the timing, and, in Chapter 9 on space communications, we look closely at many of the considerations for more effective use of space. Some managers feel that "any place is just fine for a conversation with an employee." Others feel that "when my people stop me in the halls or in the shop, I'm obligated to talk with them, listen to their problems and gripes, and give my best advice right there on the spot." Clearly, there are situations in which it is wrong to tell an employee that he or she should "make an appointment" to talk over a problem. The employee might get the idea that his or her problem just "isn't important to the boss" or that "they never have time for us!" Even moving from the hallway or the shop floor into a nearby office or storeroom may hamper the spontaneous nature of the conversation and make the employee feel less like communi-cating his or her true feelings. However, whenever it is possible, try to locate your employee counseling sessions or meetings in places where there will be a minimum of interruptions and distractions.

Don't make the mistake of a Florida manager who held staff meetings in a beautiful conference room, with ceiling-to-floor windows looking out over a lush park. While the setting was close to perfect, the combination of the meeting place and time was anything but perfect. The staff meetings always seemed to be scheduled at the same time the neighboring bank employees held their soccer practices in the park. The sight of men and women running around in soccer uniforms and enjoying themselves proved to be far more appealing than concentrating on the boss's agenda for the staff meeting.

Once you've scheduled your meeting with an employee, hold it in a business-like setting. A quiet office, a conference room, or a private lounge is preferable to the cafeteria, hallway, or locker room where interruptions and distractions can and will occur. Comfortable chairs, appropriate lighting, display or writing areas when necessary should all be a part of a good listening environment. If you don't have an office and your organization doesn't provide proper space for manager-employee counseling, arranging for such an area should be a top-priority item for you and your fellow managers. Your effectiveness as listeners and counselors will be greatly enhanced.

Know When to End the Conversation

There are two thoughts about stopping a conversation with an employee. First, it is important that a manager recognize when the productive part of a meeting or discussion is coming to an end. Carrying on any longer will usually be counterproductive. Failing to end a successful sales conversation at the right time can lead the employee to later become dissatisfied with the conclusions or agreements reached.

A meeting or discussion should also be ended when it becomes obvious that nothing is likely to be accomplished. If too many interruptions, open hostility, confrontations, or insurmountable objections have irreparably damaged communication, subsequent discussion will be unproductive and possibly even dangerous. When this happens, end the meeting or conversation as soon as possible. Be sure to set a specific time and place to resume discussions. If you don't, the employee may feel his or her problem is being "swept under the rug."

Ways to Improve Your Communication Skills

In this chapter, we've looked at listening from a number of viewpoints. Let's briefly reconsider a few useful ideas for improving listening.

1. When in conversation, keep the tone loose and informal. Use the employee's first name or surname (depending on the relationship established). Use "you" frequently also.
2. Use words familiar to the employee. A listening situation is no time to impress the employee with your technical knowledge or command of the language.
3. Be frank. When asked a direct question, give as much honest information as possible.
4. Be wary of humor that hurts or offends. You may use humor to loosen or relax tension and may unwittingly offend the employee. This can only result in blocked communication. What's funny and quite innocent to you may be offensive to another. Humor is an excellent way to reduce tension and make way for an informal rapport—if it is used wisely and sparingly.
5. Avoid passing judgment or making moralizing statements, especially when the topic is only slightly related to the main topic or problem.
6. Control your lips and eyebrows. Together, these two parts of your face convey the vast majority of nonverbal facial messages. Arching brows, sneering, contemptuous gestures are troublemakers for listeners and speakers alike.
7. Watch your talking speed. Don't go too fast, or too slow. Keep your tone of voice well modulated. Speak in a low, quiet manner, with confidence but not with overbearing authority.
8. Whenever possible, praise rather than threaten or cajole.
9. Hearing is not listening. Listening is an active process that involves understanding, evaluating, and assimilating.
10. When listening failures occur, don't automatically assume that it's the other person's fault.
11. Identify and take steps to correct your personal bad habits of listening.
12. Listen for what is not being said and for feelings as well as facts.
13. Be mindful of body language. Give approving, encouraging gestures and refrain from "negative" feedback.
14. Practice and self-awareness are needed by most of us before we can listen and persuade effectively. Often, we assume positive, self-confident roles, making decisions and giving orders. Clearly, "persuasive listening" calls for a sharp change in pace. Unless you develop the self-discipline and humility to listen respectfully, you're likely to lose touch with people, dramatically increasing the potential for misunderstanding and other communication failures.

Further Reading

For more information, you might want to read:

EDMOND G. ADDEO AND ROBERT E. BURGER, EGO SPEAK (Bantam Books)

Ego Speak is the art of boosting our own egos by speaking only of what we want to talk about and not caring about what other people want to talk about. This book is a systematic catalog of the major types of this very human form of communication problem. The authors have developed examples of the many ways in which we appear to communicate but, in fact, say nothing. The authors describe a number of the kinds of ego speak games and develop some important suggestions for handling these kinds of problems. The authors suggest that *Ego Speak* is the problem of verbal noncommunication — the thousands of ways in which we let our egos get in the ways of what we really want to say. As a result, nobody listens to us, perhaps because we don't listen to them.

LAWRENCE L. STEINMETZ, INTERVIEWING SKILLS FOR SUPERVISORY PERSONNEL (Addison-Wesley)

This book discusses in detail how to conduct a successful interview; it is specifically designed so managers and supervisors can develop their interviewing skills and select their employees more effectively. The book includes guidelines on counseling, discipline, evaluation of employee performance, and understanding employee problems.

RALPH NICOLS AND LEONARD STEVENS, ARE YOU LISTENING? (McGraw-Hill)

This book is a classic in the area of listening. The authors not only expand on the idea that we are all subject to various bad habits of listening, but they also develop some unique and very useful insights that can help a manager develop some positive listening strategies.

6

Making Meetings Work

"... meetings fulfill a deep human need. Man is a social species. In every organization ... people come together in small groups. If there are no meetings at work people will meet in Pubs after work."

Antony Jay

Few people like meetings. Most managers feel that meetings take up too much time, that they seldom seem to really settle anything. Giving a problem to a committee, they feel, is the surest way to "study" it to death. Many managers also feel that they can get more real work done if they meet privately for five minutes with each of several people than they can by calling everyone together for a two-hour meeting. Despite the feelings and hostilities that meetings seem to trigger, it is also an indisputable fact that organizations run on meetings. It is also true that people will meet together even if formal business meetings are abolished. In all organizations, meetings are events where problems are supposedly solved, where new ideas are hatched, and where communication takes place in an atmosphere of cooperation and openness. Whether we like them or not, meetings are a fact of life for organizations and their managers. Meetings present opportunities for face-to-face communication and can be valuable aids in planning and problem solving.

In the next few pages, we'll look at some of the various types of meetings in which managers find themselves, and we'll discuss some of the problems associated with meetings. As one who leads and attends meetings, you'll find some ways to improve the benefits you and others derive from such meetings.

WHAT IS A MEETING?

A meeting in an organization is a gathering of a number of people. They assemble for some purpose in a relatively formal setting. This definition ignores small group informal discussions and "bull sessions" as well as the formal and informal encounters between a manager and one other person. These other kinds of encounters are important, but the things that happen in them are quite different from what happens in a more formal meeting.

There are several different types of organizational meetings.[1] For example, there is often a daily meeting attended by all managers at a given level or in a certain area of responsibility (such as production) to discuss schedules and current operating problems. The periodic meeting is held weekly, monthly, or annually. These meetings are usually designed to bring people from various departments in the organization up to date with current activities in other departments. Of course, the corporate annual meeting is an opportunity for the top management of an organization to meet with stockholders and others interested in the organization's affairs. The agenda and the activities of these meetings vary from one organization to another, although most annual meetings do include an election of members to the board of directors. Because the annual meeting is a special kind of meeting, it is beyond our immediate concern here. Another major type of meeting is the "special" meeting. This is a meeting scheduled to deal with an unusual topic or to bring together people who don't normally have regular face-to-face contact in the organization. The most productive and least troublesome meetings in most organizations are the scheduled daily staff meetings. They are usually brief, direct, and to the point. Because there is a specific goal or target for the people attending these meetings, they can usually be finished quickly and with a minimum of discord or power struggle.

In all these kinds of meetings, there are certain formalities to be observed. There are also many reasons for holding meetings. Before examining ways to improve communication in meetings, let's examine some of the reasons for holding these meetings.

WHY HOLD MEETINGS?

Perhaps the best reason for holding meetings is that it is an opportunity for face-to-face communication. Information can be quickly given to people in a meeting, whereas it may take a lot more time and effort to get the same information to people using other media. A meeting also provides an opportunity to check the accuracy of the messages being sent. If information is sent to employees in a written memo, the writer can't be sure if every one will read and understand the message. The same message given in a meeting can be emphasized, highlighted with examples, and repeated for accuracy.

Although face-to-face communication is clearly a major benefit of meetings, meetings are not always the most effective way for an organization's management to reach its goals. In a recent "time management" seminar, several junior executives listed the "morning staff meeting" as their greatest single time waster. On closer questioning, they admitted that the meetings *themselves* were not really time wasters. Rather, it was the *way* the meetings were scheduled and run that made them time wasters. For example in one company, the staff meeting was scheduled for 9 A.M. every morning. Yet, there were days when the meeting didn't start until almost 10:00 A.M. The people at the meeting had to wait until everyone arrived before getting underway, even though the late-arriving staff people may have had little or nothing to contribute to the meeting itself. Another complaint about these staff meetings was the requirement that each person attending list aloud for the group all current problems being tackled by that person. This listing was required even when none of the individual's problems that day were critical. These complaints were included with other staff meeting problems, such as loose or nonexistent agendas, overly talkative participants, poor physical settings, and generally bad meeting scheduling. The complaints usually end with the same question, "Why do we hold meetings, anyway?"

CAUSES OF DISSATISFACTION WITH MEETINGS

While we're on the subject of general complaints about meetings, it might be useful to briefly review some of the major causes of dissatisfaction in meetings. Aside from the irritating complaints, there are some fundamental communication problems that detract from successful meetings in all organizations.

1. Anticipation of a Decision

Those attending a meeting may anticipate that a decision will be reached in this meeting. This feeling may result from being told that a meeting has been called to make a decision. It could also develop simply because the person attending *wants* a decision to result and, therefore, unconsciously convinces himself that what he wants is true. Either way, when a person believes that a decision will be reached, he or she is likely to be quite disappointed with the meeting as it actually transpires. Despite some productive outcomes from the meeting, the decision seeker will come away unhappy and possibly unwilling to again participate in another meeting.

Think of your own reaction when you attended a meeting to finally resolve a problem, only to find that no solution was even planned for that meeting. Our expectations play a major role in perception. If you expect no gifts on your birthday, you'll not likely be too disappointed if you get only a small gift. However, if you expected a motorboat or a new bowling ball, you'll likely be let down if your gift is *only* a new watch. The same principle applies to the perceived satisfaction we receive from meetings.

The best approach as a meeting goer is to learn as much as possible before a meeting about what is likely to happen. This is, of course, more important and more difficult to do for periodic or special meetings than it is for regular, daily staff meetings. As one who regularly calls other people to attend meetings, you can improve their perceived satisfaction with your meetings by letting them know in advance what they can expect to get out of the meeting. It's also a good idea to tell them what to bring to the meeting. Participation is much more likely if those attending a meeting are prepared in advance.

2. Personal Agendas

Individuals are often likely to pursue their own personal objectives in a meeting. Each person attending has a personal agenda that he or she would like to accomplish in the meeting. However, despite one's personal objectives, others attending a meeting often feel dissatisfied with the meeting if one or two persons are allowed to take over or run the meeting. Because those attending a meeting will believe the meeting to have been successful or useful if they feel their personal goals to have been met, the challenge for the person running a meeting is to give everyone in the meeting a positive attitude that ties their personal goals to the group's goals, while moving the entire group toward the goals that you have in mind. Letting the group go with one person's ideas will create satisfactory communications only with the one who gets to lead. However, if all people in a meeting feel that they've been treated fairly with opportunities to express their personal point of view, satisfactory communication for all will have been achieved.

3. Disunity Leads to Dissatisfaction

Disunity in a meeting can lead to participants' feeling dissatisfied with the meeting and indirectly dissatisfied with the meeting leader as well. Many of us feel frustrated when a meeting develops into a row over some minor point. Clearly, it is not always possible to have a meeting where everyone is in harmony and agreement. In fact, such a meeting may not be very productive, nor will it always lead to the best solution to a problem. However, it may not be the actual difference of opinion that other people perceive as dissatisfying.

Rather, research into group dynamics suggests that dissatisfaction comes from the polarization that in turn results from disunity. Indeed, the real threat to success is that productive disagreement between various groups in a meeting can degenerate into hostility and polarization.

The danger of truly democratic leadership is that it can lead to a desire on the leader's part to let open interaction in a group run its course, even when that interaction turns unproductive. As long as the meeting leader is able to keep the group on track, differences of opinion should not lead to dissatisfaction.

4. Task Versus Self-orientation

Meeting participants who are task oriented are less likely to be dissatisfied with any given meeting than those who are self-oriented. This point refers to the earlier notion that people are inclined to pursue different goals. Those persons with personal goals oriented toward the task before the group are a joy for most group leaders. This does not mean that such persons will always agree with the leader's point of view. Rather, they will be inclined to devote their attention to the task and will not likely get caught up in power struggles.

On the other hand, the self-oriented person does not see meetings as problem-solving sessions. Rather, he or she attends meetings to give and receive signals about interpersonal relationships. These people come to a meeting to demonstrate where they stand in the organization's "informal" hierarchy. They like to point out and reinforce their status roles vis-à-vis their colleagues' and co-workers'. The task or problem facing the people in a meeting is called the *content* part of the meeting. In contrast, the concern over who sits next to whom is the *relationship* level of the meeting. A good meeting leader attempts to keep the attention of the group focused on the content while in some way trying to satisfy those who consider relationship messages more important. Because self-oriented people are more likely to be dissatisfied with any meeting regardless of how the leader operates it, the key communication strategy for the meeting leader is to keep self-oriented people from taking over the meeting and distracting the content people from their mission. This can often be done by permitting relationship level people to play their games of seating arrangements as long as they don't disturb the content goals of the group.

The insurance division manager of an Atlanta-based company followed this advice by constantly changing the seating arrangements for staff meetings. She would arrive first and sit in a different seat at the meeting table each week. While the self-oriented people looked around to mentally assess the significance of this week's seating, the rest of the people (task oriented) could carry on their business. By the time the self-oriented people had the relationship messages worked out, the meeting was almost over. They had had little or no time to raise and discuss their self-oriented hidden agenda items.

PROCEDURAL VERSUS CONTENT CONTROL

Determining the reasons for people's dissatisfaction in meetings can lead us to some interesting and useful conclusions. In general, most of the dissatisfaction that people express with meetings is in the area of process rather than content. Content, as we've already noted, refers to the topics discussed and the problems solved in a meeting. Content also involves what is said in a meeting. Process refers to the way in which the meeting is run, who gets to speak, and whose rules are being followed. When people diagree, it is usually over matters of content. People form opinions and take conflicting stands on issues, which must then be negotiated and resolved in a meeting. Despite the obvious conclusion that disagreements develop over content matters, most people are dissatisfied because of procedural matters. The leader must avoid even the appearance of playing favorites, while moving the entire meeting toward a set of realistic and, it is hoped, meaningful goals.

One very good way to maintain process control over a meeting is to listen carefully for clues or signals from those who are potentially the major contributors to a possible solution. Often, when people have an *opportunity* to participate in a meeting, they have more satisfaction with both the meeting itself and the outcome or decision reached in the meeting. However, some managers interpret this to mean that we *must* have participation.

To follow through on this interpretation, the meeting leader will call on everyone in the meeting to comment on something. This makes some people uncomfortable, as they may have nothing to say. They may also feel uncomfortable if they're forced to express themselves in front of others. Despite advice to the contrary, many executives conclude every meeting by going around the table and asking each person for concluding thoughts or observations. The employees often hate this process because, after the first few people have spoken, there's nothing much new to say. They feel imposed on by their boss, who thinks he or she is improving participation by requiring participation.

A better approach to procedural control is to give people in a meeting the opportunity to participate when they feel that they have something to contribute. The leader can give such an opportunity by constantly searching around the meeting and looking for eye or hand or body signals that say, "I'd like to speak". Some people are naturally talkative and find it easy to jump in anywhere and make a comment. Others have difficulty expressing themselves, especially if they're forced to do so. When open communication in a meeting is clearly possible, those attending will feel much more satisfied with the meeting's outcome. This is especially true when the purpose of a meeting is to reach some sort of decision on an important matter. In an interview, the chairman of the board of Montgomery Ward noted that "the most useful skill for any manager is open communications. To be effective in today's business environment, you must include in decision making meetings all those who must later execute your policy decisions. You cannot constantly surprise your people and expect to retain their confidence. Whether they win or lose on a decision is not as important as recognition that their point of view was considered."[2]

PARTICIPATION AND TIMING

A good meeting leader encourages participation and pays close attention to signals from others. The process part of a meeting can also be improved by the leader's skill as a listener. National Football League Commissioner Pete Rozell is reputed to be an excellent meeting leader. He never shouts and seldom raises his voice. Yet, no matter how controversial the meeting, he's always in complete command. According to his supporters and his detractors among the team owners, his secret for effective meeting leadership lies in his almost perfect sense of timing. According to these same individuals, Rozell "does a lot of listening. He lets people debate. But his timing is impeccable. He knows exactly when to say something."[3] Process control of a meeting won't overcome the serious problems that people might have with the topic under discussion, but it can help improve both the effectiveness of the meeting and the satisfaction of those attending.

SOME MEETING PROBLEMS TO AVOID

We've already discussed many of the important causes of individual dissatisfaction with meetings, and we've explored the notion of maintaining communication control over a meeting's process rather than its content. Let's continue with a review of some problems that executives should recognize and avoid when running meetings.

1. Holding regular meetings just for the sake of meeting is the cause of many problems.[4] When employees know that nothing substantive is going to be done at the "regular weekly meeting," they're likely to become bored with the entire meeting process. Obviously, this doesn't matter in the regular meeting, because nothing was happening anyway. The problem develops when the manager must hold an important special meeting, and staff reacts to it in the same way that they react to the regular meeting. Meetings just for the sake of meeting also encourage sloppy employee habits. Prompt attendance or attention to an agenda gets lost quickly when meetings become a routine bore. Once formed, these same habits can affect the employee's performance in other parts of his or her job.

2. A related problem is that of employees' attending meetings without doing their "homework." Good meetings depend on well-prepared participants. Here, managers can use both formal and informal messages to handle the problem. If your people are habitually unprepared for discussion or if they

come to meetings with important facts and figures incomplete, impress on them privately your desire for all employees to be prepared for meetings. If possible, avoid giving such a reprimand before a group of people, unless everyone at the meeting is guilty. Above all, set a positive example by always being prepared for the meetings you attend, whether you are the meeting leader or simply an attendee. As with so many areas of managerial communication, the most effective manager is one who communicates to employees that he or she is willing to do whatever is also being asked of subordinates.

3. Avoid bad meeting sites. Some locations don't provide the right atmosphere for an effective meeting and should be avoided. Review the physical arrangements for your meetings and correct immediately any glaring deficiencies. Distractions (including windows with a "tempting" view), outside noise, interruptions, distance from the work area, and comfort of the chairs are all important concerns. Although such matters may not seem important by themselves, an unfortunate combination of several such factors can ruin an otherwise well-prepared and well-run meeting.

4. Keep the meeting under time control. Long meetings rarely accomplish as much as short meetings, simply because we all find it difficult to concentrate for long periods of time. The old expression "the mind can absorb what the posterior can endure" is very true. There are some very good reasons for holding long meetings. Often, there's simply a large number of items on the agenda, items that must be covered at a given meeting. If a group is badly divided on an issue, a marathon meeting may get participants talking about possible solutions, whereas a series of shorter meetings would break their train of concentration. Skilled labor negotiators often resort to marathon meetings to keep opposing groups from lobbying during breaks for additional support for their position. Some meetings run long simply because everyone has a lot to say and wants to say it.

Whenever possible, keep your meetings short and focused. If necessary, schedule a follow-up meeting to resolve any unfinished business, but keep all meetings within strict time boundaries. An excellent way to keep a meeting on target and within reasonable time limits is to develop an agenda for every meeting and make the agenda available in advance to those who will be attending. However, although an agenda is important to any meeting, it is just one part of your preparations for a meeting. Therefore, let's turn our attention next to some other aspects of preparing to meet.

PREPARING TO MEET

Assuming that there is a clear purpose to holding a meeting, several preparatory steps should be taken before a meeting gets under way.

Keep the number of people attending the meeting to a reasonably workable number. Generally, this means no more than eight to ten people. By restricting the number of participants, it's possible to keep better control of the meeting. It's also easier to permit more opportunities for everyone to participate if they wish. Some managers suggest that meeting leaders exercise their power by inviting certain people to attend their meetings, leaving out others who might have expected to come. If you can control who attends, don't be persuaded to change your mind by pleas from outsiders not invited. Although the most desirable situation is to hold down the number of attendees, it's not always really possible every time.

When you're forced into meeting with a large number of people, there are many useful and productive communication strategies that can be used.

1. ***Stagger Attendance.*** With a well-developed agenda, it may be possible to have some people attend at one time to discuss certain items and have others arrive later to discuss other items. For example, if you supervise people in several departments, it might be possible to have one department's staff meet at 2:00 P.M. to talk about their concerns. The other employees can be scheduled to arrive at 2:30 P.M., when matters of general concern are discussed. At 3:30 P.M., the early arrivals can be dismissed, and matters relevant to the later-arriving department discussed. With this approach, it's possible to accomplish several objectives while meeting effectively with a larger number of people.

2. ***Split the Meeting into Two Meetings.*** If there's little overlap between two parts of a group, it might be possible to hold two separate meetings. Although this approach certainly cuts the number of people attending, it also presents some problems. For example, it may become necessary to repeat a part of the meeting and, thereby, risk giving slightly different messages to the two groups. If there is a rivalry between the two sections, meeting with one group before the other may be interpreted as favoritism toward one group of employees. Also, it might be very difficult to schedule two separate meetings, especially if everyone in the large group must meet face to face to work out a problem.

3. ***Use Subcommittees.*** This approach to group problem solving is used with varying degrees of effectiveness by most legislative bodies. The U.S. House of Representatives has 465 members, too many to properly conduct effective group meetings. Thus, the members are assigned to various committees, and the committees, in turn, are divided into many specialized subcommittees. At the subcommittee level, small groups of men and women meet and discuss problems and issues in their specialty area. The subcommittee votes and prepares a report to be presented to the full committee. In turn, the full committee considers and votes on the subcommittee's recommendations and forwards those recommendations to the full House of Representatives for a vote. Managers who work through group communication and decision making

can use somewhat the same technique. By giving small committees of employees the responsibility for making recommendations, it's possible to overcome many of the problems usually associated with large group meetings. There are also some important managerial side benefits to such an approach. When small groups are responsible for certain kinds of recommendations, they're more likely to work conscientiously on meeting their responsibilities. They will also have more opportunity to actively participate in the small subcommittee than they would in the larger group. Again, we're addressing the issue of perceived opportunity to participate and its relationship to both meeting effectiveness and individual satisfaction with the meeting and the leader.

4. *Seed Planting*. Managers who rely on meetings to get decisions made or implemented find that their meetings go much smoother if they do a bit of advance groundwork. In political campaigns, candidates use "advance" people to arrive in a town well before the candidate. These people arrange for transportation, hotels, meals, meeting rooms, and services; they also try to anticipate political and schedule problems and solve them before the candidate arrives. In the same way, some advance conversations with key opinion makers and important dissenters will help you run a smoother meeting. This should not imply that the important business of the meeting be conducted privately before the meeting. Rather, advance work can plant some seeds for harmony and cooperation in the meeting, by giving the leader a better idea of what issues might be raised and how much support there might be for various positions on those issues. Such advance work can also help the meeting leader develop the all-important agenda for the meeting. Even though it's just a simple piece of paper, a meeting agenda is perhaps the single most important communication device in any meeting. Let's look at the agenda and how it should be planned and used by the meeting leader.

THE AGENDA

An agenda is simply an outline of the topics and issues to be discussed in a meeting. Usually, the topics are arranged in their order of importance, although other arrangements can be used. For example, some meeting leaders prefer to list topics starting with those that can be disposed of quickly. This arrangement saves the controversial or time-consuming topics until the end of the meeting. Often, this strategy is based on the hope that at the end of the meeting people will be less inclined to argue and rehash the issue, and therefore it too can be disposed of much faster than if the same topic were discussed at the start of the meeting. Other leaders prefer to list agenda items into natural groupings such as financial matters, personnel policies, services, and miscellaneous. This arrangement works well with a "staggered arrival" meeting, where people attend the meeting only to participate in discussion of one topic or problem area.

Regardless of how the agenda is organized, it should follow some well-established communication principles.

1. *It Should Be Specific.* The topics on an agenda should be listed in terms that people will understand. Thus, a topic listed as "training" tells people attending the meeting very little about what will actually be discussed. Instead, the item might read "Analysis of new employee training to spot and eliminate overlaps and duplication." This way, those attending can get their thoughts together, rather than having the real training issues sprung on them in the meeting. There is no general rule for the number of words each agenda item should contain. The best approach is to give an adequately detailed description of the topic, in understandable language.

2. *It Should Highlight.* People attending meetings prepare for them in different ways. Items "for information" usually need little advance preparation. Many leaders use codes, symbols, or words to indicate on a meeting agenda exactly what's to be done with a topic. This device also helps reduce the dissatisfaction that some people feel in meetings, because it keeps their expectations in line with what's actually going to happen. Thus, if Elaine is interested in the new scheduling system, she'll naturally want to attend those meetings where the system is on the agenda. However, if Elaine's only interested in voting on the merits of the new system, she is likely to be dissatisfied if the system is simply reviewed in the meetings. Her dissatisfaction will be even greater if she's made a special effort to attend the meeting, only to find that no decision is to be reached. With a highlighted agenda, Elaine and others interested in making a decision on a matter can be told in advance if the item is "for review," "update and status report," or "final decision to be made."

3. *It Should Include Timing.* An increasing number of executives are adding a new wrinkle to their meeting agendas. Alongside each item on the agenda, these executives list an estimate of the amount of discussion time that will be given. Then, during the meeting, the chairman announces the approximate time for the next item and asks if anyone feels more time should be given. When the allotted time expires, the chairman calls for someone to summarize what's been said on the matter, asks for a vote if one is scheduled, and moves on to the next topic. Executives who use this device report that their meetings take much less time than before. Also, when people know how much time is allotted for discussing a certain topic, they usually come into the meeting better prepared and get right to the point with a minimum small talk and irrelevant chatter. Obviously, it's not always possible to accurately estimate how long a topic will take, but such estimates do help the leader keep the group's attention focused. The agenda is also very useful in keeping yourself on schedule and keeping your employees on time too. By keeping trivia to

a minimum, you contribute to more effective meeting communications and reduce dissatisfaction with meetings as much as possible.

4. *It Should Include Agenda Papers (Where Necessary).* When items for discussion require those attending the meeting to read a large quantity of information, this information can be circulated with the agenda. However, it's often helpful if the person arranging the meeting can also organize the accompanying information in its approximate order of importance and with underlines or marginal notes where appropriate. It's foolish to assemble a meeting of employees and then waste their time and yours by sitting around a table reading page after page of background information that could have been as easily read well before the meeting.

5. *It Should Preclude "Open-End" Items.* Some meeting leaders insist on listing "other" or TBA (to be announced) as the last item on every agenda. Presumably, they do this to cover any last minute matters that come up after the agenda is published. However, it's not really necessary, as the meeting leader is always free to add items to the agenda or to call for additional items from those at the meeting. What very often happens is that the open-end item becomes an invitation for anyone to bring up any matter however trivial, simply because it's expected. A crisp agenda that limits topics will likely to be interpreted as unchangeable. As such, it leaves the meeting leader in much better control than when the open-end item is used.

6. *It Should Be Balanced.* A good agenda is one that gives those at the meetings a break between work sessions. This can be done by balancing or mixing working items with reporting items. Working items are topics that require active discussion and analysis. Reporting items are usually handled by one person who speaks while the others listen. By mixing these chores, the leader gives the participants some well-deserved breaks but does not interrupt the communication flow in the meeting.

7. *It Should Be Short.* Generally, the best agenda (and the best meeting) is the one that allows for full discussion of all important issues and still finishes within a reasonable time. There is no absolute rule on the length of a meeting. Still, any meeting over two hours is likely to be too long.

8. *But Don't Fear a Long Agenda.* This may seem to contradict the preceding paragraph above, but it really does not. Some managers think that circulating a long, detailed agenda will demoralize or "turn off" those attending and will keep attendance low. However, this is not usually the case. In fact, a long or detailed agenda should not be feared, as long as the items on the agenda are important and their importance has been clearly established with enough detail and support information.

9. *It Should Be Remembered that People Forget.* Agendas should be circulated two or three days before the meeting. This will give those attending enough time to prepare, read the supporting material, and schedule the meeting time on their calendars. If the agenda comes out right before the meeting, it's obviously better than no advance agenda at all—but not much. On the other hand, when agendas are sent out too far before the meeting, people tend to forget about the meeting. They tend to put off their advance reading and preparation, thinking that there's still plenty of time later to do so. You'll have to judge for yourself what lead time is best for those attending your meetings. A little experimenting with lead times and agenda formats can be quite useful.

10. *It Should Sandwich the Conflicts.* Some agenda items will predictably cause dissention and conflict among those in the meeting, whereas other items will bring the group together. If your seed planting and advance work indicates considerable argument on a certain topic, try to schedule it for the middle of the meeting. That way, you can open the meeting with some noncontroversial items and end the meeting with an item which will bring everyone together. Possible unifiers include a review of a recently completed successful project or some good news that everyone can enjoy. If it's likely that a lot of tension will develop from certain items, a light or humorous item at the end of the agenda can relieve the tension and help bring the group back together. Leaving a group in a state of discord is a poor managerial tactic. It can be avoided by some simple advance planning and some sensitivity to the human needs that develop in all interpersonal communications.

THE MEETING UNDERWAY

Once the meeting is underway, the chairman must provide the necessary direction and guidance to bring the discussion and interaction to a satisfactory conclusion. A good meeting leader should keep several concerns in mind as the meeting progresses.

1. *Keep in Mind the Effects of Space and Distance Relationships.* Generally, a meeting room should be arranged in some sort of a circle. This allows for face-to-face contact and, therefore, maximum participation. When people are seated in rows facing in the same direction, they will be easier to control but they will also be less likely to interact freely. If your advance planning indicates that several people will be taking opposing sides on an issue, you can use your knowledge of space relationships to your advantage in two directions. We know that, when people sit on opposite sides of a table looking directly at

each other, the arrangement is most conducive to discord, hostility, and argument. This does not mean that an argument will *always* break out when people sit on opposite sides, only that conditions are more favorable for such a conflict to blossom. Therefore, if you want to encourage conflict and a full airing of both sides of an issue, put the "spokesmen" for the two sides on opposite sides of the table. If you want to minimize their differences, put them on the same side, separated by one or two persons who are somewhat neutral on the issue. This way, you reduce the conditions for open hostility and keep the meeting more under your control. This kind of careful space planning can backfire. If your research indicates that two people will be disagreeing, you can make it difficult for them to get into an open conflict, but you can't eliminate the conflict completely. You may also seat opposite the antagonist persons who are neutral on an important issue and therefore are "safe buffers." The trouble is, however, that it's often difficult to predict if the "safe" person opposite will remain safe or will join the opposition and create a new kind of conflict. As with other agenda preparations, the best approach to space planning is to experiment with various seating arrangements until you find one that's best.

Another space is the prestige position of sitting on the boss's left-hand side. Many people mistakenly think the leader's right-hand side is the favored position. However, there may be a simple reason for this. "In ancient times, it was easier to stab to your left with the dagger in the right hand, than to use your right hand in trying to stab someone seated on your left, which is almost impossible since it requires a backhand thrust. It was therefore prudent to place a powerful guest on your left ... while you, of course, would be in an excellent position to stab him."[5] In some groups, people actually push to be seated in this favored spot or arrive early to get "their own seat." If you want to reduce the effects of such maneuvers, you can begin by assigning people to chairs on a sort of rotation. That way, everyone gets to sit in the "most favored position." Another approach is to ignore whoever is sitting in the favored position. The others will quickly learn their perception of a favored spot is not all that it's assumed to be. A third strategy is to follow our earlier advice about relationship-oriented people in meetings.

2. *Encourage (But Don't Force) Everyone to Participate.* Read and interpret silence as one of several possibilities. A person might be silent simply because he or she has nothing to contribute or perhaps feels satisfied with the meeting, the leader, or the progress that's been made so far. Of course, silence can also be a sign of disinterest or hostility. Don't become paranoid when individuals are silent. Do give them opportunities to speak up and participate. Be especially careful to watch those persons who are simply shy but who would like to contribute if given an opening. As a leader, you can provide those

openings and make the meeting a much more enjoyable and profitable experience for all concerned.

SUMMARY

Let's review some of the key concerns for better communication in meetings. Hold meetings with your staff on a somewhat regular basis as long as there are important matters to be discussed before the entire group. As much as possible, exercise process rather than content control over the meeting, and voice your opinions only when it is appropriate. Develop and use an agenda that reflects your plans for the meeting and is based on some solid advance work. During the meeting, search for areas of potential agreement, but don't limit or restrict open conflict; it can be counterproductive. Keep the physical arrangements as open and fluid as possible. As we've suggested, this can be done by rearranging the seating patterns from time to time, just to keep those in the meetings a little bit off balance. They'll probably pay more attention during the meetings if you do.

Finally, it should be obvious that your meetings should be a link in your overall communication strategy within your department or organization. This means that it's important to follow through on the decisions and recommendations developed in your meetings. Some experts on meeting and group communication suggest that a successful meeting requires a need for the meeting, a friendly and cooperative climate, clearly established plans and objectives, preparation and a competent discussion leader in charge. Perhaps the most important ingredient in conducting a well-run and productive meeting with your employees is leadership. You can't just cross your fingers and hope a staff meeting will come out all right. You have to define its purposes, make sure everyone has the necessary background information, conduct it efficiently at the proper pace and in the right direction, and encourage efficient and productive participation.

One final note. After a meeting, do a brief program review. Did the meeting meet all the objectives you set for it? Was your agenda arranged properly, with topics in the right order and mix? Did everyone who wanted to participate have a chance to do so? Did you take the right approach in handling the conflicts that came up during the meeting? Was everyone at this meeting sure about the decisions reached? Did everyone understand what is expected of him or her as a result of the conclusions reached in the meeting? Finally, if there's to be another meeting of the same group, did you take a few minutes at the end of this meeting to arrange the time, place, and tentative agenda for the next meeting? A postmortem is a good planning tool. You can't change what just happened in the meeting, but you can learn from it and plan for the next meeting.

Ways to Improve Your Communications Skills

1. Maintain procedural control over your meetings and give participants a chance to feel that they can participate as much or as little as possible. Don't force people to participate. Do make participation possible.
2. Don't hold regular meetings just for the sake of holding meetings.
3. Do your homework before meetings and encourage others to do the same.
4. Select good meeting sites, where participants can feel comfortable and not be distracted.
5. Keep the meeting on time, with a firm agenda.
6. Stagger attendance to keep meetings from getting to large and out of hand. You can also split your agenda into two meetings or use sub-committees.
7. Your meeting's agenda should be
   a. specific
   b. highlighted
   c. include timing
   d. distributed (with supporting papers) before the meeting
   e. "closed ended"
   f. balanced
   g. short
8. Keep space and distance relationships in mind. They can directly influence your meeting's success.

Further Reading

To follow up on the material in this chapter, you may also want to read:

MICHAEL DOYLE AND DAVID STRAUSS, HOW TO MAKE MEETINGS WORK (Wyden Books)

This book presents the interaction method for improving the quality and communication effectiveness of meetings. It provides some specific techniques for improving communication in meetings and deals with some aspects of transactional analysis as well.

7

Speaking Out
and Making Speeches

"I distrust a closed-mouthed man. He generally picks the wrong time to talk and says the wrong things. Talking's something you can't do judiciously unless you keep in practice."

The Fat Man to Sam Spade in The Maltese Falcon

They've asked you to give a speech. Perhaps you're expected to summarize the new process in your department at the next management meeting. Perhaps you have to explain the new absentee policy to your employees at a department meeting. You might even be looking forward to (or dreading) a speech next month at the PTA meeting. Some managers regularly give oral presentations to others, some managers do so only rarely. Yet, every manager can expect to be called on at some time to give some sort of presentation. In fact, as you move up to higher levels of management, the chances for such a call will really increase. The possibility of an oral presentation is a challenge by some managers and a terrifying threat by others. Giving a speech or making a presentation to others need not be a difficult process (Figure 7-1). With practice many people find they actually enjoy making such presentations. Developing confidence in public presentations and sharpening your ability to "think on your feet" can be a big asset in your other communications on the job and off.[1]

83

Perhaps the Fat Man was right. Few of us are born orators. To be effective public speakers we need, first, to learn the art and, second, to practice it regularly.[2] One expert suggests that "we think nothing of spending hours chatting with a next door neighbor over a cup of coffee, talking with our office mate about last night's game, or thrashing out the latest about guys, girls, cars, fashions, or other topics. We do not seem concerned about working with a problem-solving group ... yet, ask the average person to give a 'speech' and you turn him or her into a bundle of nerves."[2]

Unlike a casual conversion or even some of the writing we do, a formal oral presentation usually involves some period of advance notice. If your boss informs you at 5:00 P.M. that "I want you to brief the executive committee tomorrow morning on the morale problem with the new equipment in your shop," you won't have much time to do any thorough planning. However, even if time is short, some common-sense considerations and steps will make your planning efforts more productive and will help improve the quality of your oral presentations.

There are three stages in an oral presentation — the planning stage, the preparation stage, and the actual delivery. Each is important, and each involves some self-analysis and some matters of communication strategy.

PLANNING

There is a difference between the planning and preparation stages of an oral presentation. *Planning* takes place primarily in the presenter's mind, whereas *preparation* involves the physical arrangements and the actions that occur before the speech.

84

The first concern of the presenter should be the reason for making an oral presentation at all. If you've been told by your boss that you *will* be making the presentation, that is probably a sufficient reason for doing so. However, your planning should begin by fixing in your mind the reason that *someone* had in mind for using an *oral* presentation over some other form of presentation. Is the goal to entertain? To inform? To persuade? To cause some direct action? To lead to a decision? Is an oral presentation being used because a written report would be ignored or because the information must be quickly given to those who need it? Is an oral presentation appropriate because the topic is very complicated and would be very difficult to explain in writing? As in all areas of managerial planning, the desired result of any activity should be your first concern. If you fail to identify in your own mind the real purpose of an oral presentation, you risk making an unsatisfactory presentation.

Since we're on the subject, why *do* we communicate through oral presentations? We have identified some good reasons in the preceding paragraph. Some subjects are so complex that it would take an enormous amount of written information to get the message across clearly. In an oral presentation, a speaker can see when people don't understand. The speaker can respond by repeating or by using an example. Some information is timely, and an oral report is the best way to distribute the information quickly. Some subjects are very sensitive and must be handled with secrecy. Information about a new incentive program might be misinterpreted if a "leak" occurs. The need for secrecy can be stressed forcefully in an oral presentation.

In many situations, managerial briefings are designed to get some discussion on a particular idea or problem. If the same idea or problem is communicated in writing, it won't be possible to get a discussion going *unless* everyone assembles in the meeting room and *reads* the report before talking about it. Clearly, an oral presentation is more efficient. Some oral presentations are made not to transmit any information. Rather, the purpose of the presentation may well be for others to hear, see, and *evaluate* the performance of the speaker.

Many organizations use routine oral presentations as a way of identifying and evaluating people for promotion to other positions. Thus, no matter what reason is behind your making an oral presentation on the job, be aware of evaluation. You'll probably not learn until later how important a particular oral presentation might be.

The planning phase of an oral presentation should also include some thought about how you'll organize your materials. As you begin to examine the information at hand, you should be setting some priorities on that material. What are you going to tell them? What points will you tell them, and how will you support these facts? What is your most important point? Perhaps the most important question as you do your prespeech planning is simply, What thought or idea do you want those listening to you to take with them after your presentation?

The planning phase can now continue on several other matters. Because you now have a list of the key points, begin to develop the presentation either with an outline or with a list of key words. We'll make the point again later, but, in your preparation, remember that a "read" speech or "read" presentation is usually a disaster. A well-planned outline or a list of useful and relevant key words is a valuable tool for any oral presentation. Another useful tool in an oral presentation is some sort of visual aid. In planning visuals, you have several alternatives: overhead slides, $2'' \times 2''$ slides, film, opaque projectors, chalk boards, flip charts, artist pads, or props. Although the *production* of some visuals (such as films and slides) are likely too costly or elaborate for most managerial presentations, there are many excellent films and slides available for rent or purchase, often at nominal cost. Unless you're planning to make many presentations on a particular topic, elaborate visuals are not very practical. However, simple visuals are not costly and can be a big asset in your communication strategy.

When developing visuals, keep the words on any one chart, graph, or slide to a minimum. A very common error in developing visuals is to cram too much on one frame. Usually, this means that the words will be small and difficult to read. Make sure that your audience will be able to read your visuals, easily, and remember that persons with poor eyesight must be considered. If you're in doubt, it's better to err on the side of lettering that is too large rather than too small. Plan visuals with color and with plenty of blank space showing. Often, the best visuals for a presentation are a few well-designed graphs and some slides or cards with key words or phrases. Don't let your visuals overwhelm your presentation. Keep the focus on you, and use visuals to supplement and highlight your presentation. Make sure that your visuals will be introduced at the right time in your presentation. You might stir up some curiosity by leaving your charts exposed. You use them, but you may also bore your audience with them. Above all, use visuals *only* if you can effectively use them and if you'll feel comfortable with them. After a class where a professor badly botched his slide presentation, a student remarked to her friend, "If he can't handle the slides, he shouldn't use them." Good advice for anyone using slides.

From time to time, we'll see a television special about how cartoon feature films are made. When planning the film, the artists and producers work out a script and then build a "storyboard" for the entire production. A storyboard is a sheet with space on one side for rough sketches of the cartoon picture, and lines on the other side for the words that will be used. Many professional speakers use storyboards similar to the one in Figure 7-2. If you use a storyboard to help plan a presentation, you can use the visual space to list the words, phrases, or graph you'll use and match them with your text. This way, as you make your presentation, you'll have both visuals and words in one place, and you'll reduce the risk of losing your place or mixing up your visuals.

With your plans for topic coverage and visuals well in hand, you should next turn your attention to some very critical concerns. Especially if you're

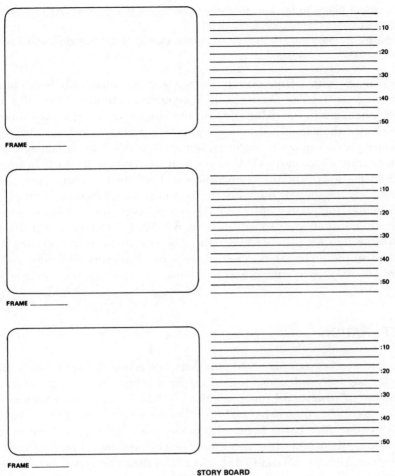

FRAME _____

:10
:20
:30
:40
:50

FRAME _____

:10
:20
:30
:40
:50

FRAME _____

:10
:20
:30
:40
:50

STORY BOARD

FIGURE 7-2

making a presentation where you work, you want to identify the key person or persons who will be attending. Does this person have any strong preferences or any major biases? If so, you'll be wise to steer clear of the sensitive areas if possible. If it's not possible to avoid sensitive areas, you'll at least be able to prepare yourself for possible objections, questions, or comments. Some other questions you'll want to consider about the key people at the presentation include:

Does he or she have any hostilities with other persons attending?
What is the key person's strengths?
Weaknesses?

87

Are there things in the key person's background that can be used to help the way your presentation is received?

How much does the key person or persons know about the topic you'll be presenting?

A manager with a large manufacturing company occasionally finds himself addressing the regular plant executive committee meeting. Every top and middle manager in the plant attends, and visitors are invited from time to time to give the committee some insights into other viewpoints. The plant manager presides over the meetings, but it is the distribution manager who seems to carry all the clout. He has been with the company longer than anyone else and has good working relationships with all the other managers. This person is also responsible for one of the most important functions in the plant. Even though the person addressing the group has no direct distribution experience, he wisely puts some distribution language and some distribution knowledge into his presentations. Once the key attendee is *interested* and *involved* in the presentation, most of the other managers attending usually follow. A bit of preplanning and forethought in this situation can pay big dividends.

PREPARATION

Preparation takes your plans and puts them into action. If you've done a good job planning, very little remains to be prepared before the actual presentation. Check out in advance the room in which you'll be making your presentation. Does it have the equipment you'll need to use your visuals? Does it have a chalkboard or flip charts? If you plan to use slides, will they be front or rear projection? (Rear projection slides must be put into slide trays backward; if they're not, all your visuals will be backward on the screen.) Are there enough electrical connections, and will you need extension cords? Will you need a microphone, and, if you do, will one be provided? Do you prefer a podium? Do you feel comfortable with a neck-type microphone (hands are free and you can move around) or do you prefer a fixed mike? On the podium? Can the lights be dimmed and where are the switches? Will windows be a problem.

Some years ago, I made a presentation to a large group of insurance company executives in Biloxi, Mississippi. The presentation was in a large room at a Gulf-side hotel. Because I was planning to use a lot of slides in the presentation, I arrived the night before to check the meeting room. All the chairs were in place, the platform was set up, and my large screen was there. Everything looked great — at least in the dark. When I came down at 8:00 A.M. for the speech, I discovered that the dark wall on one side of the room was actually a ceiling to floor glass wall looking out over the Gulf, and the morning sun was blazing into the room. The windows had no drapes, and it was impossible to darken the room enough to even see the word slides, much less the slides with charts and pictures. Careful planning could have averted this disaster. Without the visuals I'd planned, the entire presentation fell flat on its face. Fortunately, the insurance people invited me back the next year for a "second try." This time, the room had *no* windows, and everything worked. It's rare that we get another chance when making a presentation. Thinking ahead can help overcome many of these difficulties.

When placing your audience (if you have some control over where they will sit), try to avoid facing them directly into a window or toward an open door. Both the possible distraction and the incoming light can take attention off you.

If you're planning for projected visuals, you will naturally want to darken the room. It is always a good idea to have some light in the room in addition to the reflected light from your visuals. In a completely darkened room, your audience won't be able to see you or take advantage of your face and body expressions. In turn, you won't be able to see *their* faces and respond to their body language. Lights can usually be left at about half their maximum brilliance as long as they don't shine directly on your screen.

If you're planning visuals, determine in advance who will be working the projectors. If you have remote controls, there's no problem. If you find that local union regulations require a projectionist to change visuals, be sure that you have a specific, detailed, written set of instructions for that person. Indicate clearly what cues you will give to change from one visual to the next and, if possible, rehearse the visuals with the projectionist until you're satisfied that the operator completely understands your wishes.

Rehearsal

Some sort of rehearsal, by yourself or with others is a very useful preparation. Practice saying your presentation into a tape recorder or before your spouse, children, or friends. Ask for their honest comments, and use their suggestions. If you plan visuals, run through them until you're sure you know *exactly* what's coming next. Some companies are helping their people prepare for presentations by videotaping the rehearsal and playing it back. If you have such an opportunity, take it. Don't worry about being shy or overly sensitive. The best criticism and advice you'll get will be your own response to your televised image. Rehearsal doesn't mean a quick run-through five minutes before you go on. Don't delude yourself by thinking that you can "wing it" or that you know it all and don't need the practice. Even professional speakers practice, just as musicians and other communicators.

When preparing for a presentation, rehearse until you feel comfortable with the entire presentation. However, don't try to memorize the presentation. Usually, a "word-for-word" memorized presentation sounds very stilted. It makes those listening feel uncomfortable and very nervous about asking questions or interrupting while you're "on." Don't imitate the speaker who memorized his speech and had to start over from the beginning every time someone interrupted.

In your preparation, be sure to consider questions and remarks from your audience. If you plan to permit or encourage questions, try to predict what the questions will be and develop some possible answers. If you want to take questions, be sure to plan enough time to adequately answer them.

A common problem for all speakers is the questioner who "won't let go" after his question has been answered. If you try to give him the complete, detailed answer he wants, you may risk losing the rest of your audience. Most people are interested in someone else's question, up to a point. If one questioner persists (and he or she is not the key person at the meeting), ask if you can meet privately with him or her after the meeting to discuss the point in more detail. Most political leaders rehearse with their staffs before making a public appearance. Often, they rehearse only the possible questions they expect and try out several possible answers. It's better to rehearse and practice for the tough question that never comes than it is to be caught unprepared when it does.

Handout Materials

Another very useful aid to an oral presentation is to have some written materials available. Generally, this material falls into two general categories: Material to be read *after* the presentation and material to be used *during* the presentation. If your subject includes complicated charts and graphs, or perhaps a discussion of detailed points of law, administrative regulation, or company policy, it's a good idea to have copies of key charts or programs available for the listeners to follow. Some handout materials contain exercises or questionnaires to be used during the presentation. These, of course, must be prepared in advance. Often, they are distributed to the meeting participants *before* the actual meeting. If this is done, those at the meeting don't need as much briefing, and you can go directly to the discussion phase of the presentation.

When planning to distribute materials to use *during* the meeting, try to limit the information to what you'll actually need. Information not used in the meeting can be put into materials distributed at the end of the meeting. In a presentation, you want to keep the attention of your audience. Too many materials in front of your audience can distract them from you or your visuals. In addition, your written handout materials may summarize your remarks, and, if people read them before you've covered the topic, you'll have lost an important element of control over your group.

Good handouts should summarize the key points in your presentation. These can be organized into short phrases, short paragraphs, and even a list of sources of additional information. If possible have all loose sheets of paper stapled into one package. This helps people keep their materials together and is especially important when your material flows from one page to another. If a person misplaces one page, the entire handout is worthless. Three-hole punch the pages in your handouts if those at the meeting will be storing their notes in loose-leaf binders.

In some cases, it won't be wise to staple all handout papers together. When this happens, one of two approaches can be very useful. One option is to *number all the pages* so participants can check their materials before leaving and thereby avoid missing anything. Another good idea for distributing handouts is to *color code* them using different color papers. This makes it easy for participants to check their materials and have all the handouts available.

Handouts are appropriate for any oral presentation. They are almost mandatory when presenting a highly technical subject orally. One final word on written materials. Have them printed clearly. Many otherwise excellent presentations have been clouded because the written materials given participants are hard to read or lines are missing or simply because the material wasn't arranged properly. Standard ideas for good writing must be applied even to supplementary material distributed as part of an oral presentation.

Nervous?

All good speakers get nervous before getting up to speak. Some professionals even get sick or pace back and forth ill at ease. Anxiety before a speech or presentation can be a good sign, an indication that you're concerned about doing a good job. Most speakers find that, once the presentation gets under way, they calm down and actually enjoy themselves. Some professional speakers even suggest that the times when they don't feel nervous before going on are the times when their performance falls flat. However, a few people let their nerves get the best of them. These people often resort to drugs or drinks to settle them before going on. With a good stiff drink or a couple of tranquilizers, you may feel calmer before an oral presentation. However, when you get up to speak, your "helper" may actually work against you. More than a few speakers who used a drink before speaking found that, while they sounded good to themselves, they sounded terrible to their audience. The tranquilizer dulled their perception of themselves just as it dulled their nerves. Practice and self-confidence are far better nerve settlers than drugs or booze.

What Do You Say Before You Start to Speak?

Your manner in waiting to give your speech is as important as your material or your presentation.[4]

If you are the *main* speaker, sitting there at the table, you are not the Invisible Man or Woman. Whenever there's an idle moment, everyone in the room will have his eyes on the head table. If you are well known, the audience will be looking you over pretty carefully. Yet, sometimes business people seem totally oblivious of this.

During the program they may bury their heads in the speech they're going to make. Or they may simply sit like a bump on a log, looking bored, tense, or grim, and not uttering a word to anyone on either side. Then he or she is introduced. Bounding up, he or she is suddenly Mr. or Ms. Charm.

Unfortunately, if you don't look the part before, the audience won't buy that. Even humor won't turn on an audience already turned off by the speaker's actions. What you do onstage — and the speaker is always onstage — is part of the image you convey to your audience.

THE PRESENTATION

The planning has been done. All preparations have been checked, and everything is ready for zero hour. Butterflies begin to build, and your boss or the master of ceremonies is asking you to step forward and begin your remarks. What's going through your mind? Perhaps a few last-minute thoughts about your key points, perhaps a quick look at the key person attending the meeting. As you open your oral presentation, remember a few important thoughts about any presentation.

1. ***An Oral Presentation Is a Dynamic Process.*** It can't be set in concrete and done in a vacuum. Your audience will give you signals, questions, and feedback about how you're doing, and you will be responding to them. If you've done your planning properly, you probably have very little to worry about. You can't avoid all presentation problems. Unforeseen problems are bound to come up, and worrying about them won't help avoid them. Stay cool. Adjust your speaking speed and your eye contact to match in your audience.

2. ***Create a Rapport with Your Audience and Work to Get Them Committed to You.*** An oral presentation is not supposed to be a confrontation. Adopt and maintain a relaxed attitude, and relate what you're saying to the background and interests of your audience. This can be done in any oral presentation, from technical business meeting with other managers to a formal speech at the local service club.

3. ***Don't Just be Yourself.*** The conventional advice for speakers is usually "be yourself." If this means "stay relaxed, in control of yourself," it's good advice. However, an oral presentation is not a completely natural happening. Although you *can* make an oral presentation while keeping a low-key conversational tone in your voice, a public presentation usually requires that you "project" your voice much like an actor on stage. Your gestures must be much more obvious, and you will be moving your eyes around rather than keeping

them on one person. A speech is not a quiet, friendly conversation. You don't want to overdo your presentation and "showboat," but you will be most effective if you make adjustments for the situations. Be yourself, but perhaps add just a bit more to yourself in the presentation.

4. *As You Begin Your Presentation, Make Sure Your Audience Knows Your Objective for the Talk.* In these early remarks, ask and answer such questions as:

"Why are we here?"
"What is to be said?"
"How does it help or relate to me (the listener)?"

Giving such information at the start of an oral presentation serves the same purpose as a map of a cross-country trip: It gives your listeners an idea about where you are going and what stops or side trips you plan along the way. The answers to these questions also do what every good salesperson does at the start of a pitch to a client. It creates interest in the speech and arouses a desire for the listener to get involved. Many public speakers follow the "rule of 3":

1. Tell them what you're going to tell them.
2. Tell them.
3. Tell them what you've told them.

Usually there are two "master laws" that must be considered in any presentation before a group of people. They are:

1. Use your full personality to deliver your remarks, no matter how simple or informal the setting.
2. Grab your listener's attention immediately after starting your presentation. Don't wait for their interest to build as they get used to you. If you wait, you're likely to find that you've lost a large proportion of your audience without ever getting them into your topic.[5]

Humor

You can also create a rapport with your audience by using humor — if it's done properly. Humor related to the topic that you'll be presenting is almost always appropriate. Some speakers try to tell the latest joke even though they're not really sure how it goes. They stumble with it and end up blowing the punchline, ruining the story. Others simply forget how the story goes, or they tell the story properly, but with no timing. Comedy is an art, and professional comedians practice their craft just as professional doctors, lawyers, or supervisors practice theirs. If you plan to use humor, use it sparingly, use it carefully, and use it properly.

Any story that you use should relate directly to the central theme of your talk. If your audience has to work to develop a connection between the story and the theme of your talk, you'll probably lose them. A humorous story, no matter how funny, or how well you deliver it, should never interrupt the smooth flow of an oral presentation. If you break the audience's chain of thought with an irrelevant story, you may entertain them for a short time, but you may also lose the rapport you've built up. In short, don't try to be funny unless you can bring it off.

The Humor "Trap"

There are dont's as well as do's for successfully using humor in public speaking. Here are some of the more common pitfalls of amateur speakers:[6]

1. *Avoid Humor when Speaking Out-of-doors.* Even a very funny movie playing to an almost empty house won't get many laughs. Playing to a packed house, it will. The out-of-doors is something like the almost empty theater. The audience is spread out and often distracted. In that setting, even big laughs sound feeble. They won't catch on and run through the crowd.

2. *Shun Puns.* It is temptation to think of puns as performable humor. In most cases, they are not. By the very nature of its construction, a pun has the speaker saying, "Look how smart I am." That is a challenge to your listeners. You don't want to challenge them. What you want is to have fun together with them. On some television shows, writers have not been allowed to use a pun unless they have a tremendous "saver." That is a one-liner that has fun with your audience's reaction—almost invariably a groan. Audiences are conditioned to a groan at the cleverest of puns. So your saver might be, "I just threw that in. I should have thrown it out." How many times have you heard someone like Johnny Carson use that type of saver?

3. *Don't Step on Your Lines.* Storytellers who lack confidence are prone to this mistake. They don't have the courage to wait out a laugh. They pause for a split second. Then, if the audience doesn't instantly react, they plunge ahead. They step on their lines. So you have to stop, smile, and wait after telling your funny story. If you are scared, the time between telling a story and hearing the audience react seems like an eternity. But crowding a laugh is the surest way to ruin humor.

4. *Don't Be Afraid to Lay an Egg.* Inevitably, sometimes a joke will die on you. If so, don't just squirm a little and go on as if nothing happened. It is good technique to acknowledge the fact that your story bombed. Every professional, every monologist in show business, has a dozen savers memorized to

cover a situation like that. Build up a collection of your own. It will take the terror out of storytelling.

Once You're Under Way

The nervous jitters of a few moments ago disappear (or almost disappear), and you settle down into the long-awaited presentation. You've done all the planning, checked all preparations, and rehearsed until you think you could do the speech blindfolded with your hands tied behind your back. Now's the time for a few final considerations. They can make the difference between a good speech and a *very good speech*.

1. *Avoid Symbols.* In many technical presentations, there is tendency to use acronyms and symbols instead of words. If everyone present understands the symbols or acronyms, there's no problem. If you've measured the group, it's possible that some in your audience won't understand what you're trying to say. For example, in a small manager's meeting in a small organization, one of the attendees was briefing his colleagues on a new machine process being tested in his department. To illustrate his points, he was putting various production figures on a chalkboard. At one point, he wrote "$\bar{x}$." He assumed that everyone understood his meaning. After about 20 minutes, one of the other managers raised his hand and said, "I'm sorry, Harry, but I simply don't know what $\bar{x}$ means!" It meant that the average ($\bar{x}$) output of machine #12 is 185 per hour and that the average for machine #15 is 193 per hour. Yet, at least one person present didn't understand. Because of the misunderstanding, that manager had lost 20 minutes of the presentation while he was trying to figure out what $\bar{x}$ meant. The simple symbol $\bar{x}$ was jargon in this meeting, and the speaker should have avoided using it.

2. *Use Talk Words.* Your usual conversation with friends and co-workers is normally made up of everyday, easy-to-understand words and expressions. Don't fall into the trap of beefing up your vocabulary just to sound more impressive. You may succeed in sounding just a bit overstuffed and pompous. Even though you're projecting your voice, you need not resort to overblown flights of language.

3. *Speak Clearly.* Enunciate each word clearly, and don't slur your words. Many words can sound very similar. For example, you might use the words "it rained here." If you don't speak clearly, some in your audience might instead hear

"a trained ear"
"a trained deer"
"a train, dear"

The possibilities are almost endless. Some words have the same sound and are often used interchangeably or incorrectly. These include

affect versus effect
accept versus except
access versus excess

Also, try to use singular and plural forms properly. The two most common words to cause problems are "medium" and "criterion" (singular) versus "media" and "criteria" (plural). In a speech, improper usage may not always be noticed, but when it is, it can make you look unprepared and cause your listener to discount the importance of your remarks. Clear speaking isn't difficult if you remain aware of a few of the possible hazards.

4. *Slow Down.* Most of us talk at the rate of 125–140 words per minute. Although it is a fact that most people can listen and understand at a much faster rate, it is uncomfortable to be forced to do so. Talk at an even rate of speed, and use the *tone* of your voice rather than the speed of your delivery to highlight and accent your thoughts. In fact, you can often play an audience like a musical instrument by raising your voice to make a point and then by lowering it to an almost intimate level. The audience will move forward in their seats and pay closer attention when you keep your voice moving. Just as a musical selection would be pretty boring with just one note played, a speech delivered in a monotone doesn't inspire much interest. Use your voice like a musical instrument. You'll enjoy doing so, and your audience will too.

5. *Use Your Visuals Wisely.* We've examined several considerations to keep in mind when preparing and using visuals in oral presentations. With the care and work you've put into preparing them, it's wise to take equal care with how you use them in your speech. When a visual is presented to the audience, leave it up at least one minute and no longer than four minutes. If you put it up and remove it immediately, some people won't have a chance to see all the details or read the words. However, if a visual is left up longer than four minutes, it can become boring and even distracting. If it's necessary to keep referring back to a certain chart, you don't have much choice about how long the visual is up. When you do have a choice, remember the one-to-four rule.

6. *Watch for Distractions.* When you're making a presentation, try to avoid getting in your own way. Don't wildly throw your hands around, or straighten your tie, or jingle the coins in your pockets. Use hand and body gestures to emphasize your points, but don't let them get to be a distraction for your listeners.

7. *Look at Faces and Eyes.* Your eyes are the most expressive and powerful communicating parts of your body. Use them to keep your audience

interested and involved with you. Some speech teachers suggest that, if you're nervous talking before a large group of people, you can pick out a spot at the back of the room and look at it. Certainly that's better than having your nose buried in your notes, reading your speech, but it's not really good advice. Instead, move your eyes slowly from one side of the room to the other. Look at each person eye to eye. The eye contact should be brief, but it should be made throughout the presentation. If you notice someone dozing off, you can make eye contact with them and hold the contact for a little longer than usual. It's a good way to get and keep attention of your audience. The eye contact is just as important in large as in small groups. Move your eyes about the audience, and express an interest in them and their understanding of your topic.

8. *Irrelevant Questions.* Whenever possible, try to discourage irrelevant or disruptive questions. They might satisfy one person's curiosity, but they can also distract and bore large portions of the audience. As we've already suggested, ask the questioner to meet privately with you after the end of the presentation. This is usually enough to put off the questioner, and it permits you to maintain control of the presentation. In handling questions, be sure to advise your audience about your personal preferences and plans. If questions are to be taken when the entire presentation is over, let them know. If you don't, you are likely to have someone blurt out a question right in the middle of your remarks. If questions are permitted at anytime, let your audience know in advance.

Concluding the Presentation

The end of your speech should contain a brief summary of the points you've covered, in their approximate order of importance. When you are finished, be sure it's a certain finish. Don't get yourself in the spot that one manager found himself at the end of a speech. He was making a speech before the local management society's monthly meeting, and everything in the speech had gone smoothly. As he moved toward his conclusion, his voice rose and his audience started to shift in their seats anticipating the end. Finally he said "Thank you for the opportunity to speak here tonight." With that he paused, the audience started to applaud, and the master of ceremonies began to rise to return to the podium. The only problem was the speaker wasn't finished. After catching his breath, he started up again. The M.C. sat down, and the applause stopped. The speaker talked another four minutes and again appeared to be finished. This time the audience hesitated before their applause, and the M.C. didn't get up quite as quickly. Good thing, too, because the speaker *still* wasn't finished. He talked for about three more minutes, mumbled something about "thanks" and sat down. No one moved, no one applauded. Finally, the M.C. walked to the podium and asked, "Are you finished *now*, Charlie?"

The audience began to applaud and laugh, and the speech was clearly over. An otherwise good presentation was marred by a ragged finish. Make your finish clear and on an upbeat tone if possible. Don't leave your audience feeling pessimistic or "down." A short story or a *relevant* quote is a very good device for finishing a presentation.

One final bit of advice for your speech. Be careful leaving the "scene of the crime." When you retake your seat after your speech, don't spill water on your lap or stumble walking down the stage steps. Speakers usually experience a very real psychological "high" when they're through speaking. Enjoy it. If you've done your preparation and planning and have given your audience what they came to hear, relax. You've earned the applause, and the feeling of satisfaction that goes with it.

Ways to Improve Your Communication Skills

1. The first rule for effective speechmaking is to take every opportunity to give speeches. The more practice you have, the better and more confident you become.
2. Planning begins with a detailed outline and with visuals that will enhance, rather than overpower, your presentation.
3. Use visuals only if you can use them effectively. A poor showing with visuals is worse than no visuals at all.
4. Do some analysis of the key person who will be attending your presentation. Learn his or her strengths, weaknesses, interests, biases. This will help you prepare for possible problems and, in the process, help you to adapt your remarks in the best possible way.
5. Check the physical surroundings before you give your presentation. Make sure you know where the light switches, drapery cords, microphones, and other important aids are located.
6. Rehearse, rehearse, rehearse—but don't memorize.
7. Develop handouts to help those attending remember or follow your key points. However, don't distribute your handouts when they are likely to distract your listeners from your presentation.
8. Create a rapport with your audience.
9. Don't just be yourself. Project, use your voice, and remain as calm as possible.
10. Make sure that your audience knows your objective for your talk.
11. Avoid technical symbols unless the entire group is sure to understand them. Use talk words and stay away from jargon unless it too is well understood by everyone present.
12. Look at eyes and faces and avoid being distracted.
13. When you're through, make sure it's obvious. False stops can ruin an otherwise excellent presentation.

8

Changing Jobs

"As society and organizations become more complex, they will need a heterogeneous supply of human resources from which individuals can be selected to fill specific but unpredictable needs."

Douglas McGregor

One of the most important personal communication situations any of us face involves finding a new job. In some cases, we're trying to find a new job within our present organization—a promotion or a change in assignment or location. In other cases, we're actively searching for a position with another organization. If you have recently been promoted to a managerial position, you're not likely to be spending much time thinking about a *new* job. It's all you can do to learn this job. If you've been a supervisor for some time, you may be very satisfied with your present position. Either way, you're not too interested in preparing for another job.

This chapter is directed at two groups of managers: those with no plans to engage in a new job search and those either planning for a job change or actively engaged in the search process. U.S. Department of Labor statistics lead us to conclude that typical managers change jobs between three and six times during their active adult working life.

The messages you send during your active job-seeking campaign are potentially the most important of your career. Even experienced salespeople, trained in the methods of presenting products for maximum benefit frequently undersell their most valuable commodity — themselves. Assuming that you are interested in "selling yourself," let's examine a few vital considerations.

SELF-EXAMINATION

As with so many other aspects of communication, the first step in job change strategy is self-analysis. A good seller approaches a selling situation by, first, learning all that it is possible to learn about the product or service being sold. Self-analysis for an individual means developing a list of strengths and weaknesses, a list of experiences and skills, still another of education and training. These lists should be as complete as possible.

Usually, it's easy to identify our weaknesses. Few individuals are so ego involved that they assume they have no weaknesses, and most of us are painfully aware of our faults. Many of us find real difficulty in self-analysis in developing an "'objective" summary of their strengths. We've been raised to be modest in our personal statements, and we are reluctant to brag or boast. Yet, the list of strengths must be complete to highlight your unique capabilities to potential employers or superiors.

When doing your self-analysis, the first step should involve writing out these lists, with no particular order or organization in mind. Once the lists are complete, you can begin to focus your attention on some important details.

CONSTRUCT A THREAD

Look over the lists. Do you find some common elements appearing on two or three lists? Perhaps you've listed things involving mechanical skill, or dealing with people, or working with things. These "threads" can lead to adding more items to your lists and will become the focal points in your search for potential employers or in developing and writing your resume.

People, Ideas, Data, Things?

What is your main strength? If it's people, you may want to avoid areas or organizations in which you're likely to have little interpersonal contact with others. On the other hand, if you find that the common thread in your list is data, be sure that your search steers you clear of positions in which you'll be responsible for a lot of "people management."

Identifying your major strength is also useful in helping focus your job search strategy. It will also be helpful when you reach the point of actually talking with prospective employers in face-to-face interviews. You'll find that few interviewers or supervisors are patient enough to wait while you reexamine your background. They expect you to have done your "homework." Be prepared to honestly and convincingly discuss your "people" ability (or your "idea" or "data" or "things" ability) and to clearly and concisely elaborate on the reasons behind your answer.

Can You Decide Quickly?
Are You Patient?
Can You Deal with Uncertainty?

These are important questions. Negative answers are not bad by themselves, but negatives should be accompanied by some offsetting facts.

Generally, supervisors and managers find that the ability to make decisions after reasonable deliberation is a real strength. If you are a confident decision maker, all the better. However, if you find that you put off making an important decision, hoping that somehow the decision will be made for you, you may want to do some remedial sharpening of your decision skills. You can also counter your decision-making "weakness" by pointing out that your longer deliberations often lead to better decisions. Many organizations are looking not for the "hip-shooting" decision maker but rather for the manager with a good "batting average." Thus, a potential weakness, if properly identified and examined, can be turned into a positive selling point.

Patience, too, is a virtue prized by many managers. If patience is not one of your strengths, it can be developed. Be prepared to turn it to your advantage. Few prospective employers can reject your "impatience with poor quality" or your "inability to remain calm when the situation demands action."

All of us have a "tolerance for ambiguity." Those with a high tolerance are better able to work effectively in an uncertain and rapidly changing environment. Managers with a lower tolerance for ambiguity are usually reluctant to change, or to take chances. Some organizations, facing volatile and quickly changing conditions, will want supervisors able to quickly respond to change. Other more stable organizations will find little need for managers with a high ambiguity tolerance. In fact, managers with an ability to deal with the unexpected may be unsuited to deal with the demands of a largely routine kind of organization. Thus, knowing something about your level of tolerance for ambiguity or uncertainty is important when examining the requirements of various managerial positions.

Salary Versus Satisfaction

One final consideration that requires some careful self-analysis is your basic objective in seeking a new position. Some managers want salary increases in their new jobs, whereas others are reasonably satisfied with salary and other monetary rewards. These people are seeking job responsibilities that are broader or more challenging than those they now have. Either objective is sound, and occasionally both can be achieved in a single position. More likely, though, you'll have to choose one or the other in a new position. When a choice like this comes up, be prepared for it. It's an important choice, not to be taken lightly.

STRATEGY FOR THE SEARCH

The planning and personal inventory should give you all the ammunition you need to mount an effective job search. If your plans call for seeking a new job or new responsibilities in your present organization, your search process will be somewhat easier. You are a "known quantity" — your performance record is available to your prospective superiors, and they will be able to assess your qualifications easily and accurately. If your plans call for changing organizations, you are faced with a need to make your record (or at least the positive parts of your record) available to your prospective employers. Either way, the challenge is to adopt a strategy that will call attention to your accomplishments and experience in the best possible way. This is, of course, a challenge of all communication. You want to get your record and name beyond the walls of your present company or present position.

For organizational changes, many corporate recruiters suggest attending conventions, trade shows, or professional meetings, where prospective employees can be readily found.[1] Some trade and professional associations regularly conduct "job clearing houses" for their members. They list and circulate the names and qualifications of individuals seeking jobs (names are often protected by code numbers) and the positions that are currently available to members through various organizations. Private firms also specialize in executive "recruitment," matching jobs with prospective employees. These firms usually charge a fee based on a percentage of the job's base salary; they also provide career goal counseling and help in preparing for interviews and in writing a good resumé.

Fellow managers in other organizations are another good source of information about openings. In fact, one expert suggests that other managers are a much better source of career information than are the personnel departments of most organizations. In his view, personnel departments rarely know the requirements of the managers in their companies, except perhaps for the lowest-level clerical, production, and maintenance jobs.[2] On the other hand, by using what he calls the "interviewing for information" concept of visiting with managers not for jobs but for information, you develop a personal contact as well. Such an approach can also benefit you because it helps spread your name around.

Employer Literature

Most organizations, public and private, publish information about their products, services, clientele, and financial position. When you've narrowed your search to specific companies write for copies of this material and study it. Even though the material may be prepared for public relations purposes, it can still give you some valuable insights into the organization and its personnel needs.

The First Contact

The first official contact you have with a prospective employer will likely involve your professional resumé. If the contact is a "blind" contact (i.e., sending an unsolicited resumé to the company) or in response to an advertisement, your resumé will be the only "face" the prospective employer will see before deciding to invite you for a formal interview. If the contact was made through a "clearing house" at a convention or trade show or by a recruiting firm, the employer's representative will often have a personal impression to put with facts in the resumé. Either way, your resumé is one of the most powerful written communications you will ever produce. It is an advertisement for you.

YOUR PROFESSIONAL RESUMÉ

One of the most pressing problems facing today's manager is the preparation of a professional resumé. The resumé has grown increasingly important as managerial mobility has increased.[3]

The resumé should be prepared carefully and should reflect all that the individual wishes to convey to a potential employer. The resumé is an advertisement for *you* and, as such, should be planned and prepared with the same care and consideration that advertising agencies and manufacturers give the advertising and marketing of their products. To the manager, it is the most important product he or she will ever sell. Yet, too often, a good product is disastrously undersold.

It has been the practice in the past for managers preparing a resumé to merely find an example that has worked before and change the information slightly. The problem with standardized resumés is that they have a disturbing tendency toward sameness and on inflexibility that does not permit maximum exposure of the individual's salable qualities. A prospective employer looks for resumés that indicate thought and creativity in preparation. This in itself indicates much about the applicant.

Although a "form" resumé should be avoided in favor of a "tailored" resumé, there are standards that should be followed. Your resumé should be brief but complete. It is important not to omit essential information, for a poor resumé will be ignored or discarded by the person who receives it.

Most prospective employers prefer a one- or two-page resumé, but length will vary with the individual. A common rule is to prepare one additional page for each ten years of academic or work experience.

The background, education, and experience of the individual will determine the order of facts in his resumé. Facts that are particularly relevant to prospective jobs should be highlighted, whereas facts that have little or no bearing on the job should be subordinated. For example, a graduating college student who is well trained but inexperienced in a particular line of work would emphasize educational background. As a manager gains experience, the experience will gradually take precedence over education and should be emphasized.

Types of Resumés

The most common resumé is the general resumé designed for a variety of uses. It uses all information about the applicant and makes no attempt to emphasize particular experiences. The general resumé is best to begin preparing for employment. It provides an employer with a summary of the individual's experience. It can be converted to a "mass employment campaign" used by many people on their first venture into the job market. It is flexible and applicable to a variety of career positions. The main points of the general resumé will be discussed later, but, first, let's look at some other resumés that you may also find useful for other needs.

Other types of resumés have been developed to focus on particular areas of the individual's background. The first of these is the *functional resumé*. This resumé takes the individual's work experience and translates it into terms more understandable to an employer in a different situation. An example of the application of the functional resumé is the man or woman with extensive military experience who finds it necessary to translate military skills into terms that will be understood by civilian employers. It is also used for the individual who has a "generalist" background and experience in a variety of managerial problems. For him, a simple job description provides little insight into his capabilities. The functional resumé is a means for expanding upon his varied experiences.

Another resumé is the *biographical summary*. Although applicable for seeking employment, it is used primarily in situations in which an individual wishes to give a brief historical sketch of his background. The biographical summary is similar to the general resumé but follows a chronological sequence, with no separation of educational, occupational, and extracurricular experiences.

A third "hybrid" is the *introductory resumé*. This brief resumé presents a summary of the individual's academic, extracurricular, or occupational background and is a welcome service to those who are called upon to introduce him. It can also be used in situations in which an individual is not specifically seeking employment but wishes to present a brief summary of his experience to those who may in the future be prospective employers. The introductory resumé is a subtle form of informal job seeking, setting the stage for possible future consideration.

There are, of course, literally hundreds of different forms of resumés, covering a spectrum from extreme detail to vague generality. The choice of style and format must be made by the individual based on what he or she wishes the resumé to accomplish for him or her.

Career Goals

In preparing a resumé, a manager or graduating student should first ask himself or herself what career directions are appealing and the reasons for the choices. It is important that you identify your interests and abilities, evaluate them honestly, and express them clearly. Corporate recruiters continually voice concern over the number of people, including experienced managers, who have no idea of their abilities and their opportunities in other organizations. Setting a definite occupational goal and expressing this goal in clear and concise terms is of prime importance.

A major myth in seeking a new job or a change in career direction is that the jobs and opportunities go to the most qualified applicants. However, to the contrary, the best jobs and offers often go to the persons who have the best resumés or are the best prepared to conduct an effective job interview. This gives even more credence to the idea of developing clear, concise, and precise career objectives.

A clear idea of a person's goals is the single most valuable piece of ammunition, whether you are interested in advancement in your present organization or are looking for opportunities with other firms.[4] Once your career goal is clear, preparing the resumé is merely the assembling and presenting of specific biographical facts.

Your Occupational Objective

A statement of occupational objective depends on the objective of the resumé. If the resumé is to be in a general form, the objective should be phrased in general terms, being careful to avoid a "wishy-washy" image. As career plans become more specific, the objective becomes easier to write, but it should always stress a willingness to learn and gain experience.

This example may help:

OK: "A job with a company that offers eventual top-management position."

BETTER: "A management position with a national manufacturing firm, where there are opportunities for professional growth and increasing administrative responsibility. Ultimate objective, a general management position in manufacturing, with potential top-management responsibility."

Neither example is too specific, but the latter gives the impression of clear objective and indicates some thought about career plans. Obviously, in the preparation of an occupational objective, it is important to avoid inconsistencies or contradictions. For example, one does not state that his job objective is "a career as a manager in a local retailing firm" when he is applying for a job with a national manufacturing organization.

Resumés are Advertisements

It is important to remember a resumé is an advertisement — it summarizes what the individual has to offer an employer. The purpose of the resumé is to get an invitation for a formal application or personal interview. The men and women who read resumés are busy people, so a brief presentation is vital. However, in the interest of brevity, do not fall into the trap of making statements so short that they give the appearance of concealing information. It is wise to begin each statement with a past-tense verb form. For example, "directed and supervised applied research in personnel administration" or "administered enlisted training program."

Your name should be placed in prominent location in capital letters, on or near the top center of each page. If the resumé exceeds one page, but does not quite fill two full pages, it is wise to divide the information equally between the two pages. The alternative is one full page and a few lines straggling on the top of the second page. Use imagination in underlining, dividing lines, spacing, and margins. A very good layout can be designed with very little thought, and the attractiveness of the resumé will enhance its effectiveness. Although a sloppy piece of writing is unappetizing, an attractive, well-spaced, and clean resumé, on good paper, can be important in getting the resumé read.

What to Avoid in a Resumé

It should go without saying a carbon copy of a resumé should never, under any circumstances, be sent to a prospective employer. The same holds true for resumés that have erasures or unsightly smudges on them. In view of the critical mission of the resumé, time spent in retyping and reworking the resumé is well spent. Be certain that the resumé is sent to an individual who holds an executive position in a given company. The personnel office is the worst possible place to send a resumé. Their job is to provide employee services and to hire clerical and support staff necessary for the organization. A resumé sent to them unsolicited stands a good chance of being cast aside and forgotten.

There are a number of excellent sources for names of people to whom resumés should be sent. Foremost of these is the *College Placement Annual*, which each year lists some 1,200 companies, including the names and titles of individuals who do corporate hiring. The *Placement Annual* also lists companies by jobs and career positions available, regional breakouts, salary ranges, and education levels required. Such manuals are available from the placement office of most local colleges and universities.

Abbreviations should never be used in the resumé; anything important enough to be mentioned should be written out. Abbreviations give the impression of an attempt to cram information. An exception is the common abbreviations for degrees and licenses, to be used only when the prospective employer will understand the meaning of such abbreviations (e.g., M.B.A., B.S., Ph.D., C.P.A.). When in doubt as to abbreviations, the best rule is to spell out information rather than risk misunderstanding.

In preparing resumés for presentation to nonacademic people, a grade-point average is often misunderstood and therefore not beneficial in the resumé. If grades are good, it would be wise to state this by mentioning academic honors such as the Phi Beta Kappa, membership in national, honor, or scholastic associations, or academic dean's list honors. These terms are generally understood by the nonacademic public and, thus, strengthen grade emphasis. Obviously, when grades are not good, they should be avoided — however, in this case it is wise to stress other activities during school.

The resumé should not go into detail on jobs below the individual's top level of employment. Such detail, unless absolutely relevant to the position sought, tends to confuse what could otherwise be an effective presentation of experience. Finally, do not state a salary range desired. Discussion of salary is best left for later correspondence or personal interviews, at which time all factors can be included in consideration of this most important area.

WHAT SHOULD THE RESUMÉ CONTAIN?

The resumé is an advertising device. It should treat information in the most creative way possible. This does not imply that information on the resumé is falsified but, rather, chosen and presented to evoke the best possible impression. No employer will hire an individual on the basis of his resumé alone. Objections, questions, and in-depth detail that the employer desires will be answered and obtained in subsequent contacts. The resumé merely seeks to open the door for such contacts by developing an interest for the individual.

Although resumés differ, depending on background and experience, they all contain basic categories of information. These categories include:

Name, Address, and Telephone Number

Your name should appear at the top of each page in upper-case letters. On the first page, in a prominent location should be a home address and telephone number (including area code). If two addresses are used, indicate for the temporary address what period of time this address will be used.

Personal Data

Appearing near the top of the first page of the resumé, balanced with the address and telephone number, should be a brief summary of relevant personal data. You should include your height, weight, condition of health (indicate good or excellent: if neither of these adjectives describes health, it would be wise to discuss physical condition as a separate section, indicating particular disabilities and the extent to which these disabilities would interfere with job performance), marital status (if married, indicate the number of children or dependents) and birth date (optional). All of this personal data is optional, and many people feel that it gives prospective employers a basis for discrimination. Therefore, use careful and informed judgement when including personal information.

If you've had little experience, it is wise to highlight those aspects of experience that provide the prospective employer with some idea of your abilities, including a brief description of the jobs you've held.

Individuals with full-time work experience should expand upon this experience, including company names and locations, inclusive dates of employment, job description, and a summary of skills required for such jobs. Individual positions should be listed in reverse order (last job first). With the exception of the current or last job held, job detail is unimportant unless the details relate specifically to the position being sought. Other detail serves to confuse.

Education

In this section, list each college or university you've attended and its location — inclusive dates of attendance, degrees received (or to be received), major areas of specialization, and any academic honors and scholarships (e.g. dean's list). Schools should be listed in reverse order, beginning with the last school attended. For a college graduate, it is unnecessary to mention high school, unless there are extenuating circumstances. This would include unusual academic, scholastic, athletic, or leadership activities while in high school. As an individual moves away from his or her school years, the education section of the resumé becomes less a factor in employment and can gradually be reduced. Eventually, your resumé will mention only those institutions from which you received academic degrees or advanced training. For the recent college graduate, however, it is wise to list all institutions attended.

Military Service

For the individual with prior military service, this section of the resumé should include the branch of the service and inclusive dates of active duty, rank upon discharge, and a brief description of duties or responsibilities. It should include a statement of any reserve obligation. You may also find it beneficial to translate military experiences and responsibilities into civilian managerial terms.

Professional Affiliations and Qualifications

This section is a brief listing of membership in professional clubs and associations and offices held in those organizations. Also included are special certifications, such as flight licenses, radio-operator licenses, and other certifications.

Early Background

A brief statement of personal history, which may include family occupation and size, and home town. This information is considered optional but can be useful to a prospective employer in assessing an individual's background.

Personal Interests and Activities

Because employers are interested in well-rounded individuals, it is sometimes wise to list interests in literature, athletics, and activity clubs or organizations. Mention should be made of offices held in organizations and a brief list of hobbies should be included. Again, this section is optional.

References

There are two schools of thought on references. One holds that all references should be included on the resumé; the other contends that only a brief statement "references available on request" is necessary. The decision rests on the degree of flexibility you want in your resumé.

Availability

You should indicate when you can begin work. An availability date gives the prospective employer some idea of when he or she can plan to hire you. Availability should also indicate feelings toward travel and relocation. The simple statement "Travel and Relocation Unlimited" gives a carte blanche to the prospective employer, whereas restrictions on travel gives the employer notice of your relocation preferences.

Copies

The number of copies of your resumé you should prepare will vary, depending on the position sought. For general positions, you may wish to prepare 100 or more copies to be sent in a "shotgun" manner to a variety of firms offering positions of interest. For specialized work or executive positions, 35–50 copies should suffice. These copies can be duplicated by any good neat printing process.

The importance of tactile communication cannot be underestimated. In preparing a resumé, always use good quality paper—at least 50 percent rag bond—in the standard 8½ " × 11 " size. Odd sizes are difficult to handle and file, and the combination of cheap paper and unusual size may cause the prospective employer to form unfavorable impressions in his mind. If reproduced copies are used, be certain that the copy process allows for use of good paper and that the copies are clear and precise. If the copy gives the impression of a mass run, it will substantially reduce the impact of even a well-constructed resumé.

THE DYNAMIC RESUMÉ

The resumé is an ever-changing document. The best resumé is one that has been reviewed by a variety of people, each making their comments and evaluations of the resumé.

Your resumé should be reviewed and revised periodically to reflect changes in your education and experience. All suggestions of other people, while not necessarily used in your resumé, should be carefully considered as possible improvements for your resumé.

Perhaps the greatest mistake that a manager preparing a resumé can make is to assume that, once the resumé is typed and prepared, it needs no further changing. The result will be a static, uninteresting, and unrepresentative document that will, in the long run, do more harm than good to the individual's chances for successful employment. Be creative—use imagination—seek advice and guidance. The result will be an effective professional resumé.

A well-written resumé is the first stage of a job search communication strategy. Once your resumé has been reviewed by some friends or colleagues, you're ready to prepare for the next important stage—investigating job openings and potential openings.

CREATIVITY IN THE SEARCH

Many managers who would like to change jobs or organizations never do. The reason is simple. They don't look beyond the "want ads" in the daily newspaper. If no positions advertised perfectly match an individual's skills and experience, the individual concludes there's "nothing for me to do."

Go beyond the local daily want ads. If your job search involves looking at other parts of the country, you're probably already looking through national newspapers and professional magazines that would carry such announcements (such as *The Wall Street Journal*). These are also great sources even if you plan to stay in your present location. Local employers, advertising in a national market, may actually prefer hiring someone already in the area, to save on interviewing and relocation costs. Another consideration is that local "help wanted ads" seldom carry large numbers of managerial openings. These local sources carry primarily advertisements for nonmanagerial positions. Don't overlook them, but don't confine your search to any one medium.

Because many organizations regularly post notices of all job openings within the organizations, friends within a target organization can be a valuable source of "inside" information. The purpose of posting job openings is usually to give present employees the first priority for new positions. If you're not presently in that organization, you'll naturally not be given immediate attention or response if you apply for such a "posted" position. However, you may have the inside track on an opening if it's not filled from within.

The wisest strategy is to identify as many potential sources of job information as possible. Don't limit yourself to the conventional or convenient sources. Be creative in finding and using information.

When responding to a want ad or a nonadvertised opening (whether local or beyond your area), enclose your resume along with a concise, to-the-point letter. This letter should specify the position in which you're interested (or your general area of interest if you're not applying for a particular job), where you first heard about the job, and your reasons or qualifications for applying. The letter is a good opportunity to *highlight* a few of the things in your resume. However, don't overdo it. The letter should highlight, not duplicate, what's in your resume. Long letters tend to bore the reader, and the only purpose of the letter and resume is to spark the interest or attention of the persons doing the hiring. Few managers are hired solely on the strength of a letter or resume. Their mission is to interest the potential employer, and earn you an invitation for a personal interview.

PREPARING FOR THE INTERVIEW

We've learned in other chapters that the first few minutes of the first meeting with a stranger are very important. It is during this brief period that we "size up" the other person and form some long-lasting impressions of them. (Of course, they're doing the same to us.) A bad first impression can be overcome, but it's far better to avoid making the bad impression in the beginning.

Read the literature of the organization interviewing you. Knowing key facts about the organization, or asking good questions, makes a very good impression. Interviewers can be quickly "turned off" by an individual who demonstrates little or no knowledge of the organization, its products or services, its philosophy or its policies.

Dress appropriately and in good taste. In the body language chapter (Chapter 11), we examine some aspects of personal appearance and its effect on communication. Be mindful of the weight that interviewers place on good grooming. Be careful to avoid overdressing. If you're not sure about the dress, visit the organization anonymously just before your interview and note how the men and women in your prospective job level dress. Following their example is the best clue to how you should dress.

If you prefer certain "nonstandard" types or styles of dress (such as a longer hair style, beard or moustache, cowboy boots or jeans), examine the effect of these preferences on the interviewer. This does not mean that you should shave your beard or otherwise do something that's uncomfortable for you. It does mean you have to be realistic—with some employers, dress and appearance are the deciding factors; with other employers, dress and appearance (assuming they're not outrageous) are of little concern.

Ask questions during the interview. It's your chance to learn about the organization, as you'll be deciding whether or not to accept an offer, if one is made. Intelligent questions also show your interest in the organization and the interviewer. There's another benefit to asking good questions. While the interviewer is answering your question, you're temporarily off the "hot seat." It can give you a chance to briefly relax and rest—important benefits, especially in a long interview.

When you're asked a probing question that requires a negative answer (something about a past failure or difficulty), answer openly and honestly. Don't overdo the openness, however. Too much detail can be damaging. Even an innocent incident can grow to massive (and ominous) proportions if enough detail is given. It's best to give the interviewer as much of the background as necessary, but try to avoid obvious excuses. Remember that mistakes can be converted to the "positive" by looking at them as "learning experiences."

Staying Cool and Natural

The best advice for job interviewing is to be yourself. Interviewers are experts at spotting role playing. A phony image, no matter how polished your acting ability, will eventually come through under the pressure of the interview. Remain composed, and remember that an interview is a two-way communication. You are an equal participant and can, therefore, exert some influence over what happens during the interview.

Following Up After an Interview

After your interview, thank your interviewer for his or her time and interest. Later, write the interviewer a short note restating those sentiments. Don't be put off by what may appear to be a brusk send-off—the interviewer may be thinking ahead to the next interview and not really concentrating on the formalities of your departure. Be sure you know the interviewer's name — you may want to refer to it in future correspondence with the organization. If the interviewer asks for something specific (such as a transcript, article, reference), send it in as soon as possible after the interview. Doing so gives you another opportunity to make a favorable contact with the interviewer.

If, after a suitable period of time, you have heard nothing from the interviewer or the organization, it is permissible to call or write to ask for the status of your application. Be mindful, however, of the nonverbal message in doing so. You may appear pushy or insecure. Some organizations even delay contacting an interviewee, to see how well the individual handles the waiting and uncertainty. If you must recontact the organization before they contact you, it's best to use a "cover" such as an updated resume or some additional information. This will soften your inquiry but still get your name in front of the living persons.

CONSIDERING AN OFFER

Examine each offer carefully. A salary increase may not adequately compensate you for increased job tension, or added working hours, or a longer commute to and from work. Examine the fringe benefits, especially in light of your income tax situation. Look over your contract. How restricting is it? Can you quit when you wish, or are you bound to the job for some specific length of time? How much negotiation will you be permitted on various terms in the offer? Is a move involved, and how would such a move affect your personal situation?

These are important questions, and they deserve careful consideration and honest answers. Only then can you accept (or reject) the offer.

One final bit of advice. If you've decided to leave your present job, be sure of your decision *before* announcing it. If you later change your mind and stay, your boss and fellow employees will remember, and it can do lasting *damage* to your work relationships.

Ways to Improve Your Communication Skills

1. The first step in developing an overall and effective career strategy is to do some serious self-analysis and examination. Develop a list of your strengths and weaknesses. Identify your skills with ideas, people, and things. Determine what kinds of responsibilities you feel that you can handle.

2. In your career communications, start with the literature that various employers provide. Also consider newspaper advertisements, but don't limit your search for a new job to those sources.

3. Develop a resumé that fits you. Don't copy one of the resumés from the various books of "Resumés That Get Jobs." Make your resumé the best advertisement you can get for the most important product you'll ever sell—you.

4. Once you've developed a personal resumé, continually review it. When you find things you like in the resumés of others, change yours to match your changes in feelings. Also, do a periodic review of your resumé, and make sure that you have an up-to-date copy available. It would be a shame to have a job offer or a situation in which your resumé would be helpful pass by simply because your old resumé was way out of date.

5. Remember the importance of first impressions in job interviews. According to many experts, the opinion that an interviewer will have of you, and often the decision that he or she will make about you, will depend on messages and impressions communicated in the first few minutes of the interview. Don't wait for the interviewer to "warm up to you." By then, it may be too late.

6. Review the suggestions in Chapter 11 on body messages, particularly the suggestions on clothes and appearance. You should dress in a comfortable and appropriate way. Don't wear clothes that make you uncomfortable, because you'll look uncomfortable and that could hurt the impression you make on the interviewer.

7. During your interviews, stay cool and act natural. Obviously, you'll feel some pressure, but remember that the person looking at you for a position as an employee and manager is trying to evaluate how you will perform on the job. Although interviews are artificial situations, remember that the interviewer would like to have the best possible image of you.

8. Some time after your interview, follow-up on the contact. Either call or write the interviewer and politely ask if there has been any decision on your application. If no decision has been reached, be sure to tell the interviewer or company representative that you are still interested in working for the company and, if possible, ask when they think a decision will be made on your application.

Further Reading

For more information on career communication, you might also read:

ROBERT CALVERT, JR. AND JOHN E. STEELE, PLANNING YOUR CAREER (McGraw-Hill)

This book gives examples of several types of resumés, along with some useful information about planning a career strategy. The authors also include some useful information on preparing for and actually going through the job interview. They also give some information on evaluating your progress as you work through your career strategy.

RICHARD K. IRISH, GO HIRE YOURSELF AN EMPLOYER (Anchor Press)

This author takes the view that, to be successful in developing and following through on a career strategy, you must take an aggressive and forward-looking approach. This is excellent advice, and the author goes into many areas of the job search process. In particular, he deals with some of the psychological factors that are involved in such a search, and he offers some very useful tips as to how this process can be smoothed for the applicant, with more successful results.

III

NONVERBAL COMMUNICATION

9

Space and Status Messages

"There is a great need to revise and broaden our view of the human situation, a need to be both more comprehensive and more realistic, not only about others, but about ourselves as well. It is essential that we learn to read the silent communications as easily as the printed and spoken ones."

Edward T. Hall

Today's managers face challenges of space quite different from those faced by the early astronauts. Today, the challenge is to better understand the messages in the spaces where we work, play, and relate to other people. These personal spaces and the values and the status symbols that they provide can give us many clues to understanding our behavior and to learning more about the masks and goggles we all wear.

We use terms such as "status symbol" to indicate the values that we place on the spaces in which people live, or work, or worship. These values are often the unconscious reflection of the importance of the people who live in an area. It doesn't really matter how the labels or the values got attached to spaces. What does matter is that these values directly affect our behavior and our reactions toward other people when in these spaces or aware of them.

To understand how this is so, we must first acquaint ourselves with the way in which each of us uses space, distance, and territory and how these uses become part of our communications.

119

TERRITORY AS A MESSAGE

Experts on space messages point out that part of our behavior pattern is learned over time from our relationship to the physical space around us. We place value on personal spaces and territories and defend them against intrusion. And, from our relationships to these spaces, we derive nonverbal messages that directly affect the outcome of our formal and technical communications.

By understanding the many messages of space, you can improve your communications and even control the circumstances surrounding your personal relationships, such as new employee interviews, and discipline and instructions to employees, to the advantage of all concerned.

One example of the force of space on nonverbal communication is the experience of a business in a small town. For years, it maintained offices in a neighborhood adjacent to pawn shops, night clubs, and bars. Its success began to wane. The manager took steps to bolster its sagging fortunes, but the downward trend continued. Finally, the business moved its offices closer to the major banks, and it began to prosper. Surveys of the firm's customers showed that the old location caused them to feel "down and out," whereas the new location caused feelings of security and pride. These results should not be surprising. All our surroundings condition our attitudes and actions. In fact, we often find it difficult to change behavior in certain spaces even when the function of that area changes.[1]

Zones of Interaction

The relationship between space and communications involves the personal spaces and areas around each of us. These areas form invisible boundaries into which strangers and other intruders cannot come, and they often cause messages we don't consciously intend to send.

There are four principal zones of interaction (Figure 9-1) in which we conduct different kinds of interpersonal activities. These zones, in approximately four concentric circles, vary from one culture and group to another. While they are varied, studying them can give us an opportunity to evaluate the effects of space on communications in our relationships with other cultures and societies.

The *intimate* zone, extending from the individual to about arm's length, is the area in which we conduct most of our sensitive communications. Only individuals with close relationships to us are allowed to enter this zone. Strangers are excluded from it. If people do get this close to us, we usually feel uncomfortable and try to move away.

The closest we normally allow a stranger to approach us is to the boundary of the *personal* zone, from arm's length to about 3 to 4 feet from the body.

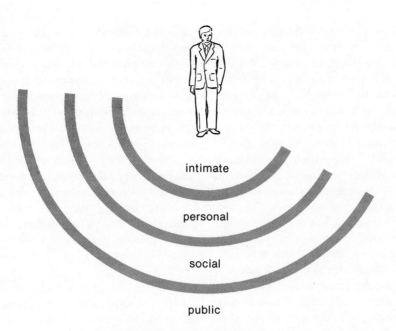

intimate

personal

social

public

FIGURE 9-1 Zones of Interaction

Even in this zone, strangers cause us discomfort unless we are able to arrange some device to reduce the threat implied when our close personal spaces are violated.

The *social* zone, extending 3–4 feet to 8 feet from the body, is the area in which we conduct most ordinary business and social activities. Usually, it is about the diameter of the circle that people take for themselves at cocktail parties or social gatherings. The arrangement of office and work space (discussed in the following paragraphs) also demonstrates the appropriate use of the social zone. Most desks are wide enough to force individuals sitting on opposite sides to maintain face-to-face distance of between 4 feet and 8 feet.

The *public* zone, extending 8–10 feet from the body, is the area over which individuals exert little personal control. Because of this, it's usually easier to ignore things happening in this zone. Thus, people in conversation groups 8–10 feet apart can effectively block out other activities around them and can concentrate on the affairs within the more comfortable social and personal zones.

When blocking out intrusion of outside activities into the social zone becomes desirable, such tactics as lowered voices to exclude strangers or raised voices to talk through intruders are used.

This phenomenon is evident in crowded elevators, in which strangers are placed in zone proximity that violates their normal territorial imperative.

Watch the next time you step into a crowded elevator of strangers that invariably someone will talk on the weather, the slowness of the elevator, or ask for floor numbers, but seldom will he or she speak about important subjects.

The speaker is reducing the implied threat posed by strangers' intruding on his or her intimate or personal zone by seeking to become more familiar with the stranger through conversation or simply by refusing to acknowledge that the other person is even there. As an experiment, pick out a person walking toward you on the street and keep holding eye contact with them for a few seconds longer than you normally do. The distance at which you feel uncomfortable is close to your personal zone boundary. The defense of territory can also be seen in the behavior of two people who are sitting on opposite sides of a table in a restaurant. No matter how large or small the table, there will be a dividing line down the middle of the table. Each person defends his or her half, often marking the dividing with cigarettes, lighters or matches, or papers and notes. If you cross into someone else's territory, you'll make them uncomfortable and even hostile.

Again, you can try a simple experiment to see how such boundaries work, and how they influence communication. Next time you're sitting across the table from a friend, begin carefully moving all the dishes and silverware over to the other side. Start by moving the salt and pepper shakers, as they're usually in the center, anyway. Then, move the ketchup, the vase of flowers, the candle, and other "neutral" objects. Then, begin moving *your* objects over the line. It won't be long before your companion will become nervous, and silences will start to grow longer and longer. Of course, don't continue doing this to the point where the other person really gets upset; continue only until you see how "invading someone's territory" can become a real threat to communication.

Although we move in on someone in this way only as an experiment, we do similar things to employees all the time, perhaps without being aware of the messages the employee is receiving. When you walk down to an employee's office, lean over his or her desk, fondle objects on the front edge of the desk, or idly flip through the employee's in-basket, you're doing the same thing. Actions that mean nothing to you can be interpreted as a personal threat to the employee. Use of such personal spaces may be viewed as a subtle form of pressure exerted by the boss.

For this reason, in our chapters on discipline and performance appraisal, we recommend that a neutral site be chosen for counseling and discipline. That way, *some* of the power messages can be avoided. Holding such meetings in your office clearly puts the subordinate at a disadvantage, because you control all the space. However, a meeting about a sensitive topic can be just as distorted if it's held in the employee's office, because you've got plenty of opportunities to use space, distance, and status to "one up" the employee.

Because we're thinking about offices and personal work areas, let's look at the office as the setting for many distance and status messages. We must be careful not to imply too much when we see the effects of these nonverbal boundaries. How people feel toward each other at the time is a decisive factor in the distance used for a communication. Thus, although zones of interaction are useful in examining our communication patterns with others, we must use this information judiciously.

Because space is such an important communication vehicle, affecting persons of different backgrounds in different ways, we can learn to use it effectively in the arrangement of our offices—its desks, chairs, equipment, walls. These arrangements communicate messages to employees and clients, conditioning them to behave much differently from how they would behave in a coffee shop. The messages that your office sends to those with whom you relate, can help—or hinder—effective interpersonal communication.

Your Office: It Reflects You

Look around you. Do you realize how much your office reveals about your attitudes, beliefs, and willingness to communicate? The way in which your office is laid out and ways in which you use your office space tell everyone who comes into it who you are.[2]

Your office communicates through what experts call out-of-awareness communication: an unspoken but nevertheless quite powerful language. You are aware of many types of unspoken language through various best-selling books that describe different nonverbal and unconscious signals that people communicate.

Serious students of body language have investigated our abilities to communicate by motions, gestures, postures, and facial expressions. They point out some important principles about out-of-awareness communication. One major conclusion, for example, is that body languages are not instinctive in human beings but, rather, are learned systems of behavior that differ markedly from culture to culture. They have been learned informally and "out of awareness," and the people of a particular culture generally remain unaware of their participation in transmitting an elaborate—and sometimes unique—system of bodily motions. Because few of us have exactly the same backgrounds and experiences, we must keep these cultural differences in mind, as these cultural differences may interfere with our ability to communicate with others.

For the most part, however, certain symbols and unwritten rules are fairly pervasive in western culture. Among these are the outward representations of status and achievement. Your office, for example, may tell people more about your position in the organizational hierarchy than your job title or salary would.

Where Do You Stand?

To begin with, the very existence of an office tells a great deal about its occupant—because, in any organization, only a relatively small number of its members occupy offices.

An office's size, furnishings, number of windows, number of occupants all provide information not only about the occupants but the organization itself. In a large manufacturing company, for example, an executive promoted to a new job was transferred to an office at company headquarters. The office to which he was moving had formerly housed a vice president, although our executive's promotion was to a position lower than that of vice president.

The new office was well furnished, including wall-to-wall carpeting, paintings, and the other amenities of a high-status business office. Before top management would let the executive occupy his new office, however, they told maintenance to cut a 12-inch strip from the entire perimeter of the carpet. Why? Because wall-to-wall carpets convey a message of position and power in this company and belong exclusively to executives of vice presidential rank or above. With a single action, the company had put the executive "in his place" and conveyed the message to all his future visitors. Individuals with power in organizations often have sofas, bars, tables, and other symbols in their offices to show their relative power and give them props for the status "games" that are a material part of space and distance communication.

Without such signals, people may feel uncomfortable in their surroundings. Many organizations take advantage of this unwritten code to arrange desks, space, and furniture.

Next to size and furnishings, location is the chief indicator of corporate status. Corner offices—and prime window views—belong only to the top managers. And status goes up—one, two, three—with the number of windows an executive can manage to snare.

Even air-conditioning—originally intended to solve the problem of working in hot, humid weather—has contributed another status problem: Who gets the thermostat? One harassed designer admits to having planted a dummy thermostat control in a particularly insistent executive's office. "Now this guy is really happy. He gets hot or cold simply by twisting the knob in either direction," the designer reports.[3]

The push button is another status symbol. Seated in his high-backed chair (as the back goes down, so does an executive's worth), an astronaut-like executive can operate a multitude of office conditions from his set of panel controls. He can change the quality of lighting, move curtains back and forth, slide away wooden panels to reveal movie or TV screens or chalkboards. He can electrically control the destruction of confidential papers, silently lock doors (any kind of lock denotes status), and switch music on. Table 9-1 outlines some of the more popular status symbols and how they vary from one level to another in many organizations.

Of course, this chart is a bit tongue in cheek, although it's also very realistic for some organizations. Of all the symbols of managerial status, the desk carries the most significance. Let's look briefly at the status and space messages often associated with desks and then examine how all these physical objects can be used to improve your communications as a manager.

Table 5 · 1 A System of Status Symbols

Visible Appurtenances	Top Dogs	V.I.P.s	Brass	No. 2s	Eager Beavers	Hoi Polloi
BRIEF CASES	None—they ask the questions	Use backs of envelopes	Someone goes along to carry theirs	Carry their own—empty	Daily carry their own—filled with work	Too poor to own one
DESKS, Office	Custom made (to order)	Executive style (to order)	Director, type A	Director, type B	Cast-offs from No. 2s	Yellow oak—or cast-offs from Eager Beavers
TABLES, Office	Coffee tables	End or decorative wall tables	Matching tables, type A	Matching tables, type B	Plain work table	None—lucky to have own desk
CARPETING	Nylon—1-inch pile	Nylon—1-inch pile	Wool twist (with pad)	Wool twist (without pad)	Used wool pieces —sewed	Asphalt tile
PLANT STANDS	Several—kept filled with strange exotic plants	Several—kept filled with strange exotic plants	Two—repotted whenever they take a trip	One medium-sized; repotted annually during vacation	Small; repotted when plant dies	May have one in the department or bring their own from home
WATER BOTTLES	Silver	Silver	Chromium	Plain painted	Coke machine	Water fountains
LIBRARY	Private collection	Autographed or complimentary books and reports	Selected references	Impressive titles on covers	Books everywhere	Dictionary
SHOE SHINE SERVICE	Every morning at 10:00 A.M.	Every morning at 10:15 A.M.	Every day at 9:00 A.M. or 11:00 A.M.	Every other day	Once a week	Shine their own
PARKING SPACE	Private in front of office	In plant garage	In company garage —if enough seniority	On company properties— somewhere	In the parking lot	Anywhere they can find a space— if they can afford a car
LUNCHEON MENU	Cream cheese on whole wheat, buttermilk, and indigestion tablets	Cream of celery soup, chicken sandwich (white meat), milk	Fruit cup, spinach, lamb chop, peas, ice cream, tea	Orange juice, minute steak, french fries, salad, fruit cup, coffee	Tomato juice, chicken croquettes, mashed potatoes, peas, bread, chocolate cream pie, coffee	Clam chowder, frankfurter and beans, rolls and butter, raisin pie á la mode, two cups of coffee

Source: Monsanto Company, *Exec-Chart: A Ready Guide for Evaluating Executives*, Reprinted with permission.

Desk Arrangement

Because space is such an important communication vehicle and affects people in such different ways, you should become more aware of the messages sent out by the arrangement of your office. These nonverbal or "out-of-awareness" messages to workers, colleagues, and clients condition them to behave quite differently from how they would if they were in a coffee shop. The informal messages transmitted from your office, in fact, can hinder your managerial effectiveness or help it.

The way you use your desk, for example—including its size and shape—will affect the images that people form about you. Remember the last time you entered an office? Where were you directed to sit and where did the person whom you visited sit? Your answer will depend on your position relative to the office's occupant and the importance of your visit to him or her.

In the standard placement of desks (see Figure 9-2a), the occupant sits behind the desk with the full width of the desk—generally 3-4 feet—separating him from a visitor but allowing the visitor within his social zone, the area in which most business is transacted. In such a situation, the office occupant controls the space arrangement. And the structure of this space says something about the occupant to the visitor.

In a more friendly arrangement (Figure 9-2b) used for those who meet regularly in an office situation, the interaction remains in the social zone—but the desk is no longer a barrier. This arrangement allows for more personal communication.

An invitation to sit at the back of the desk and beside the office occupant in his personal zone is reserved only for visitors who have close personal contact with the occupant (Figure 9-2c). Although the desk is no longer a barrier, either person can face the desk or lean on it to reestablish some degree of spatial separation.

A variation of this personal arrangement is shown in Figure 9-3a. The visitor sits in a chair opposite the desk, and the office's occupant leaves his chair and perches on the edge of his desk. Such an arrangement—with activity taking place in the personal zone and with the desk being only a slight barrier—establishes closer contact between the occupant and the visitor but keeps the occupant in a superior position. He can literally "look down on" his visitor from his perch on the desk's corner. It's easy to see why this arrangement is effective in a "selling" situation.

The occupant can structure a more neutral spacing arrangement if both he or she and the visitor move away from the desk (a barrier) and communicate at some neutral site in the office—such as a couch or lounge area over the side (Figure 9-3b). Although this device is used most frequently with high-status visitors, this kind of spacing can also be effective when you want to put visitors at ease. It allows them to personally structure the spacing of the encounter

126

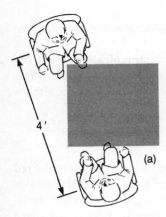

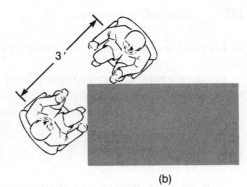

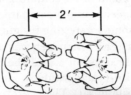

FIGURE 9-2 Arrangement of Desks

FIGURE 9-3

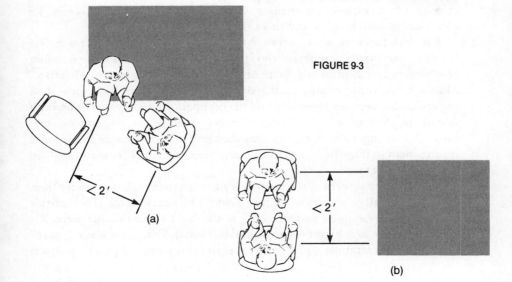

127

and control the communication—without actually being aware that they are doing so.

In this neutral office arrangement, the occupant communicates nonverbally to his visitor—while interviewing, counseling, or conversing—that the visitor is important to him and that the occupant is there primarily to serve the visitor's interests.

Office Territoriality

To learn more about office communication patterns, we recently conducted a survey of managers in many companies throughout the United States. The study turned up some interesting insights, and certain patterns of office territoriality emerged. Each manager was asked to complete a "personal space inventory" by indicating on a grid the basic outline of his office, the placement of his furniture and windows, and the positions in which he and his various visitors usually sat. Then, each respondent was asked to discuss the reasons for such an arrangement. The results did, indeed, follow a pattern.

In the most common office arrangements, the desk was either centered in the room or touching a wall. Of the managers responding, 68 percent indicated one of these two arrangements.

The desk-centered office and its variation—the throne (see Figures 9-4a and b)—revealed that the occupant preferred to maintain total control over the communication taking place in his office. They also indicated a highly structured personality—each person entering such an office must take a chair that has all or part of the desk between him and the occupant. For one respondent who indicated a "throne" arrangement, the back corners of his desk almost touched the adjacent walls—so, to get back into his desk, he had to go through a fairly elaborate maneuver. Once behind his "throne," however, he didn't budge until lunch or quitting time.

The desk-touching-a-wall arrangement (Figure 9-4c) signals a somewhat less rigid personality—someone who is willing to allow visitors more freedom to structure and control the communication that takes place in his office. Although chairs are usually arranged so that most of them have some desk surface falling between the visitor and the occupant, the space on the nonwall side of the desk permits fairly close contact. Most of the respondents who chose this arrangement indicated that they preferred it because it left more seating room in the office—and at the same time remained "conventional" in its overall appearance.

Twenty-three percent of the managers surveyed indicated they prefer their desks face a wall or a window (Figure 9-4d). Their reasons for choosing this arrangement were quite varied. Some of the most common ones were, "It makes the office look bigger" (status considerations), "it reduces wasted space" (practical considerations), and "it removes the temptation to place a physical

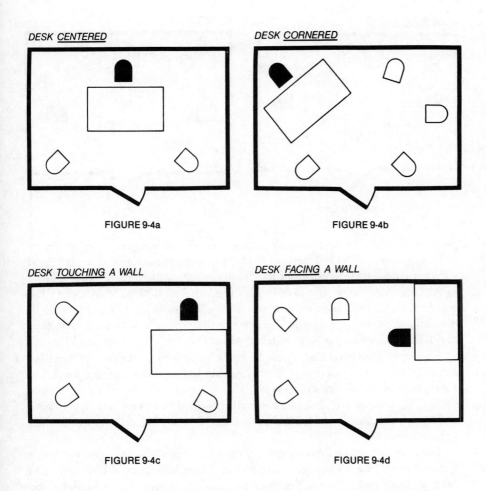

DESK *CENTERED*

FIGURE 9-4a

DESK *CORNERED*

FIGURE 9-4b

DESK *TOUCHING* A WALL

FIGURE 9-4c

DESK *FACING* A WALL

FIGURE 9-4d

barrier between me and my visitors" (communication considerations). Such an arrangement does force the office occupant to make a physical effort to move from his desk to greet visitors.

Open-ended Arrangement

The most flexible and open arrangements for offices involve choosing a "desk surrogate" (Figure 9-5a) or having no desk at all (Figure 9-5b). Each provides little in the way of a reference point either for the office occupant or for a visitor. Using something as a substitute or surrogate for a regular desk allows the office occupant almost unlimited freedom to vary seating patterns and interpersonal distances — but still allows him to maintain a hard work surface. The most common desk surrogates are coffee tables or other pieces of furniture that sit low enough on the floor to prevent an obstruction between

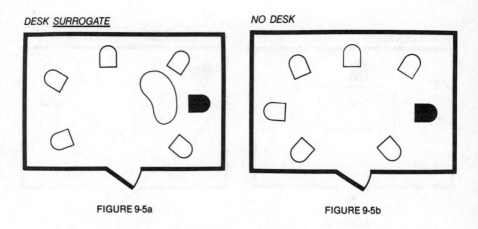

DESK SURROGATE

NO DESK

FIGURE 9-5a

FIGURE 9-5b

communicators. These free-form arrangements are not widely accepted or used, however, and only 7 percent of the respondents indicated that they used a desk surrogate. Only 2 percent had no desk at all.

Almost exclusively, the people who used the no-desk arrangement were executives who used their regular or public office only for group meetings or discussions. Without exception, however, these people indicated that they maintained a smaller, private office in which they did their paperwork.

Some top executives have gone to great lengths to establish an Olympian aura. Offices have been designed with raised platforms that perch a short boss high above his visitors or with special lighting to place the "host" in a dramatic setting. One executive's floor was actually installed in reverse: It sloped downward from the door to the table desk so that the visitor seemed to grow smaller as he approached.

Because most of us are content with the more conventional types of office arrangements, we seldom give much thought to individual differences. But take a closer look. Your office may be "saying" something about who you really are.

So What?

There are many interesting things we can learn by watching and observing the spaces around us. However, beyond our normal curiosity, what do such observations tell us? How does this information help us supervise better?

Deadwood Canyon

One manager faced a problem with employees who resented several changes in work methods and equipment. Yet, much of their attitude was actually caused by moving their offices from the main plant to an older building across the street. The new location was soon named "Deadwood Canyon" by the employees. For them, the move (and the building's name) symbolized the gap they felt between themselves and their friends back in the main building. The actual distance of the move was less than the length of a football field, but, in their minds, they might just as well be on another planet. The manager's problem was to discover what was behind the gripes and discontent, which in this case was a "space" message. Communication problems are not always a result of "space" messages. But they are usually a result of unseen or unaware forces operating beyond the conscious level of both manager and employee. Knowing the impact of such out-of-awareness forces can give you an important edge in your relationship with your people.

POWER AND SPACE

The connection between space and status messages is well documented and known to most of us. Those persons who live on the "right" side of town, or who live in "bigger" houses, or work in the "better" parts of the plant or office seem to be those who enjoy higher status. What we often don't realize is the relationship between power and the way powerful people use space. Because most of us like to keep a minimum of 18–24 inches of space between ourselves and others, a reduction in this distance, as when the boss leans over your desk or when you "move in" on an employee, usually causes discomfort. Of course, space is not the only weapon used to exercise power.

Improving Communications

Many experts suggest how you can use space to improve the power in your communications. Because we've been looking at offices, let's see what can be done there. In most of our offices, our desk is in the rear third of the room. This leaves the largest part of the room to the visitors and gives them plenty of space in which to maneuver and use "their" space to their advantage. To overcome this, try moving your desk so the space in which you sit is larger than the visitor's space. This will increase the relative freedom you have to change your posture and your distance from the other person. Also, when a higher-status person enters your office, it's a good idea to come out from behind your desk to the front edge. This tells the visitor that she or he is important. However, even though you're showing your acceptance of the other person's higher status, you can also retain control simply by perching on the front edge of your desk rather than sitting in a nearby chair. "Holding the high ground" is a time-honored military tactic, and it's just as effective in creating an aura of office power.

Another important space consideration when dealing with a group of people is to always keep group members in a position where you control the

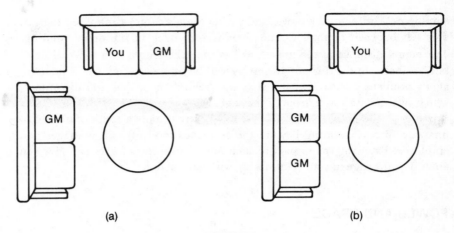

(a)   (b)

FIGURE 9-6

conversation. In Figure 9-6a, you have one group member (GM) on each side. If a real three-way conversation develops, you'll be swinging your head from side to side as if you're watching a tennis match. It's hardly a "control" or "power" position. Figure 9-6b shows the best arrangement for controlled communications with groups. In this arrangement, you can look at either person, at both, or you can have them look with you at materials on the coffee table. Splitting the group also tends to fragment your communication power in group situations.

Many managers report that they seem to be more successful in resolving difficulties with employees when the room or office where the discussion takes place is carefully arranged. By removing physical barriers between persons (such as desks or desk corners) and arranging chairs in more relaxed patterns, the psychological barriers also seem to come down. Perhaps these effective supervisors are just communicating better, and the space arrangements don't really matter. Still, there is no denying that such arrangements do help. Professional counselors always try to reduce the formality of the surroundings when engaging in their work. Even the well-known psychiatrist's couch is used to relax the patient, removing any physical barriers separating doctor and patient.

Violating Spaces of Others

Although you have the opportunity to arrange the setting for communication in your own office or work area, remember that others (bosses, employees, and others) also put value on their personal spaces. Unknowingly violating these spaces can lead to real trouble. A supervisor in a city public utility maintenance shop found himself the subject of often brutal barbs as he made his way through the work area. Employees disliked and seemed to distrust him, for no apparent reason. Yet, an outside observer familiar with spatial communications correctly sized up the problem and helped solve it.

Without realizing it, the hapless supervisor was violating the perceived "private" spaces of his workers. The workers were men of predominantly German heritage, accustomed to and preferring private work areas around their workbenches. The workers respected each other's work spaces as private and never touched tools or other materials in another man's area. Yet, the supervisor, without thinking, would touch and examine tools on a workbench as he talked to the employee. He violated an unspoken boundary and was the cause of his own misfortune. Once he was aware of what was happening he took corrective action. Things didn't get back to normal overnight, but the work relationships did eventually improve.

The effects of space messages can have many power outcomes in group situations. If you're the person calling a meeting, try to position yourself at the end of a rectangular table and, if possible, remove the chair at the other end of the table. This focuses all eyes on you and removes a potential "power drain" from the other end of the table. With round tables, power people usually position themselves with their backs to a window. This way, everyone else is looking into a glare and is likely to be uncomfortable and at a disadvantage.

A common error that most of us make is to assume that the seat opposite the boss or the power person is the "best seat in the house."[4] In fact, it may be a position where you'll be perceived as a threat to the boss's power, one who is confronting the boss as a potential rival (remember the advice about removing the chair at the opposite end?). In fact, it's possible to think about group communications by relating the seating positions to the face of a clock. On this clock, assume that the boss or the power person sits at the 12 o'clock position. Wherever he or she decides to sit, the reason for this being the pivotal position is simple — the boss or power person is the focal point for all communications in the group, regardless of whether the power person takes an active or passive role in the group's activities. All status and power communications focus on the 12 o'clock position.

Where you sit in a circle with reference to the position of the power person will have an impact on your ability to communicate your ideas forcefully and effectively. For example, in an earlier paragraph, we discussed the wisdom of sitting in a chair directly opposite the boss. This would be the 6 o'clock position and is often considered to be the position of the opposition. When you have a strong disagreement with the boss, this would be the position to take. The most powerful and therefore the most productive positions to take in a group are at the 1 o'clock and 2 o'clock positions, to the left of the boss. These positions are usually reserved for the most powerful and trusted members of the group, and this is often the impression in the minds of the other persons in the group. On the other hand, the person sitting at the 11 o'clock position is usually considered to be the "stenographer," and no matter how well dressed or well-spoken this individual is, there is a far greater likelihood that he or she will be asked to "take some notes" for the group. Because women are typically imposed on in this way more than men, women are wise to always avoid the 11 o'clock position, as it is easy for even the most enlightened male to fall back into the old-fashioned trap of thinking of all women in the meeting as stenographers and "besides, she's sitting right where I'd *expect* her to sit, so why not?" Watch a speaker at a podium. Most right-handed speakers naturally favor the portion of the audience to their left, while giving less attention to their right side. Most bosses are right handed (as are most people in the general population), so the 1 or 2 o'clock positions in a group are the positions to which the boss will naturally look more often, whereas it will take an extra effort to look over at the person in the 11 o'clock position.

As we discussed in the "meetings" chapter, there are some historical reasons for the various meanings that are attached to positions one takes in group situations. However, in terms of your communication strategies, it's wise to experiment with various seating arrangements whenever possible. Naturally, it's not always possible, for some meetings have a strictly arranged seating chart that no one violates. You can see the importance we all place on seating arrangements in such situations by watching the behavior of the people in the group when one member leaves the group, especially if the leaving member has a high-status seat in the meeting room. There will be an immediate jockeying for position, with each of the group members trying to get himself or herself into a more favorable seat. Often, such disputes are resolved either with the boss deciding who sits where or by simply assigning a particular seat to whatever person occupies a particular position in the organization. That way, the division manager's seat will always be reserved for the division manager, regardless of who occupies that position.

The fun begins in groups that have no seating chart. People will move about looking for the most favorable position, often arriving well before the meeting is to begin, simply to get the "best seat in the house." If you're the person calling the meeting, try moving your position each time you have a meeting, keeping people off balance. In time, you'll be able to reduce some of the effects of "position poker" as one manager called the space race in her organization. If you're a meeting attender, take some mental notes about where each person sits in meetings and correlate those positions with the power and influence that each person has, in the meetings and outside the meetings. You'll find that there is a "language of space" in your organization, and you'll be well on your way to developing a personal "dictionary of space."

Another strategy to follow is to avoid sitting next to an empty chair in a meeting. When you're sitting next to an empty chair, there is an image of "escaping power" about you and the person on the other side of the gap. The group members will often unconsciously assume that, regardless of who's missing or why, you're the next to go, and your power and influence in the group will be reduced. If possible, simply remove the empty chair, and fill in the space. That way, the symmetry and balance returns to the group, and the members will be less likely to focus negative attention on you.

Our discussion of the relationship between space and status messages may seem to be an exercise in trivia. Some observers of organizational space messages suggest that it's all very childish and that such status games are simply not played at the top levels of organizations. Yet, you'll find that, wherever people compete for limited resources, there is a natural competition for the marks of power, prestige, and status. In military organizations, it's possible to tell a person's rank by the insignia worn on the uniform. However, in civilian organizations, such marks of rank must be found in the way we use the spaces around us.

Although we've explored some of the space and status messages, there are countless other aspects of space and status that remain to be discovered in your organization. The interesting fact is that such messages exist in all organizations, even the military. Once you've made a survey of the status messages in your organization, you'll be on your way to a better understanding of this important aspect of nonverbal communication.

Ways to Improve Your Communication Skills

Let's briefly review the main ideas from our discussion of spatial communication.

1. Distance between people often conveys important messages of which we are often unaware. Develop an awareness of the various space zones and meaning.
2. Your personal spaces (such as office or work areas) reveal much about you and your attitudes toward your employees.
3. Arrange your desk in a way that is comfortable for you and conducive to good interpersonal relations with employees during counseling.
4. Observe the personal spaces of others. Employees have rights to their privacy. Develop a sensitivity for the unspoken messages of space.
5. Space use is a vehicle for status messages, messages that help us to develop the most productive relationships within our organizations. Some people try to ignore status messages, because they feel that they're childish. Effective communicators realize that such status messages are an integral part of any social activity and learn to work with the status and space system.

6. Power is an outcome of all human interactions, and no space arrangement *by itself* will make you more or less powerful or forceful in your communications. However, effective use of space can give you a competitive edge over your fellow managers, an edge that can make the difference between successful communication and mediocre communication.

Further Reading

For more information, you might also read:

MICHAEL KORDA, POWER (Ballantine Books)

The purpose of this book is to show that the world is a challenging game and that the sense of power is at the core of it. The author explains how to recognize, use, and live with this power. He accurately describes many of the power games that people play in the organization and develops some useful strategy for applying these power games to make our careers more successful. In doing so, he discusses communications topics that are relevant to our discussions of space, time, interpersonal relationships, and status symbols. He includes "power rules" to be applied by those interested in improving their power positions in their organizations.

EDWARD T. HALL, THE HIDDEN DIMENSION (Doubleday)

This book is the sequel to the author's earlier book, *The Silent Language*. In the *Hidden Dimension*, Hall deals with the messages of space and distance. He develops the notion of proxemics as the study of spatial communication. He also defines the various zones of interaction and discusses in detail how our culture and viewpoint vary when it comes to the way in which we use and understand the spaces around us.

10

Organizing and Managing Your Time

"There is a season for everything
A time for every purpose under heaven,
A time to be born, a time to die,
A time to plant, a time to reap."

Ecclesiastes 3, 1—2

Time is a major controlling force in our behavior. It regulates our activities and influences how we carry them out. Time also has communication implications. No matter how we use, or waste, or allocate, or invest time, we are constantly sending "time messages" to others.

TIME DIMENSIONS

Time is a commodity. We buy it, sell it, give it away. We use it, and we waste it. Thus, control of our time (time management, if you will) is a vitally important subject. Before we examine personal time use and develop some ways of better managing our time, let's first develop some ways of better managing our time by developing the communication aspects of time.

It has been said that "time talks." It talks to you and about you to others. Let's look a bit more closely at what it's saying.

137

Transitive Time

Time is transitive. Its meaning and its value changes from one person or one situation to the next. In the U.S. space program, or in computer research, time must be very accurate and measured in milliseconds. When you're visiting with friends or off alone fishing, you don't have quite the same need for time accuracy. In fact, you may even forget what time it is and not really care. Managers must deal with persons who, for cultural or other reasons, have different time values than their own. Managers raised in a culture that places a value on promptness and early rising may find it difficult to understand employees who were raised with other time values. These employees may show up late for work, or fail to meet commitments, or simply show a "why worry about it" attitude toward time. Even though the actual time differences between manager and employee may be minor, such differences can be the seeds for later, more serious, differences. When people show a lack of respect for our values, we often take their behavior to mean a lack of respect for us as individuals.

The transitive or changing nature of time can also be seen in the way we make and keep appointments. In some parts of the country, appointments are to be precisely kept. If you schedule a meeting with your boss for 10:00 A.M., you'd better be sure to be there by 10:00 A.M. Arriving late is a serious error. In fact, arriving early in such circumstances is preferred. In other parts of the country, or among certain groups of people, time is a much more informal matter. Thus, an appointment at 3:00 P.M. may actually be "three-ish" — *around* 3:00 P.M.

Time values in social settings differ from time at work. When you're invited to a party at 8:00 P.M., your host may actually assume that no one will show up until well after 8:00 P.M. Arriving early in this situation is undesirable and can even be taken as a sign of rudeness by some hosts. In simpler times, when people rarely moved from place to place, such time differences were not really very important. Today, employees and managers are constantly on the move. Different time value systems have more opportunity to clash. The potential for miscommunication because of time value differences is great.

Future Time

An interesting sidelight to the transitive value of time is the way in which people deal with the future. Most of us think about the future. Most of us think about the future as real time. That is, we have no difficulty using future time. We save for a "rainy day," we plan for eventual retirement, we take on obligations to repay loans in the future. With a conventional concept of future time, we treat our retirement benefits as a part of our overall compensation package. We assume that we'll be paid at the end of the week, or end of the month, for work we're doing today. In short, we take the future for granted.

138

Not everyone shares a conventional view of future time. For example, portions of the Navaho tribe in the Southwestern United States have had virtually no future time concept in their culture.[1] If you were to offer a Navaho a horse today, he would be excited and appreciative. But offer the same individual a horse for sometime in the future and a blank look would come over his face — he would be simply unable to deal with a gift in the future. As cultures mix, such historical discrepancies tend to fade and disappear. Still, this different concept of the future became the basis of a thorny managerial problem.

An aerospace component plant was built by the Navaho nation and operated by the Navaho on a lease-back arrangement. Although both managers and employees were Navaho, many of the aerospace contractor's traditional methods for paying and motivating employees didn't work. Because of differences in cultural time values, misunderstandings occurred. The company had to modify its standard procedures, adapting them to this particular situation.

The same kind of time differences can develop between people coming from many different ethnic, racial, and religious cultures. It's not enough to brand someone as wrong simply because their cultural time values differ from our own. Clearly, organizations must operate with some sort of common time standards for all employees. Permitting each employee to operate on a personal time would lead to chaos. Still, managers can overcome such time-based problems in two ways. First, don't quickly label as troublemakers those employees whose use of time is different or unconventional. Second, begin a personal education program to help others with different time values to see the personal benefits of adopting and working with a more conventional concept of time.

TIME AS POWER

We're suggesting that managers use some subtle strategies to help their employees develop new (and possibly unfamiliar) time habits. However, not all managers are quite so subtle. For example, it's often been said that, when Vince Lombardi coached the Green Bay Packers, he would post notices announcing the first team meeting of the training camp would begin at 9:00 A.M. on the first day. Rookies in camp for the first time would arrive 15 minutes early to make a good impression on the coach. They arrived to find all the veteran players already there and the coach running the meeting that actually (and traditionally) started at 8:00 A.M., regardless of the time posted. The veterans were, of course, delighted to see their junior colleagues subjected to the famed and feared glare of the coach. They quickly learned the difference between regular time and "Lombardi" time.

It's also been suggested that the powerless always have plenty of time and can therefore be kept waiting, whereas the powerful rarely have to wait at all.

The same manager who wouldn't think about keeping the boss waiting may keep employees waiting for a similar meeting with "their boss." Such exercises of power may be performed simply to put people in their place—without either party becoming really aware of what's going on.

BODY CLOCKS

We're all familiar with the feeling of "running down" at the end of a long day or perhaps hating to get up in the morning. Many of the influences that affect our communications with others come from our own body's natural timing mechanisms. These forces and mechanisms usually operate beyond our awareness, yet they can have a profound effect on the messages we send and receive.

Body time experts deal with what they call "circadian rhythms." These are the natural body timers that operate in approximately cyclical fashion. Today, biorhythms, body clocks, and other aspects of personal time are quite popular subjects—to be discussed at parties and in newspaper columns. However, the importance of such mechanisms to human interaction goes back many years. In the Declaration of Independence, the colonists decried King George's habit of calling for meetings of the colonial legislatures at the worst possible times: "He has called together legislative bodies at places unusual, uncomfortable and distant ... for sole purpose of fatiguing them (the colonists)." Their grievance about such meeting times became still another thorn in their side, ultimately leading to revolution and independence.

Just as the passions of the colonists were inflamed by meeting times and places, so too are all our social interactions. Suppose at 7:00 A.M. you feel like something the cat dragged in last night. You hate to get up in the morning; you do so *only* because your job requires you be there during business hours. You dress and stumble off to work and pour huge quantities of coffee into you just to stay awake. You're not a pretty picture in the morning. (Of course, you're dynamite on wheels in the late afternoon—your "up cycle" time of day.) There is no real problem with being a day person or a night person *until* you come in contact with someone opposite. If your boss is one of those people who rises at 6:00 A.M., runs a half mile, eats a big breakfast, reads two newspapers, and still gets to work by 8:00 A.M. ready to go, you're in trouble, especially if the boss calls a problem solving meeting for 8:30 A.M. The only problem you are going to solve in that meeting is the problem of staying awake.

When two persons are operating on different time cycles, it is quite possible that their attention, interest, and ability will not be equally applied to the matters at hand. Yet, changing one's body cycles to conform to a boss or a job takes a lot of time to accomplish. Why, therefore is it a topic to consider in a communication book?

Using Body Time

As an employee, recognizing your personal body time cycles is perhaps all you can do to overcome communication problems. However, as a manager, it is a different matter. When do you schedule your meetings? Do you hold meetings with your employees when it's most convenient or productive for you? If you do, it's possible you are missing some valuable inputs from people who may not be at their best. Naturally, not all meetings or conferences can be held at mutually productive times. Sales meetings may only be possible before the store opens, or before customers are available for calling. Production meetings that take key people away while the operation is going on may not be possible. Some meetings may be held at a certain time simply because that's when your boss wants them held. When you *do* have some options about the time that meetings are held, try to vary the times and watch to see any changes (positive or negative) when you try the new times. Very shortly, you'll discover the meeting times that are most productive for the greatest number of your people.

The Four-Day Week

One outgrowth of an increased awareness of how body times affect our ability to work effectively is the use of variable work times. In some organizations, variable time takes the form of a four-day workweek. This approach gives employees the opportunity to schedule their nonwork time around their personal body clocks and their social relationships. However, four-day workweek arrangements don't really address directly the communication difficulties that develop from differences in individual body clocks.

Several organizations, public and private, have experimented with another variable time system that does help overcome body time problems.

Varitime

A medium-sized city in the Midwest is in the third year of a variable time system that applies to all departments and employees except those providing vital services (fire, police, emergency medical). The plan is simple, yet effective. All city offices are to be staffed during the hours of 9:00 A.M. to 5:00 P.M., Monday through Friday, to handle public business. However, employees are free to choose to work any 38 hours during the week — from 7:00 A.M. to 8:00 P.M., Monday through Saturday. To meet the requirement of meeting the public during "normal" business hours, employees in each office or department meet periodically to decide who works when. The results are startling and apparently long lasting. Supervisors report that they get more productivity from employees in the 38 hours that the employees choose than they used to

141

get from 40 hours. Because people are more likely to choose work hours that suit their body clocks, they are at their peak and, thus, more productive. Turnover and absenteeism both declined. The city benefits, too, from increased numbers of operating hours and more efficient use of facilities. Naturally, not all these strategies for using time are available to the typical manager. We've examined them to demonstrate some interesting dimensions to time— and to sensitize you to better deal with time-based communication problems.

IS TIME MANAGEMENT A PROBLEM?

Indecision, procrastination, fatigue, lack of objectives, priorities, and deadlines share two common links: clocks and calendars. But, instead of measuring time, they waste it.[2]

Certainly, most managers occasionally wish for an extra-long day or at least one that would allow them to use their time more productively. But few appear willing, much less enthusiastic, to try what the "experts" commonly suggest: budgeting time.

Many concede that it might be worthwhile, but most wonder how much time they waste during the day. A production unit manager admits that there's a tendency to do what he enjoys—such as spending 90 minutes watching his people trying to debug an extruder when his presence is unnecessary. "I sometimes think I would be more effective if I did budget my time." But he doesn't.

Some managers see no such problems. Indeed, they neither understand nor sympathize with people who talk about having "these tremendous time problems." Some things are more important than others, and it's necessary to establish priorities, but there is always time. Thus, the view of managers is mixed.

Some aspects of time are directly "controllable" by managers. Managers who fail to manage their time quickly find that they are unable to properly handle their responsibilities. This, in turn, leads to communication problems. If you haven't time to deal with employee problems, or are constantly in a rush, your interpersonal relationships will suffer. Let's turn our attention to some practical ideas for making the best use of your time.

Making the Best Use of Your Time

Your time is your greatest resource. Your ability to control your time is your most valuable skill as a manager. Without the ability to use your time to get essential things done when they should be done, all other managerial abilities are put to naught. It is vastly important, then, for you to know how to make the maximum use of your time.

What is the starting point? The starting point is with your own thinking. The process of controlling your time begins in your own mind. It begins by your setting personal goals for yourself and personal priorities.[3]

Analyze Your Time Use

Ahead of everything else, you need to analyze, to interview yourself. Ask yourself such questions as:

What are truly the most important things in my life, on the job and off the job?
If I could be granted three wishes in connection with my profession and my career, what would those three wishes be?
What am I trying to accomplish in my days and years as a manager?
What is the most important function of my work?
What does my job hinge on?
What am I now doing in connection with my work that I should not be doing?
What am I leaving undone that should be done?

The answers to questions such as these will give you the boat and a set of sails. You will know where you want to go and why. In general, all you have to do now is to put first things first and to operate on that basis. This involves six simple, but vitally important, steps:

Step 1: List your personal objectives. Put down in writing goals that have real meaning for you in your life and in your profession. Don't just think about it; do it.

Step 2: Set priorities for your objectives. Some goals are clearly more important to you than others. So, after you have listed your objectives, arrange them in order of their importance. Set priorities on your objectives.

Step 3: List the required actions. For each of your objectives, list the specific actions necessary for you to take (so far as you know at the present time) to accomplish that particular objective.

Step 4: Set priorities on the required actions. You now have a picture on paper of your thoughtfully considered goals, arranged in order of their importance. And you have a picture of the actions required to attain each goal, arranged in order of their importance. You have a blueprint to go by. You have an invaluable working tool.

Step 5: Use of your blueprint. Schedule your daily work in accordance with your two sets of priorities. In other words, in planning your work for the day ahead, give preference to your high-priority objectives and give preference to the high-priority activities that are necessary to accomplish the objectives.

Step 6: Perform the activities as scheduled. If something unavoidable sidetracks you, always come back to your priorities when you schedule your work for the next day. Never deviate from putting first things first. Adjust your priorities as you go along, if need be, but utilize your time to accomplish those things that you know are of first importance to you and to your organization.

We cannot, of course, change the clock to give us more time. We can, however, change the way in which we make use of the available time.

Here are some practical tips that may be helpful to you in controlling your time. Some of these ideas may not fit your particular situation; some you may have tried and found unsuitable for the work you are doing. Nevertheless, there are ways in which a manager can get more out of his working hours and minutes.

1. *Be an early bird.* Get to work ahead of the gang and do first the things you may not like to do. It's often easier to perform at your best in the quiet of the early morning than it is later on in the day. And the work you do early in the morning can often result in a substantial saving of time later in the day.

2. *Answer your own phone.* Delayed messages, secretaries involved, complicated instructions that have to be relayed to you, all take valuable time from more important matters. Don't try, of course, to answer every phone call, but answer enough of them to get a firsthand feel of what people are calling about.

3. *Make your telephone calls before 9:00 A.M. or after 3:00 P.M.*[4] At other times, people will be in meetings, and you'll waste a lot of time trying to run them down.

4. *Don't be a perfectionist when it's not required.* There are times when high accuracy is required and valued. When it's not, don't waste your time working a problem out to the fourth decimal place when rounding to the nearest whole number will do just fine.

5. *Stay in shape and eat nutritious meals.* You'll feel better, and you'll work more efficiently.

6. *Don't use pencils.* They require sharpening, and the time it takes to walk from your desk or work station will use up more time than the task is really worth.

7. *Play politics when necessary.* In many organizations, moving ahead means playing political games. If you've decided that your career will be with a particular company, accept the political game as a "fact of life" and don't resist playing as well as you can. In this case, resisting the "game" may waste time, whereas accepting political activity in your organization may turn out to be a useful investment of your time.

8. *Become clock conscious.* Check frequently on the time. It is easy to ignore time for a while and then suddenly realize that it's later than you think. Don't offend people by constantly looking at your watch while talking with them; nevertheless, be aware of how much of your time you are really using.

9. *Bug yourself.* For some of your phone conversations, set up a recorder and play back the tapes to yourself later on. It's amazing how much you can

learn about your habits of repeating yourself and wasting time in unnecessary or pointless conversation.

10. *Move off the dime.* When a problem comes up, don't jump right in with the first thought or solution that pops into your mind. Invest some of your time in planning your approach to the problem. But don't plan too long. Often, some serious planning followed immediately by some movement toward a solution enables all the unknowns to fall into place and avoids wasting time.

11. *Fly to the moon.* Rarely is an important decision made on a one-shot basis. Problem solving is a process of taking some initial direction and then making midcourse corrections along the way. Time can be wasted trying to wrap up the whole program all at once. The trip to the moon was not accomplished by pointing the rocket at the moon and letting it go. Many corrections were made in the course of the flight before the objective was reached. The same holds true for your decisions.

12. *Avoid interruptions.* When you are working on a program or a project that requires concentration, put yourself in a place where you can concentrate without being easily interrupted. When you permit yourself to be interrupted a two-hour job may take six hours to do. Make it clear by your surroundings and your behavior that you don't appreciate interruptions. People will get your message.

13. *Use a tickler system.* Have some method to remind yourself of your high-priority items and to keep you on schedule. Perhaps a desk calendar or a pocket calendar will do the job — or maybe a bulletin board. But develop a system that works for you and develop it now.

14. *Be a quarterback.* Develop a good team of assistants and let them work for you. Don't try to handle all the details by yourself. Call the signals and let the members of your staff run with the ball. By giving your people more responsibility, you will motivate them and bring out the best in them. And you will save time for yourself.

15. *Keep your door partly open and partly closed.* An open-door policy, inviting anybody to drop in at anytime, can lead to a steady flow of people with problems that should be solved elsewhere. Be ready and willing to listen, but set some ground rules.

16. *Keep an open mind.* If your door is open, your mind should follow suit. Nothing is accomplished, and much time is wasted, when those taking advantage of your willingness to listen discover that you are really not interested in what they have to say.

17. *Work during working hours.* Somehow, we have gained the notion in this country that successful people are the ones who constantly work after hours. The truth of the matter is, however, that failure to get the job done during regular working hours may be a signal that you are not working productively.

18. *Spend some time with yourself.* Set up, and faithfully keep, a period of time each day or each week when you can be by yourself just to think about your plans and your performance. All the planning and budgeting in the world is wasted if you fail to set aside a time, free from interruptions, in which you can study and analyze your plans, and make necessary changes and improvements. Find 15 minutes a day, half hour, or even an hour and spend it with the most interesting person you know, yourself. You will be more creative, more innovative.

19. *Run a tight meeting.* Set strict time limits on all meetings and announce those limits to those present. Have an agenda and stick with it. Hold meetings late in the day. In our chapter on meetings, we examine in much more detail how this can be done.

20. *Gang up on visitors.* When you have planned a meeting or conference with someone you know is likely to waste your time, plan to have one of your co-workers join you. In this way, it is possible to close the meeting on some prearranged signal.

21. *Pick up speed, talk fast.* When confronted with someone who is a time waster, stay on the offensive. Keep moving. That makes you a poorer target for the time waster. As long as you are in control, you can decide how much time is appropriate for the confrontation.

22. *Avoid the tyranny of the urgent.* Don't let unusual circumstances gain control of your time. Good planning and faithful following of your plan will keep you from always being in a rush. Ordinarily, you can't perform at your best in the midst of a crisis — and letting a crisis take charge of things simply wastes time and very often leads to an even greater loss of time later on.

23. *Combine and conquer.* Combine similar tasks and activities. This is the first step in an industrial analysis of a productive process — and it is something that should be done from time to time on your job. Are you doing five routine jobs that could be combined in two operations or that could be reported on in one report?

24. *Three-for-one.* Malcolm Baldrige, a director of the Rodeo Cowboys Association and a successful manager, suggests that the time managers often waste on the telephone can be used if you'll develop the habit of doing other things while listening. Baldrige often scans newspapers, signs letters, and makes notes, all while on the phone.[5]

25. *Odds 'n evens.* We all have a tendency to think about time in terms of half hours and full hours. Because of this, we get sloppy about our punctuality. When you set an appointment or meeting time, experiment with unusual times — such as 10:05 A.M. or 3:35 P.M. You'll catch people's attention, and keep your own time on track.

26. *Don't write, phone.* Unless it is absolutely necessary to put the information or message in memo form, don't write, use the telephone instead. You can solve unexpected problems in this way; you can also save a lot of time.

27. *Keep it clear, concise, and simple.* In your writing and in your speaking, make it a habit of getting right to the point. Don't be abrupt, of course, but cut out the flowery phrases and the long-winded narratives. See to it that your main points are logical, easy to follow, and easy to understand.

SUMMARY

Time is so vitally important to you as a manager, that it is worthwhile for you to take time to decide what you want to accomplish in your work and in your life. After you have set priorities on your goals and priorities on the actions necessary to attain these goals, the next thing to do is to schedule your daily work on the basis of your priorities. Keep your priorities adjusted to changing conditions and live by them, and you will be more effective in your work and have greater satisfaction in your life.

Ways to Improve Your Communication Skills

This chapter is practically *all* points to help you improve your use of time. Try these various ideas, and discard those that don't really fit you or your situation. You'll be left with some valuable new insights and methods to make yourself a more "timely" manager.

Further Reading

For more information on time and related matters, you might also read:

GAY LUCE, BODY TIME (Phantom Books)

This book deals with our inner time clocks and new scientific discoveries about them that can change our ability to communicate as well as the way in which we live our lives. It deals with such things as how we might predict the highs and lows in our body cycles. It also suggests how the knowledge of body time may be important in the future in managing and planning in the prevention of industrial accidents and so on. It is one of a number of books that deal with the subject of internal body clocks and provides some interesting insights into the ways that we use time. The book is somewhat academic.

MARVIN RUDIN, PRACTICAL TIME MANAGEMENT (Autel Corporation)

This author gives some very helpful tips on how managers and nonmanagers can organize to make better use of their time. It is a down-to-earth book, with information obtained from a variety of executive and managerial sources.

11

Making the Most
of Body Language

"Our body language can give us a clue to how we are acting and allow us to change our behavior for the better."

Julius Fast

In the dimensions of communication diagram in Chapter 2, nonverbal communication is at the center. This was no accident. Its location reflects its importance in the spectrum of communication behaviors and skills.

Experts on the process of human communication have found that, in a typical message between two persons, only about 7 percent of the meaning or content of the message is carried by the actual words being used. Another 38 percent of the message is carried by one's tone of voice (which includes pacing, timing, pauses, accents). The majority (55 percent) of the content of a typical message is in physical, or nonword, form.

If this statistic is correct (and it appears to be), it gives us some interesting and important clues about some of our problems in effectively communicating with others. For example, when we communicate by telephone, we begin by losing the complete physical (or body message) part of the content. (Actually, the receiver loses the physical part of the message, as the sender may still be using it. Next time you see someone in a phone booth, watch how they gesture with their hands and move their bodies, even though their receiver can't see any of it.) The telephone message is further hampered by the fact that the expressive highs and lows in voice tone are lost in transmission.

The real impact of our statistic on the content of a message is felt in writing. Because a typical face-to-face message is made up of only about 7 percent word meanings, that 7 percent must carry the load for the other 93 percent. A writer must therefore choose words, constructions, and structures that are as precise as possible. A face-to-face misunderstanding about a word's meanings can often be spotted and corrected immediately, by repetition or example. A meaning missunderstanding in writing may never be adequately spotted and corrected.

NONVERBAL COMMUNICATION

Because the physical or nonword parts of a message make up the major portion of its meaning, it bears a closer and more complete look. The label "nonverbal communication" is actually an umbrella for three different kinds of communications: sign/symbol language, action language, and kinesics, or body language.

SIGN/SYMBOL LANGUAGE

Many of the most common messages we receive in a normal day come from signs and symbols all around us. Generally, we refer to signs/symbol communication in terms of inanimate objects, whereas body signs (gestures, etc.) are part of body language. Many of the signs and symbols most familiar to us are used because they are the fastest and most efficient way to transmit important information. For example, consider a stop sign. It's a red octagon, usually with the word STOP in the center. While driving, your eye will see the shape of the sign, its color, and the word (or words) on it. However, it takes much longer (in milliseconds) for the mind to recognize and interpret the word STOP than it does to recognize and interpret the message implied by the shape and color. Most state driver's license examinations require that a prospective driver be able to quickly identify traffic sign shapes, patterns, and colors. There's a sign on a busy freeway near the United Nations building in New York. On it, traffic directions are given in five languages: English, Spanish, French, Japanese, and Russian. It looks like giant multiple-choice question in the air. Imagine a driver seeing five languages on a stop sign and having to find his or her own language before responding to the order. It would make for a dangerous intersection. Obviously, we can't afford to rely on verbal (word-meaning) message in traffic situations.

There's a growing movement in many countries to develop and use standardized traffic symbols. With these symbols, persons who speak any language will be able to quickly and accurately get information they need.

In factories, stores, and public places, symbols are replacing or supplementing word signs. We now have symbols on the doors of many public restrooms, in airport and bus terminals, and for motels and restaurants. Safety symbols (along with the more familiar traffic symbols) are becoming increasingly popular in factories and shop areas.

Corporations, foundations, trade associations, and government agencies also use symbols (logos) to identify themselves or their products. Once a symbol has been firmly placed in our mind, we think of the organization every time we see the logo. Such symbols help to create recognition that is useful in helping sales and in maintaining a visible public image. In one well-publicized search, the NBC television network spent $1 million on its new logo, and Exxon spent $100 million and three years converting to its new name. (Its old name was Standard Oil of New Jersey.)

Sign and symbol communication also extends to many of the practices and customs in which we engage. The annual department Christmas party and gift giving at the time of child's baptism or bar mitzvah are also filled with symbolism.

When a tall building is completed or "topped out," a small pine tree is hoisted to the highest point on the building. Today, it symbolizes the turning point in the stages of construction and a free party put on by the boss. However, the origins of this custom date back to the time of the ancient druids. They were worshipers of trees, and the ceremony was filled with religious significance. Customs such as deference to the elderly, certain foods eaten on holidays or special days, and organizational "status" considerations such as office size, location, furnishings, color, and decoration are all highly symbolic forms of nonverbal communication.

We all recognize symbols of authority (police uniforms, badges, emblems, etc.). On the street, we respond to these authority symbols in many ways, including a cautious pullback on our speed when a police car comes into view. Managers often try to acquire symbols of status or authority, such as more privacy, or better parking spaces, or control over some money matters. With these symbols, their ability to manage is supposedly enhanced because their employees already accept the manager's power or importance. Every organization, of course, has its own "language" of symbols and their meaning. In some organizations, wearing a dress shirt and tie symbolizes "management," whereas, in other organizations, managers wear coats, and shirt and tie dress is for the employees. In some organizations, managers who take work home with them every night are admired as dedicated, hard workers, whereas, in other organizations, the same behavior symbolizes low status and importance (the manager who has no staff to do paperwork or can't get the work done during normal working hours). People who change jobs, even if the change is just from one department to another in the same organization must be careful to remember that the symbolic language is different in the army from that in a business corporation or a hospital. We often forget that symbols, like words, mean different things to different people. These meanings change from time to time, place to place, and person to person. The famous "V for Victory" gesture of World War II became the "peace sign" of the Vietnam era, only to return to its former meaning in the mid-1970s. Upraised fingers, arms, or noses have a variety of symbolic meanings quite apart from their role as elements in body language.

Some of our symbols serve dual purposes. For example a wedding ring may be a symbol of marital status, just as in some cultures a flower behind a woman's left ear symbolizes her marital or relationship status. Apart from their status implications, these symbols may also guide other individuals in their choice of behavior (as in making courtship gestures). Morse code, semaphore flags for ships, colored lights on cars, airplanes, and boats are all practical symbolic forms of communication. A thermometer-type device used to indicate how a company is progressing toward a profit or productivity goal and a city's using a similar device for its United Fund drive are other functional symbols.

Some symbolic communication is emotional, as with the reaction most people have when they hear their national anthem or see their flag being carried in a parade. These symbolic forms of communication help to express complex emotions and to evoke those emotions from others at appropriate times.

It is interesting to watch the status symbols of those who travel to far-away places, only to return home to find that no one knows they've been gone. One subtle form of travel-status indications is the midwinter tan in Chicago (travel to the Caribbean or at least Florida). Other devices, such as automobile rear-window or bumper stickers advertising exotic ports of call, perform the same function, although it is a somewhat *obvious* way of showing where you've been. Hotel ashtrays, matchbooks, towels, and other memorabilia at least indicate that you've stayed in (or been in the lobby of) some fancy places. The desire to identify one's travel destinations even leads chain hotel managers to imprint the name of a particular city over the company's standard matchbook. You can thus get a matchbook from Holiday Inn Dolthan and an identical one from Holiday Inn Monte Carlo. All that changes is the city.

Evidence of broader travel is also plentiful. Thus, midwinter ski racks appear on cars in New Orleans, 1,000 miles or more from the nearest skiable snow. The same goes for surfboards tied to roofs of cars in Kansas City. It used to be that a T-shirt from an unusual locale could only be purchased in that locale. Today, you can buy a T-shirt anywhere with anything you want printed on it. The end of a symbol. Of course, handbags, strawgoods, and other paraphernalia still bear some status, as do "tourista" stickers affixed by Mexican immigration officials to cars traveling south of the border. Stamped passports, if we could flash them around, would do the same thing.

Although not the ultimate, the attire of two men in the Phoenix airport arriving on a flight from Los Angeles gives a clue as to the importance of such symbols. They entered the terminal from their plane still proudly wearing their newly acquired Hawaiian hibiscus leis. This is significant, as they changed planes in Los Angeles and could no longer be identified by the casual passersby as recent emigrés from the islands. Best bet is that, once they'd reclaimed their baggage, they reattach their old, battered (but still status-laden) claim tags they picked up going over — the ones proudly proclaiming HNL (Honolulu).

ACTION LANGUAGE

Earlier we defined informal communication as communicating with the examples we set for others. This might also be called "action" language, especially when the examples involve nonverbal actions or movements. Action language is not restricted to nonword messages any more than symbolic language is word free (in fact, things, or places, or people, or ideas). One can, with action language, show a child how to tie a shoe and use words to reinforce the message and the learning. However, when words and actions are used jointly, the actions often have a more powerful effect on another's actions than do words. Thus, we say that "actions speak louder than words" and supervisors tell employees to "Do as I say, not as I do!"

The distinctions that we've made thus far between action and sign/symbol language may be difficult to understand fully. We do so to impress upon you the wide range of communications covered by the title "nonverbal communication."

In this chapter, we will consider some other parts of body language that are only indirectly related to the subject. For example, the clothes that we wear play an important part in our communications with others and their impressions and responses to us. We'll also bring into our discussion some additional aspects of space and distance messages, even though we've already examined much of the last chapter to this topic. The broad subject of nonverbal communication is too interconnected to make neat, clean breaks between one chapter and another. With this thought in mind, let's turn our attention next to the most popular part on nonverbal communication: kinesics, or body language.

Before we proceed, try your hand with the following quiz.[1] We'll discuss the answers throughout the chapter and summarize the quiz at the end of the chapter.

WHAT DO YOU KNOW ABOUT BODY LANGUAGE?

1. When attempting to lie, people will avoid eye contact. (True/False) _T_

2. Eyebrows are one of the two key dimensions that communicate our emotional states. (True/False) _T_

3. There is a definite ritual of nonverbal behavior that occurs between men and women when courting. (True/False) _T._

4. Red-headed people blush more than other people. (True/False) _F_

5. All movements and nonverbal behaviors have meaning associated with them. (True/False) _T_

6. Most nonverbal communication contains information about our sexual feelings. (True/False) _F._

7. Most nonverbal communication is a result of unconscious intent and, therefore, is really the best cue about how someone feels. (True/False) _T._

8. In which of the following situations is a person most likely to *adapt* to nonverbal communication? _A._
   a. giving a presentation to 25 or 30 people
   b. talking face-to-face with another person

9. When a mother scolds a child in a harsh tone but smiles at the same time, the child will tend to: _E_
   a. believe the nonverbal message
   b. believe the verbal message
   c. believe both messages
   d. believe neither message
   e. become frustrated

10. When you are sitting in position 1 in the diagram below, which of the following seats would present the most cooperative position nonverbally for another person? _5._
    a. 2
    b. 3
    c. 4
    d. 5
    e. 6

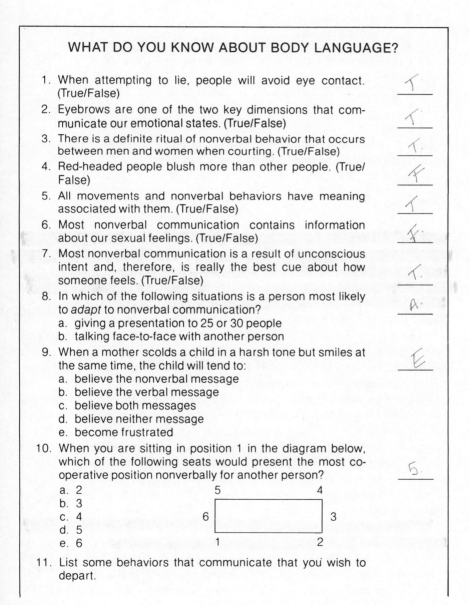

11. List some behaviors that communicate that you wish to depart.

12. People's reaction to you depends on the kind of image you
    communicate to them. (True/False)
13. You make a better impression on people when you
    a. refrain from "talking with your hands"
    b. avoid prolonged eye contact
    c. only occasionally smile
    d. all of the above
    e. none of the above
14. Nonverbal communication has many advantages over
    spoken or written communication. What are some of
    them?

Now that you've tested your knowledge of body messages, let's turn our attention to some of the finer points of the subject.

KINESICS

The word *kinesic* comes from the Greek and means "movement." Therefore, kinesics is the study of communication through body movement. Experts note that we communicate by our manner of dress, physique, posture, body tension, facial expressions, degree of eye contact, hand and body movements, tone of voice, continuities of speech, spatial distance, and touch—as well as by our words. Over the past few years, it has become a popular and well-written-about subject, with many books currently available. All experts seem to agree that different gestures or postures have different meaning to different people at different times. Thus, rather than looking for absolutes, try to begin developing an appreciation for kinesic patterns.

When an employee or other person uses a particular combination of gestures, postures, and expressions each time that he or she is in the same situation, you can begin to generalize some meanings that can later be useful in analyzing that person's behavior. For our brief study of kinesics in this book, however, your best bet is to focus on your own body language. Learn to spot your kinesic patterns and try to determine if your boss, your employees, your family, or friends are reading you correctly or if you're giving them false, misleading or conflicting signals.

Kinesics is an elaborate, nonverbal code. We understand (or at least responds) to the code even though we're not always aware of doing so. Some years ago in Germany, a horse called Hans was astounding people with his apparent ability to add and subtract using simple arithmetic. Given a math problem, Hans would stomp his right hoof until the correct answer was counted off. Apparently, he deserved his name "Clever Hans."

Suspecting that Hans and his trainer had some signals between them, however, critics would have Hans perform without the trainer giving the commands or even being present. Still, Hans still performed admirably, correctly solving all the "problems" given him. More study revealed that the critics were right. Hans couldn't do arithmetic. He had the uncanny ability to "read" the cues of those who were watching him perform. When given a problem, Hans would begin to stomp his hoof. As he approached the right answer, his audience would begin to give him anticipation gestures. They would lean forward, eyes wide open, breath held in. When Hans reached the correct number of beats, the audience would respond by exhaled breath, leaning back into their seats, eyes lowered. Sensing this, Hans would stop beating, and the audience would break into applause. Hans couldn't really do arithmetic. He did what managers and employees do, often without realizing they're doing it. He was reading and responding to body language.

Professional interviewers use all sorts of body language in much the same way to get interesting and often revealing information from their guests. A Miami-based television talk-show hostess uses a variety of conscious and unconscious techniques to encourage her guests to reveal themselves. As *TV Guide* reported, "On the air there is a determined tension in her. She leans forward, gazes levelly into her guest's eyes. She will tilt her head quizzically (I am interested), pin him quite pleasantly to his chair and pop the question. 'All right, now ... ' Those big starry eyes and that gorgeous smile help, too."[2] This interviewer also revealed that she isn't afraid to leave unfilled air to smoke out her guests. She allows a silence to build, as a way of making her guests uncomfortable and perhaps say something interesting. In our chapter on listening, we suggested the same techniques, such as giving the other person plenty of time and opportunity to form his or her thoughts and then answer a question, rather than filling a silence with unnecessary or even counterproductive chatter.

Employees also "read" their managers for signs of approval or disapproval or for indications of what you really know but are perhaps not telling. Thus, a hand on the shoulder may be merely a gesture of contact, but other employees seeing it may assume the person being touched is favored or that the touched person and the boss are sharing secret information. Because you hold a status position higher than your employees, the gestures and other nonverbal message that you use are observed and "felt" by the employees. Properly sensitized, you can learn many nonverbal messages and use them to motivate and influence your subordinates.

For example, persons with a higher status determine the degree of intimacy in their interactions with that of a lower social or organizational rank. The higher-status person must initiate the closer relationship, and the territorial rights of the higher-status person are much more important than are those of the subordinates. This, in part, explains the behavior of many employees

FIGURE 11-1

when one of their colleagues is promoted to a supervisory position in the department. The space, distance, and territory relationships that used to be appropriate won't work anymore. The new supervisor is not approached as often by the employees. Instead, he or she must make the first move now to establish the communication contact.

A newly appointed supervisor in the Boeing company was perplexed by the behavior of his new subordinates (and former colleagues). They never invited him to share lunch and were reluctant to come into his office for "bull sessions." Yet, just six months before (before the supervisor's promotion), such lunches and discussions were commonplace, and the supervisor was always included. What changed, of course, was the relative rank of the supervisor and his employees. It was now his prerogative to set up the interactions. Failing to realize this, he sat isolated from his employees, growing more and more resentful about their "standoffishness." He simply failed to understand how body language signals are interpreted when status relationships change.

Body relaxation, too, is an indicator of high status, whereas body tension is supposed to be a fear reaction indicating lower status. Watch your reaction the next time you spot a traffic cop while driving. Your body will tense, a response to the fear (however minimal) that you'll be stopped for speeding.

The same reaction is typical when an employee enters the presence of his or her boss. However, consider the opposite effect. If a manager is tense in a confrontation with an employee, the employee is in a position to take the upper hand (i.e., to assume the higher-status role) and influence the outcome of the confrontation. Some managers even report that such a situation led them to make unwarranted or unearned revisions in their employee's performance appraisal ratings.

What you don't know about your body language can be used against you. It is important to establish the proper attitude between yourself and your employees if real communication (and productivity) is to occur. Use distance and timing as a barrier between yourself and your employees, or do away with barriers, whatever you feel is productive. Either way, try to hold informal meetings in your work area, where you can stand or sit in the middle and be surrounded by employees.

Johnny Carson uses his desk to create a barrier between himself and his guests, thus maintaining a certain formality in the show. Other talk-show hosts (Mike Douglas, Merv Griffin) use only a semicircle of chairs. They apparently feel the informality of this arrangement helps set the mood of the show and contributes to its success. Clearly, the approach depends on many factors, not the least of which is an individual's own attitudes and preferences.

When dealing with two or more persons, try to keep from "splitting up the team." Although it may seem like good strategy to get yourself right into the middle of the group, such an arrangement has decidedly negative effects. Group members can divert your attention by forcing you to look first in one direction, then another. No matter how you use furniture in your dealings with groups, always try to put yourself in a position where you can address the entire group or simply one individual without moving your head more than a few degrees. That way, you remain the focus of the group's attention and can more easily get and retain control of the communications.

Height is an important symbol of superiority and control. We talk about "looking up to" certain persons, and it's thus natural to translate the physical act of looking up into the emotional response of respect for admitted superiority. Many people know this and try to gain and hold the higher ground by standing on a platform, sitting on a high stool or high chair when talking with subordinates or customers. Some people even go so far as to wear "heightening" clothing (thin vertical stripes, solid colors) or to stand in height-accenting postures (hands firmly set on hips, back straight, chin up, and eyes level and forward. Some people try to extend the notion of height as a control device by choosing a comfortable chair (a high one) for themselves, while putting the employee in a shorter, less comfortable chair. If the subordinate's chair faces a window, with outside glare shining directly on his or her face, so much the better.

A Florida import/export company supervisor always interviewed employees by seating them in direct sunlight on a hard, straight-back chair with one leg a quarter of an inch shorter than the other legs. With this arrangement, the employee can never be completely at ease, and the supervisor maintains the upper hand. This may be too manipulative for you, but it gives you an idea of how far these attempts at body messages can be taken. A female manager is another company solves a common "height" problem in a unique way. Because women are generally shorter than men, they're constantly put in the position of having to look up to them, implying admiration. When there is only a few inches difference in height between persons, such looking up poses very little problem. However, this woman is only 5' 1" tall, and her male employees *average* 6'1" tall, with one employee standing 6'5". Her solution is to stand face to navel or face to chest with her employees, forcing *them* to come down to *her* eye level. For the really tall guys, this means talking in a full crouch, and obviously establishes the boss's control. "For people I really admire," she says, "I look up. Only now, it's *my* choice."

Some managers, of course, are better at using body signals than others. An undisputed master of the nonverbal message is the National Football Commissioner Pete Rozell. His supervisory job is made more difficult by the fact that, while he works for the team owners, he must get them to agree on changes in policy for the good of the game. This puts him in a position of having to persuade in a way that will motivate the owners group to move in a particular direction without antagonizing them. Thus, in an owner's meeting, Rozell seldom raises his voice. Instead he gives small but unmistakable signals about his feelings. "When he needs time to think, he'll search for his cigarettes, then a cigarette holder and finally a match. Sometimes he doesn't get it lit right away and has to try again. But, when Rozell stands up, everybody knows the fun and games are over."[3]

Despite our goal of exploring better managerial communications, don't limit your study of body messages to strictly managerial applications. "Communication-sensitive" managers practice their ability to "read" and properly respond to body language. This practice can be had off the job as well as on. Don't let an idle moment go by when you're not watching other people, trying to relate their body messages to their true feelings and attitudes.

Some body language is very easy to interpret. A firm grip handshake or a finger pointing in the direction of the water cooler or exit gate usually need little or no explanation. It's been said that a big, broad smile carries the same message anywhere in the world. Some common body messages become easy to interpret simply because they are used in one particular way by so many people. Thus, an upraised middle finger is an obscenity to North Americans, an exposed shoe sole is an insult to Arabs, and "abrazo" or hug a greeting and expression of happiness to Latin Americans and Eastern Europeans.

On the other hand, seduction signals can and will change frequently. Many young men have their faces slapped or their advances turned away to young ladies giving nonverbal signals that were interpreted.

Some body language must be studied carefully if one is to get the complete, correct message being sent. The hula and other folk dances (including the ballet) can thus be viewed on two levels: these dances are interesting and beautiful to watch "as is" and yet far more interesting (and communicative) when one knows the meaning of each gesture, each hand, finger, arm, leg, and foot movement. The same technical nature of body language is also found in hand signals of some Indian tribes and in the sign language used to communicate with the deaf. Football referee and baseball umpire signals must also be learned (although the hand signals used by unhappy coaches and managers usually need little or no deep interpretation). Whether highly technical or common-sense simple, body signals are a fascinating source of new information about human behavior.

Let's turn our attention here to some of the individual facts of body language and how a supervisor can put this information to productive use.

EYES

According to body language experts, our eyes (and the face area around the eyes) are the most expressive and power parts of the body in terms of sending nonverbal messages. Many managers feel that persons who can't (or won't) make eye contact with them are somehow not to be trusted. We talk about "shifty-eyed" people, or about "bedroom eyes" or "the evil-eye" — all expressions representing the importance of our eyes. Look at the six faces in Figure 11-2.

FIGURE 11-2

Imagine each of the six faces saying the same thing (use any old line: "You've got a problem with what?" Or "You think the statements are false?"). You'll find six different meanings, one from each face. Yet, all we've done is change the set of the eyebrows and the shape of the lips. Critics of television news broadcasts contend that newspeople make editorial statements often by simply raising an eyebrow.

Although we may well appreciate the power of eye messages, we also can fall victim to misunderstandings of these same messages. Some persons with physical defects may be unable to look you straight in the eyes while talking to you. As we all become more sophisticated about all kinds of body messages, we find that the old notions about eye contact and truthfulness don't always apply. Today, the skilled liar can look you straight in the eyes and with all sincerity "lie like a rug." Eye messages (and misunderstandings) may also be culturally based. Some black persons (particularly older, southern blacks) have been culturally conditioned to lower their eyes when talking to their bosses or even to white people in general. In the Middle East, direct eye contact between adults is considered rude and uncouth. In either case, the lowered or averted eyes may be misread as "shiftiness" or "dishonesty."

Eyes as Strategic Tools

Since ancient times, Chinese jade dealers would haggle with their customers (often for hours) and finally agree on a price for some gems. Observers could never figure how the final "clearing" price was finally reached. Once kinesics became a subject for scientific investigation, however, the secret became obvious.

It is a fact of human physiology that, when an individual is excited or aroused, the pupils of the eyes will dilate. When haggling over price, a buyer will unconsciously signal an alert seller that a particular price is acceptable. By watching for such a signal, the dealer knows when to stop haggling and begin closing the deal. Candid, slow-motion movies of people in grocery stores showed various eye pupil dilation levels when individuals looked at different color, shapes, and designs of packages on the store shelves. Some colors or shapes caused more excitement than others, and the reaction registered in the shopper's eyes. With this research information, marketing people redesign their products to better appeal to buyers in a competitive environment. Good poker players watch the eyes of their fellow players as new cards are dealt. The pupil dilation very often will show if the card being dealt improves the player's hand.

The Telltale Eye

When two persons shake hands, their pupils will normally enlarge. If, however, one's eyes get smaller, the other person will often develop a negative attitude toward the person. This is, of course, a reaction we usually can't consciously control. It does suggest some of the many messages we send and receive with our eyes. The old bromide that "gentlemen prefer blondes" does have some basis in fact. Blond-haired persons frequently have blue (or light-colored eyes). Change in pupil size is more easily seen and, thus, an open "wide-eyed" expression is more noticeable.

An interesting eye-response test was run recently, when a group of supervisors were shown pictures of men and women. Some faces were retouched to make the pupils large, other photos of the same persons had small pupils. Those looking at large-eyed pictures usually described the persons with such words as "warm," "loving," or "sincere." The same faces with small eyes were most often described as "hard," "insincere," or "insensitive." The importance of eyes was known in Western civilization even during the Middle Ages. Women would put a drug called "belladonna" into their eyes to make the pupils dilate or enlarge. In fact, the Italian word "belladonna" means "beautiful woman!"

Eyes Can Be Used by Managers, Too

Although it may not always be possible to know if someone is lying or telling the truth simply by looking for eye contact, we can use the principle of "pupil dilation" as a good indicator. When talking (and listening) to employees, look into their eyes and become aware of changes in eye-pupil size. Changes can be caused by changes in lighting, and they will also occur when a person's emotional state changes. Thus, a person trying to lie, or one emotionally caught up in a complicated story, will give himself away with his eyes. Watch, too, for shifting of eyes or for a faster rate of blinking (caused by a drying of the surface of the eyeball, which happens when stress levels change).

Eye Movement

Another interesting (and useful) idea for managers is to watch for the direction a person's eyes move. Studies show that right-handed persons tend to look to the left when they are emotional (or when they are trying to deal with an issue on an emotional level) and to the right when they are rational[4] (the directions are reversed for left-handed persons). This knowledge can help you "read" people and better understand their mental processes when working out a conflict. It is usually difficult to use logic and rational arguments on a person who is operating on an emotional level. If you sense an emotional tilt to the employee's behavior, a change from one sort of logic to another tack may well help resolve some of the conflict.

Another useful insight is to watch for "eye-locks" between people during management meetings. Catching and holding another's attention while you (or other people) are talking may be a sign of collusion. The same is true about the "too-long" smile and body postures such as leaning forward. During meetings, try to become more aware of who is looking at whom. You'll be in a better position to understand and effectively deal with the informal organization in your department.

TOUCH

Touching is a tricky subject in body language, primarily because so many conflicting messages are possible. If you refuse to shake hands with your boss, one of your employees, or even with a stranger, you'll be considered rude and very ill-mannered. Yet, if you hold on to the other person's hand too long, you'll end up offending them (and quite possibly cutting off any chance of getting your message across).

Because a handshake is the most acceptable form of contact between people (at least on the job), it is interesting to see some of the variations and examine some of the possible nonverbal messages. The "normal" handshake is a firm grip and up to five "shakes" before breaking. If the grip is too weak, or too strong, we may form an unfavorable impression about the other person. A two-handed shake (where the left hand covers the gripped hand, or supports the elbow, or grabs the arm) is often used to indicate sincerity. Politicians use this form of handshake, perhaps explaining why many nonpoliticians think of it as being a bit "phony." There's no need for a long discussion about how handshaking got started. Suffice to say that it is an acceptable, even required, form of body communication.

Touching in Business

Consider your own reaction to other kinds of touch messages. Suppose that you are sitting next to another person (at work) and that he or she puts a hand on your knee — or an arm around your waist or shoulders. Would this change your assessment of your relationship with that other person? Would such touching make you nervous? Clearly, these touches are not as common in most organizations. (A female supervisor in a communication seminar suggested recently that, if it's Paul Newman or Robert Redford doing the knee touching, "what the heck!")

Yet, no matter how "unbusinesslike" such touching may seem to you, it is done by many people in organizations. Some forms of touching are culturally based: Italians, Spaniards, the French, and many East European persons are cultural "touchers"; blacks, and an increasing number of whites and browns who copy, go through a ritual of hand, elbow, and even body touching whenever they meet, or depart.

How do you react to such touching? If you appear uncomfortable when given a "soul grip," you may be telling the "gripper" that you find his manner (or even him) unacceptable. You'll be viewed as insensitive to other behavior patterns, which can cause difficulties with your believability. Although female managers rarely make this error, some male managers will put an arm around a female employee while giving her instructions. Many women, including those used to such actions by the boss, feel very uncomfortable with this sort of "familiarity." Even when the woman knows the male manager means nothing by his gesture, it can seriously interrupt the listening process for the female employee and lead to later breaks in communication.

Touching as Power

Frequently, touching is used to define power relationships. Thus, a manager who wants to emphasize an order will grab an employee's arm while issuing the order. In contrast, few employees would touch their bosses in the same way, unless they were looking for a fight. Some managers who really believe they manage in a participative way confuse their employees by issuing orders or explaining their positions while using such power signals.

One such example occurred in a bank. The manager took pride in his open, participative relationship with his staff. Yet, his staff perceived him as something of a "two-faced tyrant" who asked for employees' opinions and then rammed his own ideas down their throat. At least part of this employee perception can be traced to his unconscious habit of grabbing an employee's arm and poking the employee's chest with his pipe whenever he tried to express his viewpoint. Once he became sensitive to the "power message" he was sending, he kept his hands to himself while discussing ideas with his people. Within a short time, much of the dissension and complaint about the manager's "two-faced behavior" stopped.

PHYSICAL ATTITUDE

The combination of gesture, posture, and face and hand signals is commonly called physical attitude. In many medical schools today, young doctors are studying kinesics. They are aware that very often the "bedside manner" of a medical practitioner is as important to a patient's recovery as is the technical, medical skill. Doctors, nurses, and technicians must try to communicate hope and avoid giving negative or confusing messages to patients and families of patients.

Management is a "sales" profession, whether or not we're in selling. We sell our ideas and our honesty, on the job and off. Because we're always trying to convince others, it is possible to learn some useful body message strategy by watching and learning from salespeople.

In an interview with *Sales Management* magazine, Julius Fast (the author of *Body Language*) stated ways that a salesperson can use body language to help him in sales.[5] Fast points out that a good salesperson leans forward in an aggressive way when making a sales pitch; the prospect usually leans back. Also, a salesperson may use body language to spot certain facts about the prospective buyer. For example, sitting with arms folded is a traditional sign of resistance. When the prospect unlocks his arms and legs, he may be coming to the salesperson's side. Other traditional cues may be the prospect's uneasiness, displayed by juggling his foot or drumming his fingers, or doubt, displayed by holding his hands under his face. As we said earlier in some detail in our listening section, be careful of your own unconscious body messages when you're "selling" your ideas and watch for revealing information about your "buyers." The answer to question 7 of the body language quiz is indeed True. We do give clues about our true feelings and attitudes in our nonverbal behavior.

In interviewing applicants or present employees about job matters, a wise manager is aware of body movements, not to judge the employee or applicant, but to determine how the applicant's statements relate to how his or her body movements. If the supervisor is busy writing notes, he will miss everything that the person may say with his body.

BODY LANGUAGE IN LEADING

The influence of body language on leadership can be seen in the results of a study of teachers and low-performance, low-IQ students. The teachers were told that the students had exceptionally high intelligence. During the test, the students' performances gradually improved, leading to the conclusion that the teachers' behavior was a subtle nonverbal influence on the performance of the students.

By what a teacher says, how it is said and when it is said, by facial expressions, posture, and perhaps by touch, the teacher may have communicated to the children of an experimental group that he or she expected improved intellectual performance. Such communications, together with possible changes in teaching techniques, may have helped the child learn by changing his or her self-concept, his expectations of his own behavior and motivation, as well as his cognitive style and skills.[6]

For you as a management communicator, the message should be clear. We can, and do, influence the behavior of our subordinates. Our expectations, as expressed in our nonverbal actions, can directly control employee reactions.

CLOTHES MESSAGES

The way we dress also contains nonverbal messages about us and causes certain reactions in other people's behavior. Today, many employees express themselves nonverbally in nonconforming manners of dress in an effort to be "different" from the ordinary John or Jane Doe, but this identity crisis can often cause adverse reactions from others. The effect of clothing on behavior can be seen in a test using persons dressed in "high-status" or "low-status" clothing.

In one study, a dime was left in a phone booth, and, when a person entered the booth a few moments later, the "well" or "poorly" dressed person would come up to the booth claiming the dime was his, and ask if it was still there. Seventy-seven percent of the people returned the dime to the well-dressed person, whereas only 38 percent returned it to the poorly-dressed person. In another similar study, persons dressed in uniforms and persons dressed in civilian clothes would give orders to passers-by on the street. Eighty-three percent obeyed the person in uniform; yet only 46 percent obeyed the person in civilian dress, clearly indicating that people perceive authority in certain manners of dress.[7]

Dress and Grooming

Clothes may not make the man or woman, but the way that we dress and groom does have an influence of the attitudes others form about us. A New York clothes consultant conducted a very revealing survey some years ago. He selected two white male actors, both in their mid-forties, with greying hair, and had them go into a large insurance company and select 50 men and women at random. Each employee was given a simple order (such as, "Please get me the Jones information from your files"). One actor was dressed in a "tacky" outfit — frayed cuffs, shiny suit, socks falling down over the tops of unshined shoes, loud hand-painted tie, plenty of gaudy gold-colored jewelry. The other actor was dressed in what might be called "executive contemporary" garb — subdued, quality fabric, over-the-calf socks, brogue shoes, off-white shirt, polka-dot tie.

The man in the executive outfit succeeded in having 42 of the 50 people he addressed follow his instructions. The man in "tacky" outfit was successful with only 13 of the 50 he contacted. When the two actors later switched outfits, their rates of success were almost identical — about 40 for the conservatively dressed man, about 12 for the "tacky" dresser. Clearly, the response that people have to each other is based in part to how each person is dressed.

Most managers are aware of dress codes. Some are strict, others are not. We ourselves may have no set dress code, but, then again, we try not to have people running around in horse blankets either.[8]

Dress codes today are seldom, if ever, put in writing. Instead, management usually sets them by implication, and not always subtly. To this day, mention a dress code to nearly anyone in business, and he or she will likely cite IBM.

How one dresses may stamp that person as more or less moral in the eyes of others. Studies have shown that some purchasers of computers have chosen IBM over its competition because of a belief in the moral superiority of IBM people. That image of morality is largely attributable to "the IBM look." Yet,

IBM spokesmen insist there never has been a dress code per se. "All we ever said was that businesslike appearance, which includes appropriate clothing, is an important factor in the impression employees create with customers, suppliers, other employees, and the public," one spokesman says. "Appropriate clothing depends on the type of work the employee performs."

If there never was a stated dress code at IBM, one nevertheless developed. To this day, IBM employees tend to don the cut of clothing that continues to instill confidence in others.

The image a person conveys, or wants to convey, can be bolstered or weakened by certain choices in clothing. Make the right ones and promising new vistas may emerge. Make the wrong ones and nagging questions may haunt you for years: "I wonder why I was never offered that job"; "I wonder why my career leveled off when it did."

One key choice involves colors. As a rule, bright colors convey vibrancy, whereas muted colors connote trust. In general, the paler, more subtle shades of color give off sparks of upper-middle class; the icy, shiny, darker, harsher colors suggest lower-middle class.

Specific colors can emit specific sparks. Some fashion experts offer the following conclusions: pastels: the paler, the better, but loud pastels are gaudy; pink: gives off negative, nonmasculine associations; gold, green, or gray: generally, colors not flattering to the skin; light shades of blue, gray, beige: can minimize the presence of people who are physically domineering—you are more apt to be liked than respected in these colors; black or navy: the supreme authority colors—they exude power, competence, and authority.

Most of us, by the time we are able to purchase our own clothes, have become "fixed" on certain colors that will be more or less characteristic of our dress. It may be that we have learned some of the above lessons, such as that "loud pastels are gaudy." Or, personal taste may dictate what colors we choose to wear.

A clinical psychologist points out the fixation that many have as to certain colors or styles of dress. "We reach a maturation age, and we fix our dress on that," he says. Some never change their dress habits one iota after having "fixed" on that certain age, he suggests. Life, and the suggestions of life, have just never been as pleasant for them as they were at that particular time, he says. "And we associate certain colors with the sensations of that time, clinging to the memories." Hence, the high school look of some adults.

Others have their favorite colors or styles but deviate once in a while in an effort to change their image, suggest some psychologists. Example: buying a green suit even though blue is more flattering or more acceptable. Green may be the choice because someone looked good in green in a flattering situation, and a person strives to emulate that other image. But sooner or later, most of us return to the colors we know by experience are safer—or more comfortable—for us.

Power Stripes

Besides colors, patterns can also help or hinder you. Fashion experts believe that the pinstripe is still the most psychologically powerful suit made, followed by the solid and the chalk stripe (wider than pinstripes). And cut can be important. Too fancy is chancy. Thus, the wearer of a European-cut suit may be trusted less, respected less, and promoted less.

With color, pattern, and fit, the wearer projects certain images that other people are conditioned to like or dislike. But most of us know, at least subconsciously, what is right in most cases. Another expert suggests that "people will buy things that they feel look right to others, but more importantly, what looks best on themselves physically." "And you experiment," she says. "The tall person comes to realize that stripes are not advantageous to his or her appearance. The fat person learns very quickly what is right for him." (Advisedly, not bold plaids.)

Perhaps most important for your "clothing communications," you should choose clothes that will keep you comfortable in the circles in which you're moving. If you aren't comfortable, you portray an image that is not secure, and you are on the defensive. You don't blend in with the other people in your organization. You stick out, and you don't need that in business life.

HOW ABOUT YOUR KNOWLEDGE OF BODY LANGUAGE?

Earlier in the chapter, we asked you to answer 14 simple questions about body messages. We've discussed some of the answers in the chapter. Other answers lap over into other chapters. Either way, let's briefly review the questions, so you can compare your answers to the "correct" answers, as given to us by experts on kinesics.

Question 1. *When attempting to lie, people will avoid eye contact.* This is false, mainly because we've become so sophisticated. Many of us know that shifting eyes might be taken as dishonesty. Thus, the best liars are those who can look you right in your eyes while lying. We need better signals to learn if someone is lying or telling the truth.

Question 2. *Eyebrows are one of two key dimensions which communicate our emotional states.* This is true. Our eyes (or more correctly our eye "areas") are one of two most powerful communicators, and lips are the other. Look at the six faces in Figure 11-2; you'll see how they make up important parts of a message.

Question 3. *A definite ritual of nonverbal behavior occurs between men and women when courting.* Also true. The behavior may change from one generation to another, but nonverbal communication is an important part of the courting process.

Question 4. *Red-headed people blush more than other people.* False. Red-heads and light-skinned persons in general blush just as much as darker-skinned persons. The only difference is that, with the light-skinned person, the blush is easier to see. (Assuming, of course, that we define blushing as a rush of blood to the face. If we define blushing as a reddening of the face, the answer could be true.) Once we've defined blushing as we have, it's possible to see why we often label red-haired persons as "volatile" or "easily excited." Perhaps, because we can easily *see* changes in their emotional state, we infer something about their behavior in general.

Question 5. *All movements and nonverbal behavior have meaning associated with them.* The answer here is a qualified true. We may not intend to send a message with every gesture, but we can't avoid another's watching our gestures or movements and forming meanings from them. After all, even lying on the floor, hands folded over your chest, not breathing, you are sending a message — dead! You don't even have to be conscious to communicate or at least to have others form messages about us.

Question 6. *Most nonverbal communication contains information about our sexual feelings.* False, false, false. In the past, we became so taken with Freud that we began to associate everything we do with some hidden sexual meaning. Most psychologists today seem to agree that, although many messages have sexual overtones or undertones, most of our nonverbal messages are quite unrelated to sex. Sorry!

Question 7. *Most nonverbal communication is a result of unconscious intent and, therefore, is really the best cue to how someone feels.* True. Enough said.

Question 8. *A person is more likely to adapt to nonverbal communication when (a) giving a presentation to 25 or 30 people.* The reason is tied to our answer to question 2. When talking to a group, you have 25 or 30 sets of eyes and lips to which you respond. The power of these two powerful nonverbal signals (magnified as they are) are much more compelling than the same signals from only one individual at close range. Also, because we often feel uncomfortable looking eye-to-eye with a person standing or sitting directly in front of us, we're likely to look away from time to time. Consequently, we lose some of these strong nonverbal cues to the other person's true feelings or attitudes.

Question 9. *When a mother scolds a child in a harsh tone while smiling, the child will (e) become frustrated.* Even though the nonverbal signal (the smile) is stronger than the verbal (the scolding words), the combinations of harsh tone and smile will result in confusion and frustration. The smile implies reward, the harsh tone punishment. Children are more sensitive to such conflicting messages, but even adults can become frustrated when repeatedly given such opposing nonverbal signals.

Question 10. *When you're sitting in position no. 1, a person would be most cooperative and open to nonverbal communication if he or she were seated in the no. 6 position.* This is a subject we discussed in our space communication chapter.

Bodies at angles to each other are more likely to engage in cooperative interaction than those seated either side by side (1–2 or 5–4) or completely opposite each other (1–5 or 1–4). With a corner of the table between them, 1 and 6 can move closer to the corner or farther from the corner, thereby decreasing or increasing the distance between them. Thus, in negotiation, the individuals in 1–6 are much less likely to be affected by space messages, because each person is free to move and thus change his or her relative position.

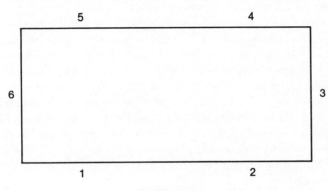

FIGURE 11-3

Question 11. *The best known "leave-taking" gesture is taking a peek at your watch.* Of course, if you really want to say it's time to go, you can take a dramatic wrist-shaking, shirt-jarring look at your watch. Other common leave-taking signals include standing, slapping the thighs while slowly standing, shifting from one foot to the other rapidly (as long as it's not a hop or a dance), inching toward the door, or leaning on the door frame. These body signals are often accompanied by blank stares, long sighs, and an occasional ".... wellll ...." If you give enough of these signals to someone, he or she is likely to take the hint—eventually. If someone else is giving you these signals (especially if it's your boss and you're in his or her office) pay attention and be prepared to move.

Question 12. *The reaction other people have toward you does depend on the image you communicate to them.* In our section on dress, we discussed the effects of one's clothing image on other people's behavior. We pick up adaptation cues from people and unconsciously respond to these signals. Remember the story of Clever Hans. His behavior was based on the messages that others sent him. In much the same way, we all respond to the image and the messages of others.

Question 13. *You make a good impression on people when you hold eye contact, smile, and act naturally.* For some people, acting naturally means a few hand gestures. For others, it means hand all over everywhere. There have been many studies about the image created by "too much" hand talking, but they've all been inconclusive. The damage is done when people used to using their hands when they talk try to avoid doing so. They look stiff, unnatural, and just a bit uncomfortable. When you convey this impression to someone else, they may think you feel that way toward *them*. Stay natural, loose, and "do your own thing" so long as it's not a distraction to the person or persons with whom you're speaking. Naturally, the answer to question 13 is (e): None of the above.

Question 14. *Nonverbal communication or body language has many advantages* over written or spoken messages. They usually make a stronger long-term impact on the receiver. They help convey sincerity, trust, and other emotions in a way that words cannot. They are subtle and can be transmitted when more obvious messages cannot be transmitted. Nonverbal messages can give us insights into the true feelings and attitudes of other people. Because they are usually formed out of our awareness, nonverbal messages can help express feelings that we have difficulty expressing any other way. There are, of course, some serious disadvantages of nonverbal messages. They can reveal. They can be easily misunderstood. They are subject to "cultural interpretation." And they take a long time of repeated exposure to get across a point we may be trying to make.

In this quiz, and in this chapter, we've examined some interesting aspects of nonverbal or kinesic communication along with some of its dangers. If you find these ideas useful and would like to examine them in more detail, check some of the books listed at the end of this chapter.

APPLYING BODY MESSAGES TO MANAGEMENT

The true test of the value of body messages is the way they influence the things we see around us. Words and body movements taken together are much better indicators of a person's true feelings than either words or gestures taken separately.

The accuracy of the applications of body language interpretation is totally subject to the nature of the situation in which it occurs. All experts on body communication warn that no body position or movement, in and of itself, has a precise meaning. Body movement interpretations are useful *only* when viewed as part of the larger pattern of communicative behavior in one's work area.

SUMMARY

An awareness of kinesics is important because it provides managers with another powerful technique to use in reaching his or her personnel and organizational objectives. In certain circumstances, this awareness can be a decisive advantage. All managers at all levels in an organization are in competition for resources and rewards. With the increased popularity and use of body language, it is safe to assume that every manager's competition is beginning to pay attention to the subject. You need the "body messages" just to stay competitive. If your competition isn't using "body messages" as well as they could, so much the better for you.

Ways to Improve Your Communication Skills

1. Remember that only a small fraction of the total message being communicated between two persons is carried by the meanings of the words the persons use. Watch for and begin to interpret the nonverbal or body messages that are being communicated and develop a sensitivity for the messages that you may be inadvertently sending to others.

2. When we interview others, we can help them feel comfortable and, thereby, improve the quality of information we're getting by leaning forward, using good eye contact, and generally giving the other person the feeling that we really care about his or her point of view.

3. Eyes can be important indicators of a person's emotional state, particularly if the eye pupils dilate during a conversation or if the blinking rate increased markedly during a particular portion of the conversation.

4. Touching messages often carry "relationship" overtones. When working with employees especially, watch to see if your usual touching messages may be having an adverse effect on your verbal communications and on your relationship with those employees. Some people are "touchers" and like such contact. Others are not touchers and resent intrusions by their superiors, especially when they feel they can't retreat.

5. When dressing, choose styles, colors and patterns or combinations that help you present the kind of image you want to present. Use clothing as an "adaptive" tool by selecting those outfits that best match the dress of those with whom you're communicating. You'll be more successful as a communicator if you can minimize the obvious differences in clothing between yourself and the other person.

6. Develop an appreciation for "patterns" of nonverbal communication. Don't become convinced that a particular gesture or posture or physical attitude *always* means the same thing to all people. It does not, and, if we begin making such assumptions, we are likely to encounter some unfortunate miscommunications.

171

Further Reading

Some books you may want to read for more information are:

Julius Fast, BODY LANGUAGE (Pocket Books)

In this book the author examines the subject of kinesics and explores each of the various movements involved in the subject of "body language," including the subjects of territoriality and space, personal masks, posture, gestures, eye and hand behavior, and symbolic communication.

Gerard I. Nierenberg and Henry Calero, HOW TO READ A PERSON LIKE A BOOK (Pocket Books)

The authors of this book, experienced labor negotiators, have observed how the signals that we send are very often better indicators of our true feelings and intents than are our spoken word. This book contains a wide variety of drawings of various body postures, gestures and signals, and the ways in which these signals can be interpreted. The authors point out that certain gestures are very often interpreted in a certain way and that by using these gestures others may unconsciously be misreading our true intent. This book is very easy to read and contains practical suggestions for improved body communication.

John Molloy, DRESS FOR SUCCESS (Warner Books)

This book uses clothing as a tool to help get what we want. The author has done extensive research on how various costumes and clothing uses are perceived by other people and how these messages can be used to make an individual more successful. Although this book primarily deals with clothing, it also has such factors as self-selling development of a corporate image and strategies of dealing with job interviews.

Nancy Henley, BODY POLITICS (Prentice-Hall)

This book is a well-researched and well-documented examination of the political implications of body language. The author has developed a book for people who are curious about nonverbal communication as it is used to exercise power over others. This book also examines how nonverbal, or body, language has been used to keep woman in a submissive or a subordinate role and presents strategies by which this process can be reversed.

IV

PROBLEM SOLVING COMMUNICATION

12

Persuasion and Negotiation: Getting Your Points Across

"Everyone sells—all the time. It may be refrigerators, or clothing, or Buicks, or cosmetics—it may be ideas, or information or political positions—but it's selling. No matter what the setting, no matter what the stakes, it's getting your point of view across that counts. If the word 'sell' bothers you, say 'communicate.'"

Ralph Nelson

In the two previous sections, we've discussed some of the specifics of verbal and nonverbal communication. We've learned some of the important strategies for communication orally, in meetings, in job interviews, and in groups. We've also examined some of the finer points of space, distance, time, and body communication. In doing so, we've considered some of the ways that we can be misunderstood and how it is possible to reduce some of this misunderstanding. We have also considered strategies for doing a more effective job of communicating, using both the verbal and nonverbal aspects of communication.

In this chapter, we will pick up on many of these ideas and put them together. We'll look at some body signals and combine them with some word strategies, or presentation strategies, or arrangement strategies. We'll develop the "selling orientation" that Ralph Nelson talks about. As persuaders, negotiators, or communicators, we are constantly selling others, and to sell effectively, we must use all the resources at our command. In this chapter, we'll also look at some of these resources, and we'll develop some new combinations from previous chapters to help us get our ideas across to others.

175

AVOIDING THE POWER STRUGGLE

When we communicate, we do so on two distinct levels.[1] The *content* level of communication deals with the subject, topic, or problem that concerns us at a particular time. We usually think of communication problems developing because two people can't agree on the content of a particular message. In a persuasion situation, therefore, a power struggle develops because they can't agree what should be done, or they can't agree about who is responsible for what, or they can't agree with each other's definition of the problem itself.

Clearly, there are situations in which this is true. However, most experts in communication feel that real communication difficulties develop not in the content part of an exchange but in the relationship part. The *relationship* level of communication involves the way in which two individuals themselves define their relationship. When we accept the ideas, products, or "sales pitches" of another person, or when we resist their attempts to persuade, we are probably responding to relationship messages.

Whenever we enter any sort of persuasion transaction, the relationship between the persuader (for convenience, called the "seller") and the person being persuaded (the "buyer") is determined in advance. In all persuasion situations, the buyer is one up over the seller because the buyer can pull out of the transaction at any time. In some persuasion situations, a power struggle develops when the seller attempts to take the upper hand and gain control over the buyer. This can be seen in the use of phrases like "you must" and "you should." It can also be seen when the seller uses a buyer's questions as a chance to become an expert and thus take charge. For example, if you're trying to persuade your boss about an idea you think will save your firm money, you're the seller, he or she is the buyer. If the boss asks, "What are the problems you see in such an approach?" You could respond with a simple list of potential problems, perhaps with your assessment of how these problems can be solved. In this case, the boss's question is an invitation to move from the "one-down position" and communicate as an equal. Your reasoned and direct response shows that you accept the offer to communicate as equals. In transactional analysis, we'd call this a complimentary transaction, one adult to another. However, you *could* respond to the boss's simple question about potential problems by citing grand and elaborate claims, broad dismissals of any problems, and so on. For example,

Boss: "What are the problems you see in such an approach?"

You: "Hey, not to worry, boss! I've thought through every angle, figured every catch, and there's absolutely no problem at all. Trust me, boss, this is a sure-fire, 100 percent success idea that can put this company on the map, ..."

176

If this sounds like high pressure, you're right. The employee (you?) hasn't heard the question as a question or an opportunity to talk as equals. He or she views the question as a perfect chance to take control of the boss. If the boss accepts your take-over attempt, there will be no power struggle, although there may be some resentment over your "high pressure" tactics. However, when dealing with the boss, there's more involved than just buyer and seller. There's also the role relationship of boss and employee, and in this relationship the boss is clearly on top. Because of this second relationship, there's a much greater chance for a power struggle to develop, especially when the seller (the employee) fights for the upper hand.

Consider another case in which the relationships aren't quite so clear. Suppose you are trying to motivate or persuade an employee to do something, to accept your idea, or to behave in a particular way. As the boss, you can *order* the employee to *buy*, but let's assume that you feel such an exercise of managerial power is unwise. Therefore, you decide to persuade, and, in so doing, you again become the "seller" (one down) communicating with the "buyer," who's one up. Although this is a "crossed transaction," no major problems will develop as long as you keep in mind that the "buyer-seller" relationship takes precedence over the "employee-employer" relationship. As the seller, you must listen for the buyers real needs, for the doubts and uncertainties the buyer feels about your proposition. You'll also be listening for signals about changes in the relationship. Some of these signals include:

Employee (Buyer): "Could you tell me more about _____?"
"I'm concerned about the _____."

These are direct questions and suggest that the buyer is looking for straight answers. Your best response is to give those straight answers. In the process, you're responding to the relationship signals and communicating as equals. No power struggle is involved.

Employee (Buyer): "We've had some real problems with similar ideas. It won't work this time!"

Here, the employee is suggesting that he or she wishes to remain in the dominant position and that your persuasive argument needs some more support before a position of equal communication is appropriate. Often, this is the point at which bosses try to overcome their one-down position by reverting to the argument "Look here, I'm the boss, and you do what I say!," which is really no argument at all. Instead of working within the relationship of buyer and seller, the boss tries to change the relationship to one in which he or she is clearly on top. The employee is then put in the position of having to either go along with the boss (in which case, motivation has been replaced with force) or resist the boss. Because the boss holds many other "cards," such as poor work assignments, firing or disciplining, or simply displeasure, the employee will likely find it difficult to resist. However, when this change in positions does take place, the employee is put on notice that the boss wants to motivate and persuade *as long as the employee goes along with the boss's wishes.* In the long run, this will not create a motivating climate.

> Employee (Buyer): "You make a good case, boss. Since you're more experienced than me in these things, I'll go along with your judgment."

In this situation, the employee (or buyer) is saying that he or she accepts the boss's expertise and is willing to reverse the roles and let the boss resume the dominant position. This is similar to the way most of us respond to medical advice from a doctor. As "buyers" of medical advice, we can accept or reject what the doctor tells us we should do. However, recognizing that the doctor has the professional expertise that we don't have, most of us are willing to trust the doctor to tell us what to do. However, even doctors find that they are more successful in selling a particular kind of treatment or medical solution when they assume the "seller" role rather than the dominant "expert" role.

Although we've been suggesting that successful persuasion involves listening and responding to the relationship messages that others send us and accepting the one-down position of the seller or persuader, we are not suggesting that to persuade you can't be aggressive. When you listen and respond to comments about the relationship and communicate as equals in the transaction, you can aggressively present your points of view. If you've done your homework before trying to persuade, you'll have the best answers to each of the buyer's objections already at hand. As long as you resist the temptation to respond to questions with a one-upper, you'll be able to present your strong and valid arguments and more than likely avoid the power struggle that gets in the way of your primary goal, which is to *persuade the buyer to buy.*

There are, of course, techniques that can help you become a more successful persuader. In our chapters on meetings, oral communication, body messages, and others, we've explored many of these techniques. In the next section, let's review them in one place and tie them specifically into the objective of getting your points across effectively.

DO's AND DON'Ts OF SUCCESSFUL PERSUASION

In addition to the relationship messages of communication and the importance of listening and responding to these messages, there are some techniques that you can use to become a more effective persuader.

In meetings, especially with your superiors, try to avoid direct confrontations with the "power" people. You'll usually come out on the short end of such a confrontation, even if you have the "right" answer or the "weight" of evidence on your side. In those rare cases where you *do* win in a direct public confrontation with a power person, you'll probably create a dangerous situation for yourself in the future. By forcing a powerful person to lose "face," you'll create a potential opponent on future problems. This does not mean that you should passively submit to the boss's authority. It means choosing the appropriate time and place for confrontation. Usually, a public attack will be put down with a full show of power. However, in private the leader may be able to look more objectively at your proposal without all the "role playing" involved. Once they've examined your proposal, you can use their reaction as a guide to taking it further, or going back for more study.

Although it's wise to avoid confronting power people in a meeting, the same advice doesn't hold for *others* at a meeting, with one important condition. If the powerful person or persons are on your side, or are generally favorable to your position (or to you), go ahead and confront your opposition head on. You will likely want to use tact and stay on the subject (the content level) rather than attacking your opponent personally (the relationship level). When the persons opposed to you are not the power people or the central characters, keeping on a content level is relatively easy to do. However, with power people or key figures in the organization, their opinions and their personalities are intimately tied together. When you threaten or question their publicly held positions, you are in effect threatening or questioning *them* and creating unfortunate relationship messages.

When persuading, don't be excessively negative or start from positions of weakness. In sales, this often translates into "don't knock the competition," as this form of persuasion is usually a reflection of an individual's confidence in his or her own product or position. Putting your ideas into a negative position (ours is better than theirs, because theirs is "crummy") gives the buyer a choice between two worsts. Instead, present ideas and positions in a positive way, and respond positively to comparisons.

Thus, if the person being persuaded asks, "Don't you feel that the idea Sara proposed is better than yours?," don't respond by suggesting that "Sara's idea is all wet, 20 years out of date, and based on faulty assumptions besides." If the person doing the buying is already committed to Sara's idea, you've again created a position in which you might be interpreted as attacking the buyer's competence. Hardly a strong position from which to argue. Further, you've also put yourself in a position to "one up" the buyer, by suggesting that you've developed more insight than he or she has been able to muster. This strong one-up bid also personalizes your opposition, by at the very least implying that Sara hasn't done her job in making her proposition.

A more positive way of responding to the buyer's question is to suggest, "I'm familiar with her plan, and it is generally strong. However, there are key areas in which the plan I'm proposing is better and would result in more favorable results for the firm." This opening line can then be followed by a detailed and well-reasoned point-by-point comparison of your plan and Sara's, with your strengths clearly demonstrated. By taking this positive approach, you're protected in case the buyer has already made a tentative decision to go with Sara's plan, and you're also showing that you've done your homework and have made a thorough study of *both* plans before making your presentation. Resist an attempt to downgrade your competition even when the buyer makes a statement that is clearly critical of the competition. This statement may merely be a way of testing you to see if your position will stand on its own merits or if you'll find it necessary to resort to "smear" tactics to make your sale.

When confronting a potential buyer, be sure to use constant and direct eye contact, without staring at the individual. Keep your eyes frank and direct, but not cold and expressionless, and try to watch for subtle changes in the buyer's eyes, such as pupil dilation or increased blinking. These signals may indicate that the buyer's emotional state is changing and that you should "go for a close" or summarize and complete your presentation. Also, watch for and evaluate facial expressions for similar signs.

Keep your voice controlled, low but well modulated, and above all keep your voice relaxed. In a perfume commercial, the message suggests that you should "whisper if you want to get his attention." Whispering may not be an appropriate managerial communication strategy, but changes in the tone and level of your voice will accomplish the same thing. When you lower your voice, you can often see the listeners moving in toward you, to better hear what you're saying. You keep them from focusing on your monotone voice by raising and lowering it. However, if the person with whom you're talking has a speech problem and clearly wants you to "speak up," don't lower your voice too far, or you'll lose more than his or her attention. Women should try to avoid the high voice ranges, as their voices tend to get shrill when excessively raised. Both men and women sound demanding when their voices are too high, but soft and wavering voices should also be avoided as too passive and nonauthoritarian.

When persuading, keep your body as still as possible, thrust slightly forward. When seated, keep your hands in sight, but not folded across your chest or behind your head. Don't rock or swivel in your chair. Keep both feet firmly and flatly on the floor. Crossed legs tend to create more barriers and may look sloppy.

When standing, maintain a balanced stance, erect but not rigid. Avoid "storking" (standing on one foot with the other tucked behind your leg and your foot on the tip), leaning, stooping. Try to avoid excessive head nods. All can be interpreted by your buyer as signs of weakness. However, do remember the positive effects of occasional and aggressive signals, such as hands on the hips, arms folded tightly across the chest, or feet wide apart. These are often viewed by buyers as domineering signals, and they can be interpreted as attempts by the persuader (you) to take a dominant, one-up position in the transaction.

The amount of hand movement that each of us uses is somewhat controlled by cultural and learning factors over which we have little or no control. In general, it's wise to avoid excessive hand fluttering, although some hand movement is natural and very effective as a means of emphasizing your points. When persuading, avoid playing with beards, moustaches, long hair. Avoid clenched fists, finger pointing, and table pounding. All these gestures can and are frequently interpreted by buyers as dominance gestures and are, therefore, seen as threats to the buyer's one-up position.

When persuading in meetings or in one-on-one situations, maintain good bladder control. Leaving a group meeting, even for the best of reasons, gives your opposition a chance to relax and marshall their forces. It can also be viewed by your buyer as a sign of weakness. Also, when a break in a meeting *is* called, don't be the first one to bolt out the door, even if you're in pain. A controlled, calm, and easy-going image will be more effective. In general, your persuasive messages will be more successful when you convey to your buyers a sense of competence, self-assuredness, and strength. Combine this with an attitude that you really care about the buyer and his or her problems and that your proposals or plans are aimed at satisfying the major needs of your buyer. Unless you are with intimates, avoid sarcasm or flippancy when trying to persuade, as these messages often imply an equality position that usually is not present in a persuasion transaction, even after the sale is complete. Don't overdo "superiority" messages or exaggerated shows of strength or knowledge, although you're wise not to shy away from them either. In the final analysis, a strong content and a strong relationship message is the best communication strategy for successful persuasion.

Because the strength of a persuasive appeal depends on some adaptation to the person being persuaded, let's examine some important factors to consider when trying to persuade your boss about an idea or proposal.

PERSUADING THE BOSS

Selling a good idea to the boss may be one of the most difficult tasks a manager faces. Not only must the subordinate decide on the merits of the idea, but more often than not there's also the question of timing and approach.[2]

How do you approach the boss? The first answer, for many managers is simply to pray. But the wise manager spends time analyzing the boss and goes in with an approach that lets the boss retain his dignity and authority.

Approach is especially critical in an autocratic or hierarchical environment where the boss either is unapproachable or at least seems that way. In that case, standing up for what you believe is likely to be more effective if you couch your suggestion within the goal structure, belief system, sensitivity, or needs of your manager or boss.

You won't be able to express your idea if you get all hung up by an emotional confrontation. The manager must adopt a problem-solving orientation. He has a better chance if he focuses on the rational completion of a task.

Before you take an idea to the hard-to-reach boss, make an effort first to understand the boss's goals, values, and self-concepts. Present your idea in the context of what's important to the boss and try to understand his or her overall objectives and needs. Then, try to find some component of your idea that fits into his thinking. You must be able to postpone your own self-gratification if you want to persuade.

When knocking down the boss's idea, the approach should be quite subtle. Even in a bad idea, there are some components that aren't bad. Talk to those first. It helps present the criticism in a better light. After building on the constructive components of an idea, you can then make suggestions. It can be a positive way to suggest a negative thought.

Another way of telling the "always right" boss that she or he may not always be right is to beg time. Ask the boss to let you take the idea and test it out on your people to see if there might be some negative reactions.

That way, flaws that you see can be reinforced by worker reaction without flatly disagreeing with your boss. When a person finds it hard to express his or her ideas to the boss or continually fails to win acceptance of his ideas, it's often because of the wrong approach.

Change Your Approach

If you are naturally boisterous and active, you could easily rub someone the wrong way. In that case, you are wise to go in conservatively and have a plan well-organized and outlined on paper—things that will impress an orderly planner. Your aggressiveness should come out in a clean presentation. And it should indicate that you have considered other options.

When you do have an idea, your boss will likely want "background and a concise presentation."

A manager also has greater force if he or she can say—and say in truth—that he or she represents a team. And you try to give the man upstairs some options, so that you don't run into a stone wall of opposition on just a few points.

When you disagree with the boss, it's important to make sure it's in private, on a one-to-one basis that doesn't undermine his or her authority. If it's a violent disagreement, tackle him or her behind closed doors with the understanding that my boss is still *the* boss. Tell him or her, "This is what influenced your thinking, but this is what influenced me even more."

Criticize, but Don't Ridicule

If you don't ridicule and if it's understood that none of it is being done on a I-know-more-than-you basis, then there won't be any problem, and no one will feel his or her job's being threatened. However, when the final decision is made, it's final and you should support it whether you like it or not. The most you can productively do then is that, if you feel there are areas in a plan that are critically weak, you can work to strengthen them in the plan's implementation.

The other side of the coin is how you as a boss consider ideas from your employees. First, you have to ignore your natural unwillingness to hear bad news. Yet, it's better to have someone tell you the bad news than have that someone tell everyone else. When listening, give the employee enough time to explain his thoughts, and then, when you have to reject an idea, at least you've listened at length. Make sure that there's feedback, whether it's good or bad. One thing that will cut off criticism and ideas is no feedback.

Hearing the worker's reasoning also enables a manager to make a more valid decision. The employee may have additional facts that may change your mind, and, if not, you'll be able to explain your reasoning to him or her because you've found out what he or she knows.

Blunt or Tactful?

Managers who must reject ideas are divided on whether to be blunt or not. "When the boss brings something to me, he or she is not looking for praise; the boss wants constructive criticism," declares one typical manager. "I try to be as constructive and as brief as possible. He'll let me know if he wants more information by his reaction."

"There is too much concern on how you phrase things," agrees another. "There is no substitute for frankness," as long as it's in private and not at an open meeting.

Others, however, think it's best to move into the bad news slowly. "You start off with the good points and then proceed to your points of disagreement." Also, be very specific in explaining why it is not a good idea. No matter how you tell someone that his or her idea has been rejected, it's important that you *do* tell him.

Rejecting Tactics

When discarding an idea, don't do it out of hand. At the worst, ask the person to put the idea down on paper and let you think about it. What usually happens then is that either the employee doesn't bother to write down the suggestion or in putting it on paper finds out himself "that the idea isn't as good as he thought."

Another tactic is to tell the employee, "That's a great idea, check back with me on Friday." This allows time "to separate the employee from his or her emotional involvement with the idea. It helps the individual think out the idea and also makes him or her more willing to listen to a factual exchange on the idea's merit."

Directing the individual to the person who'd be responsible for implementing the idea also helps remove the emotional involvement and makes the idea man strive for improving upon his idea before actually submitting it. Recognition of the employee is extremely important, even if just a small part of the idea is accepted. Give the employee credit, and don't let him or her see it turn up as your idea or in someone else's larger plan. This is an important strategy in overcoming the negative effects of phony feedback.

This honesty and feedback can take on even greater importance for the middle manager. A middle manager can't take every request to management, or he's merely a funnel. He or she must sometimes disagree with requests as nonlegitimate or he'll lose the respect of those who report to him. But, if they're legitimate, the manager should be just as strongly compelled to forcefully present the idea in an advocacy manner.

Personal Rights

The same principles apply, it seems, to obtaining personal freedoms on the job.

Too often, when a worker seeks a favor (possibly flexible working hours, time off, or a variation on the dress code), it appears that what he's actually saying, "If I get what I want, I'll do the job." When this happens, place yourself in your boss's shoes if you want to obtain a deviation from the norm. Most people don't think about the customer who may not understand why you're not there when he calls—or about others who depend on you to get them started. A manager must demonstrate that the change will not affect the jobs of others or any customer relationships. If you can point out that the change will enable you to do some extra things, that's even a better selling point.

Otherwise, the boss will think you may not be carrying as heavy a load as you can, such as the salesman who claims he could produce more if he worked on commission. Similarly, if you want to take on new tasks or get rid of some, you must first achieve your own objectives. If you want to get rid of a task, first do it well yourself and then present a plan that would make it easier to do, less time consuming, and more productive.

Getting Workers to be Assertive

It's up to the boss to encourage such open communications. If you don't, you run the risk of developing managers who are ineffective, nonproductive, and waste time fussing with their frustrations. A lot of good ideas may slip by the boards. Yet, you can't just tell an individual to be more assertive, especially in the case of a worker who simply does his job due to personal problems that make job security his top priority. In this situation, it's best to help him appreciate his stature more. It is a management task to bring out the best in workers, to nurse them along. It requires an inordinate amount of sensitivity. You must be sincere, and you can't be phony. You have to encourage disagreement by the behavior of the supervisors.

Managers themselves have various techniques they can use to elicit ideas from their people.

1. Talk to individuals in a positive tone, and let them know that you want to hear their ideas—even if you disagree. Give them confidence first in a private meeting in your office and then solicit their views in an open meeting.

2. Encourage employees to take good ideas directly to the manager in charge—even if it's the president. It makes them develop better ideas and also makes them feel more important in the company's eyes.

3. Have your workers take the time once a month to write a paragraph or so of just what's on their mind. That way, the dialogue starts with them. Then, we sit down and talk about it, and the significant points are openly discussed in depth.

4. When you're wrong, admit it, and then the boss or employee usually will, too. Moreover, "that clears the air, and you're on to the next move."

5. If you have an unapproachable supervisor, it requires a considerable amount of courage, real understanding of the supervisor's belief system, and an ability to look at the task from the supervisor's point of view.

GETTING YOU ACROSS—OR UP—IN YOUR ORGANIZATION

In our chapter on career communication, we looked into some strategies that you can use to sell yourself in the job market. In this chapter, let's assume that you've decided to try for another job higher up in your present organization. Most of us move up the management ladder by staying with our present organization and working from the inside to get that next promotion and the power and rewards that go with it. Again, the notion of "selling" comes into our discussion, although in a much more subtle way.

When you're in the job market, you are selling yourself, complete with advertising (your resumé), performance claims (your references and past work record), and personal salesmanship (the interview). However, when you're working for a promotion in your present organization, only your performance record and the way you personally handle yourself are important. Because we're assuming that your performance record makes you a likely candidate for promotion, the only variable left is your method of persuading others that you're the person for the promotion. You can't use the more direct selling methods of resumés and job interviews, and you must therefore communicate in a way that gets your points across persuasively, but in a soft-sell manner.

ADAPTATION

The surest way to succeed as a communicator is to adapt your message to the language and experience of the receiver of the message. In this way, you have reduced as much of the potential for distortion as it is possible to remove, and the receiver can concentrate on the merits of your message. In promoting yourself in your organization, you have the same objective in your communications. You want to send your persuasive messages to your superiors in a way that they can understand and evaluate you and your record with a minimum of distortion. To do this, you must adapt your message and yourself as much as possible to the thinking and value system of the management group you wish to join.

The person who is upwardly mobile, the one who wants to get ahead badly enough, is usually astute enough to learn what the value system of the corporation is.[3]

This means acting like those who have made it in the company, right down to the striped ties, dark-blue suits, and wingtip shoes. This is usually the first form of adaption, and we've discussed some "dressing for success" ideas in our body messages chapter. If you get to work and find that your supervisors come in before you, before the normal starting time, you'd better take that as a cue that they consider the goals of the organization so important that they are willing to spend some of their own time furthering them.

So you must send out a signal of your own: "I understand what you're telling me, and I'll accept and imitate it." Start coming in early. If the boss takes work home in his briefcase, you do the same—even if the briefcase is never opened at home. The point is that you will look like a member of the management team, and this is precisely what you want.

Unless your father owns the company, don't expect to reach the top by lingering over two-hour lunches and taking off early for a round of golf. Most executives are so wrapped up in their jobs that it's a part of their personality that they couldn't feel good while the corporation is going down or feel bad while the corporation is going up. This is why they are so intolerant of people who treat a job as only a job.

Upward mobility has tended to be associated with identification with the organization. People at the upper levels of organizations tend routinely to be more motivated, involved, and interested in their jobs than those at lower levels. An aspiring executive has to have an enjoyable experience in coming to work and doing his or her job.

Your boss probably lives his or her job. Identify with him, and he'll love you for it. He's human, and, if he sees some of himself in you, he can't help but compliment your good judgment and think as highly of you as he does himself. This is a subconscious reaction known as "halo effect." We choose a value system and we tend to measure other people by how closely they mirror that value system. It's a very natural thing.

It is possible that you may have no respect for the boss or the values of the company. In that event, compromise yourself or move on. That's why we have people dropping out of the organizations; they feel they cannot stay there and maintain their personal integrity. Generally, money-motivated employees are best able to substitute the company's values for their own.

Once you have identified the value system, get busy applying it to your job performance. You are not ready to begin negotiating until you have somehow made yourself visible to the corporate powers—either through outstanding performance or, more difficult to do, by acquiring status through political action (aligning yourself with the comers on the fast track).

THE MENTOR

If you can attach your career to that of someone above you in the organization, special advantages will be yours. You will, for example, be privy to inside information that may allow you to cut red tape or go around the hierarchy and get things done more visibly. Most employees are capable of doing more than their positions allow them to do; if you can enlarge your sphere of influence through association with someone up the line, making it appear that you have influential backing, the power to get things done is yours. This is known as "reflected power," and it can come even through a social relationship with a higher up. Get yourself an office uncle (so what if you have to take up golf to do it?).

Higher status may allow you to claim a measure of autonomy over your corner of the corporate world. Autonomy is rare in today's complex and impersonal business structure. With it, you can gain some discretion in doing your job, and it is good performance, using discretion, that is recognized. Most employees routinely do what is expected of them; the edge is held by the one whose behavior is not charted, and whose work can therefore become visible. People who look like comers seem to have an instinct for doing the visible.

There are also pitfalls in office alliances, whether in the selection of a sponsor or targeting a person higher in the organization whose job you want. Careers often turn on a single incident of bad judgment. Associates of the senior manager you have targeted may regard you as a threat to them as well and join forces to protect him or her. You can encounter two supervisors with power over your career, be forced to make a choice, and pick the wrong one.

Some people's careers come to a bad end when, through no fault of their own, they get into a role-conflict situation.

In choosing a supervisor to line up with, pick the one whose values are closest to those of top management. If the corporate goal is production, you would be unwise to align yourself with a supervisor who is always jousting with others over quality control. Lean toward supervisors who delegate authority, train subordinates, and allow a bit of autonomy. This type is promotable because there are others who can fill his shoes. And, if you are on the supervisor's team, he will want you to be in those shoes. Bosses who are restrictive generally anticipate no growth for themselves. They keep control to show that they are the only ones who can do their job. If you are capable, you will be a threat to them.

Let's assume now that you've identified the value system and have been performing well under it, that you have formed alliances and enlarged your influence and gained some autonomy, which in turn has made you more visible. What remains before the start of negotiations is getting together your end of the deal. What do you have to offer the company—the boss—in return for that raise or promotion?

In approaching the boss for more money or a new position, you won't win by stressing the past. He knows the past. What he's interested in is buying for the future. Be prepared to sell yourself with a program based in large measure on future performance. Tell the boss what your goals are for the job at hand, but do so in general terms. Avoid knocking the competition, avoid overselling, avoid specific references to the company's problems and suggestions that you are the one to solve them. Remember that a free consultation from you on company problems is an insult to the existing management, an indictment of its inability to solve the problems. Moreover, if you've given them the answers, they may not need you in the job. On the other hand, speaking generally of common goals allows them to know that you're both on the same track. Take the time to gain a thorough background before seeking an interview. The worst time to make a mistake is when your every word is being weighed.

HOW ABOUT A RAISE, BOSS?

Try to learn what your peers are earning before barging into the boss's office to contend that you are being underpaid. If you're near the top of the scale for your job, you'll have little bargaining power. If you are near the bottom of the scale, be prepared for some criticism. The boss may take the opportunity to enumerate your faults by way of explaining why you're at the bottom. The best plan is to offer a program for greater accomplishment and try to get an agreement on a reward if those goals are met. This will mean a delay in getting more money, but it's probably a lot more acceptable to the boss who has salary budgets to deal with and is responsible for getting the company the most for its money.

Develop a case for yourself based on demonstrated performance. Look to the future and try to change. Always work through your immediate supervisor, he or she will fight if you go over his or her head. Get agreement on specific levels of job accomplishment. If it's money you want, nail down a commitment to a figure; if it's a promotion, ask for specific criteria under which you will be evaluated. Ask for more responsibility in either case—quiet, dependable, shrinking violets never go anywhere.

There are situations, too, in which your best tack may be to request neither a raise nor a promotion but a transfer to another department. Many companies have fast-track departments out of which the majority of executives rise. Don't dawdle in personnel if the fast track is in production. Sniff out where the power is and try to get there. And, if your boss hasn't been promoted in three years, try another department.

Remember that the goal of your negotiations is to satisfy you and the company. Although it is never wise to describe the ultimate that you hope to attain (your boss doesn't want to hear your plan for replacing him or her), you should start high, above your immediate objective. That allows room for compromise. Be assured that, particularly in the case of money, the boss will come in from the low end. A successful negotiation would be one on which you ask for $3,000, expecting $1,000, and the boss offers $1,500, having been prepared to pay $2,000. You win, he wins. When you're in salary talks, take a strongly positive attitude into an interview but avoid overuse of the first person pronoun, which can be tiresome to listen to and conveys a self-centered attitude. Come off as a team player by using the editorial "we." By acting as though a decision has already been made in your favor, you give the boss advance credit for having the intelligence to recognize a good thing when he sees it. On top of that, managers are trained to be optimistic; they relate best to displays of optimism and confidence.

If you expect to get more money by demanding it, be prepared to be told, "If you're so good, maybe you'd better try your talent somewhere else." The best approach is a soft one: Come in and say, "I think I've been overlooked. I've done a good job, what do I have to do to get ahead from here?" With this approach, you are more likely to get a sympathetic hearing and not be looked upon with disfavor. Notice too that this request is based on future performance, with no demand for an instant raise.

Remember that sex is a factor in your success as a negotiator. There is a recognized male bias in management, where the rules of behavior are made and controlled by men. As latecomers to the corporate world, women tend to miss the cues to advancement that require a knowledge of how one moves up the corporate hierarchy. They need to think in terms of career goals rather than short-term planning, according to Margaret Hennig and Anne Jardim, psychologists who wrote *The Managerial Woman*. It helps, too, to target departments where there are few women managers, and the company can be persuaded of this fact.

Most negotiations succeed or fail less because of the formal elements of the transaction than by "the actions, inactions, habits, idiosyncrasies, blunders, insights, and clever strategic moves" of the parties. There is a requirement for learning, expertise, and common-sense thinking (see the following section for more specifics on strategy).

In any event, your dealings with management must be held in confidence. Your case will be seriously weakened if word spreads through the office that you're seeking a raise or promotion. Organizational politics is an endlessly fascinating topic of conversation for employees, and they watch for signs of favor and inclusion. If you succeed and divulge terms, you could be the source of serious discontent among less favored colleagues and ruin your career on the spot.

How much time, energy, and anguish you are willing to put into this process will depend on your personal values. Getting to the top will mean devoting a big chunk of your life to the company. The financial rewards are there, but there will be limited time to enjoy them. The pressures of the job can be physically detrimental. You wouldn't be the first to leave the kitchen to get away from the heat.

Ways to Improve Your Communication Skills

If you're going to persuade and negotiate, it's best to learn the rules:

1. Let the other person make the opening statement; you may learn the company's needs and be able to satisfy them on your terms.
2. Phrase questions for a positive answer. That gets the other side used to saying "yes," which is what you want said.
3. Make an early concession on a minor point; the other side may feel called upon to reciprocate.
4. Never promise unless you can deliver.
5. Never suggest a range of values; the other side will choose the end that suits it.
6. Defer key issues until the end, when you know most about the other side's stance.
7. Take a position of prominence. Stand up when talking, if necessary; don't let them stare down on you.
8. Pick the right time of day. Don't hit the boss when he or she is thinking of the next appointment.
9. Have the strong points of your case on the tip of your tongue, ready to be unleashed strategically.

10. Guard emotions. Never show anger unless you know it will carry your point. Avoid gleeful expressions that could alienate.
11. Avoid snap decisions that you may regret. Better to insist on a delay to think it through.
12. Never underestimate the other side. It is already in a position of strength or you wouldn't be negotiating.
13. Remember that the boss is under pressure and faced with a decision that will reflect on him or her. Don't crowd.
14. Take along your sense of humor and be open and friendly.
15. Tell the truth. Exaggeration reduces your credibility.
16. Be yourself. Posturing is transparent.
17. End on a positive note regardless of the outcome, if only to express thanks and say that both sides have learned from the bargaining.
18. Adapt your messages to the receiver. Talk his or her language, and use examples and values that the receiver can appreciate.
19. Apply the "body messages" that strengthen your persuasive message.
20. Listen for the "relationship" messages when you negotiate or persuade. Don't simply rely on good content to bring about the persuasive goal you have in mind.

Further Reading

For more information, you might want to read:

MARVIN KARLINS AND HERBERT ABELSON, PERSUASION (Springer Press)

This book summarizes all the important research over the past few years on the subject of perception. It is a very readable book that develops all the important persuasion research. As such, it is a very interesting summary for those interested in the subject of persuasion.

LYNDA BLOOM, KAREN COBURN, AND JOAN PEARLMAN, THE NEW ASSERTIVE WOMAN (Dell)

These authors contend that for some time women have been afraid to assert themselves because of "fear of success" syndrome. This book describes a new kind of female behavior and is a how-to manual aimed at curing passivity and powerlessness in your personal relations. Although written from a woman's point of view, this book can be applied successfully to interpersonal communication and relationship by both women and men.

ANTONY JAY, MANAGEMENT AND MACHIAVELLI (Bantam Books)

Machiavelli was a medieval advisor to an Italian prince. In a book called *The Prince*, Machiavelli suggested ways in which a person in power can consolidate that power and maintain an effective leadership position over others. This author discusses various Machiavellian concepts as they relate to power, interpersonal communication, organizational strategy, and group behavior and develops some interesting comparisons between Machiavelli's advice for success in the Middle Ages and people's behavior in modern organizations.

13

Those "Bad News" Messages: Saying "No" and "You're Fired"

"You make a guy a manager, and right away he turns into a crabby old man."

—*Lucy in* Peanuts *(Schultz)*

Everyone likes to say "yes," and no one likes to be thought of as crabby. Saying "no" is unpleasant, it's negative, and it often feels unproductive. Even worse, saying "You're fired" is a terrible burden that most of us will avoid at all costs. In some organizations, managers so dislike sending these "bad news" messages that "no sayers" or "hatchetmen" are hired to take away the burden. This may make you feel better, but it won't make the problem of bad news messages go away anymore than the ancient Greeks were successful in disposing of bad news by disposing of the courier who simply *brought* the bad news.

Negative messages involve a degree of disconfirmation. This is the notion that we are telling a person that he or she doesn't exist, or that he or she is unworthy or unimportant. Yet, often, the negative is designed to help the employee change behavior and improve. Of course, there *will be* some disconfirmation in a "you're fired" message. However, even with this extreme example of a negative message, managers usually don't want to embarrass or humiliate the discharged employee. Because part of any manager's job is the communication of "bad news" messages, let's look at two such messages. First, the "no" message.

HOW TO SAY "NO"

Favors, raises, jobs, help. Managers are forever being asked for something. Sometimes the proper answer is, "No." But there is more than one way of saying no — just as there is more than one way of saying goodby.[1]

Management and tact are almost synonymous. It's no accident that some of our top diplomats came to the government from industry. Going from supervisor to executive increases the awareness of the need to say "no" gracefully — as gracefully as saying "yes."

TAKE A MEMO

Cold, impersonal "nos" are very defeating. They leave no room for doubt. Nothing can be salvaged. They range from the "F" on a report card to just plain being ignored. Being passed over for promotion time and time again is being ignored on a grand scale. Form letters of rejection to job applicants are equally crushing.

The key to understanding the impersonal "no" lies in its use as a means to avoid responsibility. People tend to back away from being held accountable for the results of a "no" answer. It's a rejection of responsibility. If those people would explore their impersonal behavior, they would see that they are literally afraid to confront a situation. The ultimate effect of this kind of behavior is continuing ineffectiveness.

A communications manager with Dow Chemical Co. looks on the impersonal "no" as a door closer. "Never say 'no' unless you leave a way out for the employee. There is usually some component of the employee's request or proposition that has merit."

Why trample a person with a flat "no?" Leave him or her some dignity — some way out. Another manager suggests that "the main problem is the distance, both psychological and physical, that the impersonal manager sets up between himself and his or her people. The ability to motivate people is severely handicapped by distance. Impersonality becomes a managerial example to the staff. They, in their turn, begin to avoid responsibility — to build distance. Ultimately, a vast empire of mediocrity evolves. People engage in the game of communication rather than the real thing."

Personalizing a "no" answer isn't an automatic diplomatic passport. It is possible to destroy a man personally as well as impersonally. It is the approach, the basic honesty in the personal answer, that is the foundation of maintaining a successful relationship while denying a request.

THE "EMPATHY" PRINCIPLE

Think in terms of the "empathy" principle, that is, put yourself in the other fellow's place. Ask yourself, "How, in a similar situation, would I like to be treated? Would I prefer to be patronized—or would I want the situation laid on the line?" It is possible to say "no" in a manner that leaves no doubt as to why you said it, yet, because of a basically honest explanation, does not forever end a relationship. Never let an employee walk away from you with your "no" answer unless he or she is aware of exactly why you felt you had to say "no."

Developing an awareness of the need for honesty in interpersonal relations sometimes comes suddenly—even to those who have been practicing it daily. "Some years ago, at the company," says an Eastern consultant, "I was given the job of collecting and assembling technical information required for a proposal. As it came in, I noticed some contradictions. Investigating further, it became evident that we were going to offer our customer something we just couldn't produce. I went to my manager and told him I thought this was less than an honest approach. His reply was, "What does the truth have to do with this job?" From that day on I have tried to ensure to myself that all my relationships with people, whether I have to say 'yes' or 'no,' are honest."

WITHOUT FEAR OR FAVOR

Intelligence is a factor in promotion to executive and managerial rank. That same basic intelligence will allow you to recognize when you are being worked on for favors to which you must answer "no." "Good employees are usually discreet employees. They don't ask an everlasting string of favors. Good managers are equally discreet and usually can't be fooled into a compromising situation. After all, a favor is a relative thing. The employee who is performing at or above standard and who needs a rare special consideration is not really asking for a favor. He or she is, in every way, entitled to the same good treatment that he or she has been giving management. This is rarely a "no" situation. Conversely, the marginal employee who constantly finds need for special treatment is a drag on both himself and his management—probably a "no" is the way out.

As managers, we do give favors. We do favor some employees. If we didn't, we wouldn't be ensuring management succession. We wouldn't know who to train. As managers, we cannot avoid making some value judgments. Consider that, even in this freest of democracies, we make a value judgment every time we step into a voting booth. Although it is an uncomfortable feeling and we are sometimes accused of "playing God," we do have to select and promote some people over others. It is a managerial responsibility and it has to be faced—as objectively as possible.

THE OBJECTIVE CASE

"It's a matter of perspective," says another manager who attacks the problem of why a "no" is sometimes not communicated. "Employees to whom we must say 'no,' are often lacking in perspective; they don't have the tools to understand. They are psychologically incapable of viewing a problem from the perspective of top management. Whether you like it or not, I insist that this is a management failure! We have for too long looked at communications as a one-way street. We have assumed that we must communicate with the employee and have ignored the fact that he has a responsibility to communicate with us. We have failed to insist on behavior that will allow the employee to adopt the perspective of management.

"To state it in the simplest terms possible, we have not furnished the employee with means to match his goals to ours. As managers, we need information to develop our own careers and to reach company objectives. Self-motivated employees with integrated goals provide us with information. When an employee is on our side—shares our goals—we rarely have to say no to him or her.

"We too often tend to accept all the guilt—to let the employee off the hook. We need his information and his thinking and we should never stop working until his goals and ours are compatible and leading to what Peter Drucker refers to as 'upward and outward thinking rather than inward and downward thinking!' "

LET GEORGE DO IT

Every time you have to say "no" to a request for your time—to serve on a committee or to take on an extra assignment at work—you have probably been able to think of at least two people who could accept the request to serve or take on the assignment. It's much like the old adage, "To get something done, give it to the busiest person in the company." Yet, busy people often learn the art of the gracious 'no.'

There is also a bad way of passing off a "no" message. Managers often rationalize the postponing of a well-deserved "no" as "not wanting to hurt people." For instance, they begin to find specious reasons for a totally ineffective employee's staying around. Reasons such as "the organization needs his type of person" lead to the creation of jobs that are really only titles. The sad thing is that, when times get a little tight top management may be forced to do what the manager should have done long ago.

Action by top management relieves the lower echelons of the necessity of facing their duties and still preserving their psychological defenses. Letting go of a whole troop of people who should not have been there in the first place becomes a way to perpetuate a lower management who never learned the diplomatic 'no.' Developing an ability to say 'no' gracefully and effectively is important in your trip up the management ladder.

Although "no" is difficult, "you're fired" is positively devastating for some managers. We've already looked at some issues involved in "you're fired" messages; let's next consider some other dimensions in more detail.

SOME ULTIMATE "NOS"

Big "nos" are given in hiring, promotion, firing, and evaluation situations. On these occasions, particularly rejection of an applicant and at termination, there is one great pitfall. Often, our "no" answer is not understood as an attempt to explain that someone else was selected and another rejected. By the same token, we have not analyzed our reasons for letting an employee go. The failure to conceptualize — to think through what we are doing and saying — leads to a blind, emotional stab at effective management.

Unfortunately, many people have never been taught to stipulate to themselves the reasons for their actions. How, then, is it possible to explain to someone in a diplomatic, tactful way that which you yourself do not fully understand?

It's probably correct to say that nobody wants to be rejected, disconfirmed, or psychologically frozen out of the mainstream. A person senses this and gets anxious. In turn, you may get anxious about the situation. Stress and guilt begin to grow. To relieve this stress, one day you simply blurt out, "You're fired." It seems sadistic; indeed, it may be accompanied by behavior that reinforces a judgment of sadism. But what else is sadism but a reaction to guilt?

In our culture, we have preserved the idea that a bad condition automatically means that blame is due. We cannot conceive of a deteriorating situation in which someone is not guilty of sin. How much better if we could look at things objectively and say, "This is not working out. Your job is over here — we both know that. How can I help you?"

HOW TO SAY "YOU'RE FIRED"

Firing an employee is a nasty business. We declared the effect on the person earlier, and clearly he or she has a severe problem. Yet, too often, the effect on the company hasn't been considered — loss of morale in the remaining staff, financial commitments to the departed executive, replacement problems. These things must be considered before, not after, termination.[2]

The first step in firing an employee is to know exactly why you are doing it. Dipping in the till and chasing secretaries are good reasons, but they're not that common. Three usual reasons are — dead-end job, oversupply, incompetence. The euphemism for all three is "personality conflict." Breakdown in interpersonal relations is a symptom — not a cause.

Dead end means that a person is receiving pressure from below. Competent subordinates are waiting for promotion, and the person on top has reached his or her limit. Personality conflicts here show up from below as complaints against promotion policy and against the boss— the one in the dead-end position.

Incompetence means not pleasing the boss. This is the case in which firing comes in stages. First a talk, then a warning, then out. At each stage, there is hope that job performance will change.

TO FIRE OR NOT TO FIRE

Alternatives to firing aren't hard to find. Transfer, demotion, leave of absence, retraining, early retirement are all possibilities. When should you consider these courses of action?

Organizations under the gun to cut costs can get away with a harder line, especially in downward turning economy. But that's not necessarily to their own best interest. Firms should look carefully before lopping off talent as a fast, effective means of decreasing cash outlay. Yet, some managers get carried away and lose good, irreplaceable people in the name of cost cutting.

Dead-enders may be that way because of bad job person matching. Oversupply may be temporary. Incompetence may mean that you have not tried to help an employee improve. It is entirely too easy to overlook reductions in travel, postponement of capital expenditures, and other economies and seize on termination as a *panacea* for rising costs. Thus, it is important to determine that the person being fired for cost-cutting reasons cannot be used in any other capacity.

HARD LINE, SOFT LINE

No alternative? Then the second step is the actual firing. How do you go about it? Two methods are common. Some managers say, "Get the person out—and now." The other side says ease out the employee and help him or her find another job. Both sides agree that firing shouldn't be disguised or approached obliquely.

Sometimes, firing procedures seem designed to make the situation as unpleasant as possible. People are transferred to jobs for which they have no background, are ignored or harrassed by their superiors, or are simply passed over again and again.

Tactics designed to freeze out an employee or encourage him or her to resign only extend the unpleasantness of the situation and damage corporate efficiency and morale. This is the notion of "dehiring" that we'll discuss in the performance appraisal chapters.

A five-point program for termination developed by Wytmar & Co. stresses getting the person off the job quickly with the least disruption to the company and to the person's life.

1. *Make sure that there is no alternative.* Under no circumstances should an employee be kept on the payroll simply as a reward for seniority, loyalty, or as a balm to the company's conscience. The problem certainly will not be remedied by transferring the person to a responsibility beneath his or her actual or imagined capabilities—it will only aggravate the situation. Consider first the twin responsibilities of the dignity of the terminated employee and the best interests of the company.

2. *Face the situation squarely.* Inform the individual directly, candidly, and factually that he is being terminated and tell him exactly why. Don't try to freeze him out.

3. *Do not prolong termination.* In most cases, it is wiser to determine a fair severance arrangement and terminate the person immediately. It is rarely wise to retain the employee on the payroll until he or she relocates. The person's interests and energies will obviously be directed to job hunting—not to his or her job duties. This was the position of Admiral Stansfield Turner in his well-publicized reduction in the work force of the CIA. Early in 1978, Adm. Turner swiftly and effectively fired a large number of employees. Despite the initial shock, such an action is far better for employee and agency alike than the more "humane" approach of a slow firing. Slow firing is about as "humane" as snipping of a dog's tail one inch at a time!

4. *Provide what help you can.* Write fair letters of recommendation. Offer the services of the company psychologist for counseling if appropriate. Make sure that the person carries away with him or her the same version of the termination as the company's so as to avoid difficulties in reference checking.

5. *Maintain friendship.* It is to your advantage. Poor handling of an employee termination can tarnish a company's reputation along with the manager who actually does the firing.

ANOTHER APPROACH

It is logical that the reasons you have for firing an employee are exactly those that might lead him or her to quit if the whole situation were visible to the employee. Stress this point when it comes to termination. It may not only remove some of the trauma from the situation but will eliminate any implication of lack of personal worth on the part of the terminated individual.

If you allow an employee to resign in the face of termination, make sure he or she understands that you will be truthful about his or her strengths and weaknesses in recommendations. If you can afford to wait, give the person time — even a few months — to find another job.

Be specific when evaluating performance at termination. Make sure that the person knows exactly why you are dissatisfied if the termination is for unsatisfactory performance.

FIRED, BUT NOT FORGOTTEN

Hard-line firing or soft-line ease-out — either way, there may be repercussions. First, there is the loss of investment in the person who has left. Training time and money are lost. Many companies are paying the costs of relocating certain executives who have been dropped because of merger or acquisition. Many companies are preserving their reputations by trying to be as nice as possible when an executive just can't be kept, even though the story is just an excuse for firing when poor performance is the real reason. These companies (and their managers) are not going to fare well in the eyes of those who had to go.

However, there are other, less apparent costs. An employee who has had a relatively short tenure has not paid off his or her recruitment and relocation expense to the company. The cost of hiring a replacement will probably be higher than it was to hire the person who was fired. One bright spot (maybe) is that the company that picks up the fired employee will probably put out more money to get him or her than it cost your company to fire him or her.

If firing is absolutely necessary, an analytical approach to the problem is best. Analyze your attitudes toward this investment in human talent with as much vigor as you would approach capital investments.

Morale is rarely a cost item when a firing is clearly deserved. However, there can be some horrible examples. For instance, a company was trapped by circumstances and morale did suffer badly. An executive with a lot of seniority, a good reputation, and a good work record was suddenly found to be, let's say, a drug addict (which wasn't really the problem). He was fired immediately. But, to protect him and the company's reputation, no one was told the exact reason. Needless to say, it looked like a good man was bounced arbitrarily. Fortunately, that kind of incident is rare.

The real cost of firing is to the concept of management continuity. Management continuity is a basic and important function of all organizations. Accordingly, you should conduct a careful and thoughtful analysis of your management "talent" depth prior to any decision on employee firing. Is the decision to eliminate the person absolutely necessary? Is the decision being reached in panic? With an upturn in business, would the terminated person's talents be sorely missed? Employee firing must be considered in terms of its long-range impact on your department's growth.

SCARS

For many, firing is the ultimate rejection. There are six important consequences for the fired employee.

1. Loss of income. Financial security is threatened. Living habits have to change.
2. Change in the routine. No job means no commuting, no lunch with friends, no need to get up on time in the morning. Total disruption.
3. Family tension. Spouses get upset during job hunting. Family quarrels that develop can result in scars that take a long time to heal.
4. "Masculinity" crisis. The feeling that the manly role is not being fulfilled. Sexual problems among the fired are frequent.
5. Public humiliation. There is a feeling of being held up before the eyes of friends, relatives, and the public at large as a loser.
6. Job hunting. Searching for another job can be a demoralizing proposition. Rejection seems to follow rejection, making it harder to keep up the pace.

Somehow, compared with saying "no" or "you're fired," the following problem may seem trivial, or at best not worth the time to read and think about. Yet, like the other two bad news messages we've discussed in this chapter, it too contains the possibility of disconfirmation and rejection and must be handled with care.

HOW DO I GET RID OF THE "UNWANTED VISITOR"?

There are many times when you find yourself "trapped" in your own office, or even in a public place, by a person who either thinks he or she is really entertaining you or who fails to pick up and respond to your leave-taking signals. Often, the person who puts you in this sort of spot is involved with some personal problem and probably isn't aware that the conversation from your point of view has come to an end. Perhaps the best way to handle this sort of imposition is to directly confront the individual. Tell him or her that you simply don't have the time to continue the conversation and that you would appreciate their leaving (or permitting you to leave).

If it is convenient for you to meet with this person at another time, or if you want to avoid giving the individual the impression that you never want to talk with him or her again, you might also suggest that this individual make an appointment to visit again at a later time. If you know a time when your schedule would permit a more in-depth conversation, you can even suggest the time and make a firm "date" at the time the message is given. However, although this is the best way to handle such problems, some individuals may react poorly to such a message. They feel that your request for them to leave is a personal putdown, and they will feel rejected and even angry with you for putting them in this spot. With these individuals, other more subtle approaches may work, although you must always be prepared to go to the "confrontation" option should the subtler approaches fail.

In our time management chapter, we suggested that an effective way to handle chronic time wasters is to "gang up on them." When you have to visit with a person whom you know will take far more time than you have to spare, you can arrange with a secretary or fellow worker to break in on you and the visitor and "remind you of a previous appointment" or something similar. This works if you can prearrange your signals, and, if it's done properly, the visitor will feel that this is a legitimate reason for stopping the conversation and, therefore, will not feel put down. Some managers who have chronic problems with unwanted visitors even have a buzzer installed under their desks. When the visitor gives signs of settling down for the winter, the manager simply buzzes the secretary, who then interrupts or rings the telephone. This way, the manager can make up his or her own excuse, and make a quick get-away.

Another useful approach to give visitors a signal without directly "discon-firming" them is to use the various "leave-taking signals" we discussed in Chapter 11. These signals include slapping the thighs and rising (when seated), edging toward the door, stuffing all your papers into your briefcase and walking toward the office door, leaning on the office door, and of course the ultimate leave-taking gesture of them all—simply leaving. Although these signals may seem rude, they have to be weighted in light of the time the unwanted visitor is taking and the problems that the person's staying may contribute to other matters. Like so many managerial decisions, this one involves some conflicting options, and the best choice may not always be the easiest to implement.

SUMMARY

In many parts of this book, we've examined the importance of looking at all sides of an issue or a message before communicating. In doing so, we can reduce the possibility of being misunderstood or of taking an action that will have unfortunate consequences in the future. This is clearly a major factor in communicating "bad news" messages. When "no" or "you're fired" must be communicated to an employee, have as many of the related issues as possible in mind *before* you communicate. What will be the effect on the person's morale? On his or her future performance in the company? On the company's reputation, or its relationship with other employees?

No one likes bad news messages, either as a sender or a receiver. Nonetheless, such messages must be communicated. Developing a sensitivity to the related issues and an ability to apply some effective communication techniques can have an overall impact on your performance as a communicator.

Ways to Improve Your Communication Skills

1. When giving negative messages, try to separate the message from any personal comments about the individual. This, of course, is difficult to do when firing a person. However, in other "no-saying" situations, make sure that the other person realizes that you are giving a "no" to his or her idea, not to him or her as an individual.
2. Avoid putting yourself in a compromising situation—where saying "no" becomes difficult.
3. When giving a "no," try to take the time to explain why such an answer is necessary. You'll be much more likely to improve an individual's outlook than with a single harsh "No!"
4. Don't pass off saying "no" to someone else. This can be viewed by others as a sign of your weakness as a manager and can seriously erode your standing in the organization, both in the eyes of management and of your employees.
5. When firing, be sure that there is no reasonable alternative.
6. Face firing squarely and without game playing.
7. Do not prolong a termination.
8. Provide, or at least offer to provide, as much assistance as you can to help the fired person readjust to the new situation and to find another job somewhere else.
9. As much as possible, maintain your personal relationship with the fired individual. Offer friendship and do so in a genuine, rather than a condescending, way.
10. When faced with unwanted visitors, remember that your choice is wasting time *or* having to be a bit rude to the other person. It's a priority matter, and, when tact fails, bluntness may be your only alternative.

14

Managing the "Unmanageable": the Problem Employee

"In coping with the problem employee, the manager has a distinct responsibility to communicate to him precisely what is expected of him and his performance on the job."

Lawrence L. Steinmetz

Perhaps the greatest and most frequent communication challenge for any manager is to effectively manage the "unmanageable" employee. It's often because employees are difficult to handle that managers throw up their hands in disgust and proclaim "it's impossible to manage *those* people!" In earlier chapters, we dealt with the notion of impossibility, suggesting that the "impossible" label is itself a real barrier to effective communication and effective management. Therefore, let's turn our attention to these so-called "unmanageable" employees and see if better analyses, better understanding, *and* better communication can help overcome some of the problems.

WHO ARE UNMANAGEABLE?

Broadly speaking, an unmanageable employee is anyone whom a particular manager finds difficult or "impossible" to manage. It could be the person whose cultural background, language, or behavior is quite different from that of the manager. This employee may have different views about responsibility, punctuality, or unconventional notions of honesty and fairness. It could be a person who speaks a language with which you are unfamiliar. The unmanageable employee could be the one who causes trouble, or refuses to work with others, or who drinks or uses drugs on the job. He or she might be unmanageable because of a fundamental difference in how he or she is motivated or in how he or she relates to the department and the organization. The unmanageable employee may be resisting change or may feel (rightly or wrongly) that "the organization doesn't care about me, so why should I care what goes on around here?"

The unmanageable employee may not be so much unmanageable as different. If he or she fails to conform to the manager's expectations of appropriate employee behavior the "unmanageable" label is attached. Many male managers even feel women are unmanageable, and many female managers share the same view about their male employees. Thus, the problem of unmanageability is relative. It depends on exactly who is the manager and who is the "unmanagee."

In this chapter, we will examine many communication issues related to such problem employees. Some problems—for example, those related to employees from other cultures—can be handled by a change in your assumptions and attitudes. Other problems—for example, discipline or motivation problems—can best be attacked head on. In other chapters, we've outlined some appropriate prescriptions for managerial action for these problems. Now, we also address the often thorny issue of involvement and motivation of employees that perform the so-called "unenrichable" or "dead-end" jobs.

THE WILL TO WORK

Instead of claiming that problems of motivation and leadership might be solved by better communication, some managers suggest that their employees simply refuse to work. Other managers suggest that, by improving the flow of communication *from* employees, they could set up a purposeful and motivating dialogue.[1] This dialogue, they argue, would help uncover latent problems and thereby improve morale and productivity. Motivation expert Fred Herzberg suggests that employees do have a will to work.[2] In his view, what's *missing* in the workplace is what's causing problem employees to be problem employees. Herzberg's "missing" factor is a meaningful relationship between the employee and the product or the customer.

For too long, Herzberg suggests, managers and communication experts have focused their attention on the relationship between employee and management, the so-called "hygiene" factors of motivation. These hygiene factors include pay, working conditions, benefits, and the quality of supervision. Although these factors must be supplied to employees by their management, supplying them will not make employees happy or motivated, nor will these factors prevent problem employees from developing. These hygiene factors serve employee-replenishment needs, just as bread or water temporarily satisfy one's need for food or drink. Just because you had a great meal at a friend's house last week doesn't mean that you'll never be hungry again. You were completely satisfied after that meal, and yet, today, you can be as hungry as you've ever been in your life. In the same way, the pay raise you give an employee this week may satisfy his need for money, but today's raise will not keep the employee from asking for more money in the future. All the things that Herzberg identifies as hygiene factors are involved in the relationship between supervisor and employee. They keep an employee from being too much of a problem, but they don't make the employee productive.

What does contribute to motivation and to the correction of "unmanageable" employee problems is what Herzberg describes as *motivators* — those factors in the job itself that contribute to the employee's personal sense of accomplishment and identity. Motivators include recognition, opportunity for advancement, peer visibility, evaluation, and support. They also include the fulfilling nature of the job itself and the degree of contact that the employee feels that he or she has with the customer or the final product. Thus, in a restaurant, the waiter or waitress usually has the highest status because he or she deals directly with the customer and, therefore, influences how the product (the meal) is perceived and consumed.

In many organizations, employees who have contact with customers have greater status and, therefore, a better opportunity for some measure of self-fulfillment and satisfaction. In an auto dealership, the salesperson has the highest status, whereas, in a hospital, the nurses have a higher status than the orderlies. (Of course, such status rankings are also clearly related to the type and amount of professional or technical training an individual or group of individuals has had.) In an aircraft engine company, the highest-status employees (and, therefore, the least likely to be "unmanageable") were those who worked directly with Defense Department officials (the customers) in proposing design changes and performance standards. Clearly, a great many jobs cannot be redesigned to permit those doing the jobs to feel a greater sense of participation or involvement with the customer and the finished product. However, in a classic story about "problem employees" aboard wartime U.S. Navy ships, we can see how a bit of creativity, coupled with a basic understanding of communication and human behavior, led one manager to a novel strategy.

FIVE EXTRA KNOTS[3]

The story is about a Navy battleship on duty in the Pacific during World War II. The captain had tried in vain to get the engine room to give him an extra five knots speed. The engine room wouldn't do it — first, because it was above the specified maximum limits and, next, because of boiler scale. Obviously, they just weren't cooperating. Obviously, morale was bad. So the captain turned to the executive officer and said, "I want you to build up morale down there." The executive officer went to the ship's library and found a book on building morale. This gave him no help at all, so he decided to get the chaplain in on the problem.

The chaplain recommended a face-to-face approach. Let the captain go down and inspire them personally. So the Old Man tried. He suggested they do a little better planning, that they get organized for a little more speed, that they improve their coordination. It was apparent that he was getting nowhere. The chaplain took over. "You know why we're here and what we're fighting for," he pleaded. "For home and hearth, for God and country." He got nowhere either.

They gave up and went back up the ladder. The chaplain hadn't really given up, however. He was determined to get to the bottom of this thing. So he stuck around and kept his eyes and ears open. He noticed that, in the mess compartment after a strenuous engagement, the above-deck's crowd was comparing notes on what it had accomplished. "Boy, did you see us get that Zero coming in on our starboard bow?" "That ain't nothing. What about those three planes ... ," etc. The engine room men ate silently. What did they ever do that was worth bragging about? What recognition did they ever get?

The chaplain had the answer. He went to the captain and suggested that they find an officer who had had news or sports broadcasting experience and that they give him a microphone on the bridge and have him relay a complete account of the battle as it unfolded to the men down below. During the next engagement, the officer did his job well. When it was over, the captain took the microphone and said, "This is peanuts compared to what we could do if we could overtake a squadron of destroyers directly to the west of us. To do it, though, will take an extra five knots."

He got the five knots. They overtook the squadron and clobbered it. The Old Man grabbed the microphone and shouted, "Men, we did it. And it goes without saying that without those extra five knots, it would not have been possible." That night the engine room boys did join in the conversation. I doubt if they ever mentioned boiler scale again.

The point should be obvious. If you want that extra effort, you have to talk the language of motivation, not the language of production and efficiency. This is a pretty good thing to remember if communications are not getting response. After you communicate with your employees, review your message from their point of view. You'll doubtless find your messages more effective and your difficulties with so-called "problem" employees significantly reduced.

SOME EMPLOYEE TYPES

Today, almost everyone who researches human behavior in organizations develops a series of models of types of managers, supervisors, or employees. Some of these models or "types" are vague and general and serve no useful, practical purpose for managers. Other models, such as those we'll discuss briefly in the following paragraphs, are very useful. To be of any value to a practicing manager, a model of personality types must:

1. Be realistic. The manager using the model must be able to identify those people in his or her department who fit into the various categories.
2. Be based on research and intensive study. Obviously, anyone can develop a model of *human* behavior, with various categories. The key issue is whether the types and categories actually reflect the way people behave.
3. Be prescriptive. The model of employee types must permit the manager to learn what to do with each of the different types of employee to reach some goal or objective. If we were interested in examining various types of employees to learn how to overcome motivation or behavior problems, a model of various types of employees wouldn't be of much use *unless* it also contains some "do's and don'ts" for supervisors.

In looking at the "unmanageable" employee, let's briefly consider two such models that fit our criteria for a useful model.

THE ACHIEVEMENT MOTIVE AND BEYOND

Some years ago, David McClelland, a social scientist, developed a test to determine if individuals were motivated by a desire to achieve, a desire to have good interpersonal relationships with people on and off the job, or some combination of the two.[4] McClelland found that about 25 percent of the managers he tested were indeed motivated by a desire to achieve. These people he labeled "ascendants" or "achievers." Another 65 percent of the managers studied really didn't care much for achievement or advancement on the job. Instead, these people preferred to enjoy themselves off the job. They viewed their jobs as merely a way to get the money necessary to do what they really wanted to do. These people were labeled "indifferents." A third group of people (about 10 percent) were described as "ambivalent." These people really couldn't decide if they wanted rewards on the job, off the job, both, or neither. They had what many psychologists call an "approach-avoidance" conflict going on within them. Perhaps the best way to describe the approach-avoidance conflict is to picture a person on a diet standing in front of a table of "goodies." The desire to diet and to enjoy are pulling from opposing directions.

Robert Presthus, another social scientist, described these three types of employees in much more detail.[5] He also developed some supervision issues for each type and predicted where and when problems with each type might arise. Let's briefly examine what Presthus called the upward mobile, the indifferent, and the ambivalent types.

The Upward Mobile

The upward mobile employee is the person who wants to move up in the organization and is motivated by a desire to achieve. This person wants the rewards that such achievement can bring and he or she is willing to pay whatever "price" is required for such achievement. The "price" of upward mobility in any organization will vary, but it usually involves working long hours, at lower pay, with a consequent loss of family time or time to pursue personal interests and hobbies. The "price" that many organizations require usually includes loyalty and commitment to the organization and its goals, objectives, and policies. The upward mobile person is willing—even eager—to respond in a positive way to the demands of the organization.

Clearly, this sort of person should be very easy to supervise and, in fact, most are. They will usually do anything their manager asks, and they will often find ways to improve on the methods and procedures currently being used. The manager blessed with this employee type must remember that the upward mobile is motivated by achievement. He or she is therefore constantly looking for indications that others are aware of his or her skill, ability, performance, and dedication. Managers should give positive feedback often and should also give negative feedback when necessary, as the upward mobile person wants to make whatever corrections are necessary to improve his or her chances for achievement. As we develop further in our chapter on communication in performance appraisal (Chapter 16), such criticism should be sandwiched between positive feedback and should also be accompanied by suggestions of specific things that the employee can do to improve. In short, communication with the upward mobile should be open, honest, and direct, more so than with either of the other two employee types.

Although the upward mobile employee must seem like the ideal, problem-free employee that all managers dream about, some problems do arise. The upward mobile is often ridiculed by other employees as a "company man" or the "house errand boy." In some situations, the upward mobile is clearly the "person on the way up" and is resented by employees who may fall into one of the other groups. Also, because of their dedication and skill, upward mobiles are often paid more than less motivated employees. This can create friction within the work group and can pose serious motivation problems for the manager.

Upward mobility poses another familiar problem for managers in departments where employees are organized by a labor union. Because the upward mobile employee is motivated to move up in the hierarchy, a good question is "which hierarchy?" If it's the company, few real motivation or communication problems result. If it's the union, the upward mobility of an employee can lead to a variety of conflicts. As in management, an employee who wants to move up in the union organization must be committed to the goals and policies of that organization. He or she must develop visibility within the union. Visibility usually requires that the employee stand out in labor-management disputes, taking the strong union position against management. An ambitious shop steward or local representative can serve his or her interests by maintaining an obvious state of agitation and will eagerly capitalize on supervisory errors, slips, and miscommunications. Thus, employee upward mobility isn't always a bed of roses for a supervisor.

Another problem for supervisors is the upward mobile who has reached what Lawrence Peter calls the "level of incompetence." In his *Peter principle*,[6] Peter suggests that individuals who are upward mobile will continue to move up in an organization until they finally get themselves into a job or position in which they're incapable of further upward movement. This last position becomes the individual's level of incompetence. When an upward mobile "taps out," he or she is likely to pose something of a motivation problem for management, as the individual still wants to achieve but cannot go any further. This often causes the individual to change from an upward mobile to an ambivalent, presenting new difficulties for his or her manager. Faced with such an employee, managers can motivate by putting the individual in situations in which his or her *past* accomplishments and contributions can be recognized.

A manager of airline personnel faced just such a problem with a cabin attendant whose upward mobility had been halted. The employee had advanced as far in the airline organization as it was possible for her to advance. Her performance on her present job was adequate, but it was obvious to both her and her superiors that any further mobility was out of the question. As this fact began to sink in, the formerly upward mobile employee began to change into a "problem" employee. She was too valuable for the airline to lose, but she could not be motivated with the prospect of future advancement. Her boss took our advice and began to involve the employee in developing training programs for new flight crews. By recognizing the employee's past accomplishments and wide experience, the manager was able to redirect the employee's efforts in a productive but clearly nonmobile direction. Once upward mobiles cease to be upwardly mobile, they need to have their egos soothed. They need confirmation that their past efforts were valued and that their experience and present contributions are important to the organization. With this form of upward mobile employee, a manager's communications should be in the form of counseling, with emphasis on the manager's use of listening skills. At this stage of his or her career, the upward mobile needs to feel a part of the larger organization. Wise managers provide this contact with an open, willing-to-listen attitude.

One final problem that upward mobiles sometimes cause their managers is competition. Because an upward mobile wants to move up, the logical next step is to take the manager's job. Hopefully, this won't happen until the supervisor is moved up to a more responsible position, and a vacancy is left for the upward mobile employee to fill. However, some managers feel threatened by competent upwardly mobile employees. They do everything possible to confuse, confound, and otherwise restrict their best people from getting visibility in the organization. Managers who feel the pressure of competition from their employees will often do everything in their power to avoid hiring people who present any sort of challenge to their managerial position. This can, of course, work against you, as many top management people look at such actions as signals that a manager is on shaky ground.

The top executive in a large manufacturing company in Indiana once observed in a management seminar that the only supervisors he would promote were those with enough confidence in their ability to hire people better than themselves. Clearly, it takes a lot of self-confidence to hire upward mobile employees. However, despite the potential threat there is also a benefit for the manager who does. As the upward mobile performs his or her job well, such performance helps the department meet and exceed its performance standards. This will make his or her boss look good and improve his or her chances for promotion and recognition.

Although the upward mobile employee seldom causes any severe management problems, the same unfortunately can't be said about the other two types of employees. Let's briefly examine each of them.

The Indifferent

The indifferent employee is quite different from the upward mobile. He or she presents some interesting and perplexing problems for supervisors. The indifferent person is motivated by a desire to have satisfactory interpersonal relationships, although this individual usually prefers to maintain and enjoy such relationships off rather than on the job. The indifferent personality type rejects both the rewards and the pressures of the organization. In fact, many indifferents really have no strong feelings about their organization, for *or* against. They aren't committed to the organization's goals, and they reject the usual ego rewards that the organization can provide (such as advancement or recognition or power). They don't dislike their organization either. What they do want from their organization is a clear and understandable set of job performance standards, an acceptable wage, and the mental freedom to pursue nonwork interests.

The indifferent person will likely reject any attempt by management to involve him or her in the decision-making processes. Instead, the indifferent usually prefers to be told what to do and then be left alone to do it. The indifferent is not always a problem employee, only one who won't respond positively to the usual organizational reward system. Some indifferents are found in highly skill positions, and they may take great pride in their achievements. However, they are not interested in any organizational reward except the salary, benefits, and quality supervision that the organization usually provides.

Indifferent employees are far less willing to communicate with their superiors than are the upward mobiles, except when relating as a person to another person. Indifferents are unlikely to offer suggestions or to share perceptions or personal feelings with management. They do value their interpersonal relations with others. They are best motivated by having their boss maintain as much as possible a tension-free environment in which the job can be done as painlessly as possible.

Because the indifferent rejects competition for advancement, he or she is far more likely to take a somewhat callous or suspicious view of the manager, especially if he or she is perceived as an upward mobile. Thus, the stage can be set for some severe personality clashes.

To combat or avoid such clashes, you should be aware of the need most indifferents have for structure and order in their work assignments. Also, you should realize that, although the indifferent may reject symbols of status, he or she nevertheless wants to be treated as an individual, not as a member of a faceless herd.

This attitude can lead to many communication problems, brought on by the indifferents who seem to want plaudits for simply doing their regular, routine jobs, even if those jobs are done in a sort of average, run-of-the-mill way. And this attitude often antagonizes managers, who may feel that it's not appropriate to commend or praise a person for simply doing the expected or the mediocre. Because of an indifferent attitude toward work and the workplace, manager and employee are likely to clash over various job standards, including absenteeism, lateness, and personal behavior on the job. Indifferents don't really care whether or not they come to work, so their absenteeism and tardiness exceeds that of either of the other groups. Yet, just as they are likely to not show up for work, they'll often give an indifferent excuse for their failure to come in. For an upward mobile manager, the indifferent can be both a challenge and a mystery.

The Ambivalent

Managing the ambivalent personality often requires a manager with the listening and counseling abilities of a professional psychiatrist or analyst. The ambivalent is the person torn between a desire for personal freedom and an unwillingness to "pay the price" of upward mobility while reaping the rewards of such mobility. Left alone, an ambivalent person can become quite mentally ill, in effect pulled in two directions at once. Yet, although the true ambivalent remains a constant source of problems for most managers, a degree of ambivalence can be found in the personality of all individuals, yours and your employees. In effect, few of us, no matter how upwardly mobile, are willing to pay an unlimited price for organizational rewards. Each of us at some point ceases to be upwardly mobile. However, just because a person reaches his or her limit does not mean the individual will not be motivated by additional rewards from the company or the boss. Instead, frustration sets in. This condition is similar to that of the upward mobile person who reaches his or her level of incompetence while still wishing to maintain upward mobility.

The ambivalent person presents some new problems for managers, by resenting upward mobiles for their success yet maintaining an aloofness toward the indifferents. The ambivalent person often "enjoys" poor interpersonal relationships in much the same way that the hypochondriac "enjoys" poor health. The ambivalent also tends to believe that those who achieve some measure of success on the job (upward mobiles) or off the job (indifferents) do so because of blind luck. The ambivalent is often unwilling to admit that talent, and hard work, or dedication have any part in such success, especially success earned by the upward mobile. Ambivalents are often more intelligent than either their upward mobile or indifferent co-workers and frequently like to display their intelligence, especially at the expense of their co-workers. In short, the ambivalent employee is one who must be managed with a firm hand, but with some sensitivity as well.

The problem facing managers is often a reluctance to face up to demands of the ambivalent for "special considerations" due him or her because of real or imagined feelings of being "underpaid, underloved, and underfed." The ambivalent can and often does resort to immature behavior and requires that managers maintain close communication contact and control over this individual.

THE BOSS AS A COMMUNICATION MODEL

When looking at the link between manager and employee, we find an interesting reaction of employees to various forms of job enrichment. Regardless of the job enrichment strategy used by an organization, employees usually judge the quality of their job by the quality of their boss. When the boss helps create a positive climate in a department, demonstrates competence, or manages in a way that the employee can appreciate, employees express satisfaction with their jobs. When the boss is "inappropriate," employees appear unmotivated and complain about the need for some sort of job "enrichment." This notion lends further emphasis to the importance of analyzing your employee's personalities and adjusting your management and communication strategy to fit.

Employee Personality Types

Many of the costly programs designed to improve morale and communication in organizations seem to fail for no obvious or apparent reason.[7] One possible approach to solving this problem is to analyze employee personality and behavior in terms of six broad types of individuals. With these types, it is then possible to develop and use communication strategies directly suited to the individual's needs and motivations.

Not everyone agrees with this approach. Some experts have difficulty "pigeonholing" people according to some arbitrary set of personality types. One psychologist even goes so far as to suggest that, when you establish jobs with different complexities, you must set up different work systems for all. It simply doesn't work if you push them into slots without any options.

Throughout this book, we have consistently rejected the notion that all people are alike. Nevertheless, it does managers little good to study communication and human behavior if no generalities can be drawn. Therefore, when we look at various personality types and the appropriate communication response to them, we assume that such generalizations are merely guides for appropriate managerial behavior.

An assumption made by most managers is that there is bound to be some measure of clashing or hostility between individuals in any work situation, no matter how harmonious the manager tries to make it. Because of this "fact of organizational life," you may find it useful to make yourself aware of how to communicate with various types of employees. The importance of this communication relationship between employee and manager is underscored by our earlier observation that most employees judge the quality and desirability of their jobs in terms of whether they feel that they have a good boss or *a bad* boss. Thus, even when you try to provide employees with growth opportunities, many such employees may simply choose to ignore them. In short, they are indifferent to such involvement attempts.

We have already examined how certain groups or types of employees are motivated by different things. Let's consider a more detailed set of employee types. Recognize, however, that, just as with the personality types we've already discussed, no one individual fits neatly or completely into any one category, even though most of us have one set of "type characteristics" that predominates.

1. *Tribalistic.* Although accounting for one fourth of the population, this group includes some 40 percent of all hourly production workers. Most comfortable with an established ritual, members of this group take pride in working for a prominent company like being in a strong tribe.

They generally have little or no ambition to rise out of their group, and they interpret most of their job in the context of whether they have a good or a bad boss. They will attach themselves to a good one and often will go to him for assistance — even after he has been placed in a different job.

213

The most effective way to motivate tribalistic workers is to provide them with a boss they will respect. Or, if you are their boss and can't relate to them, find their natural leader and get him on your side. You can't ask them to make decisions, but, if you work out a procedure together, they will follow it.

They will also interpret working conditions as a sign that management cares about them. Thus, they will respond to a modern office or shop. Because their "future" extends only a few weeks out, meaningful compensation means money, not retirement or deferred payments.

2. *Egocentric.* Although dominant in only about 10 percent of the manufacturing population, this group's traits are found in some degrees in almost all people—and a few drinks will usually reveal these traits. Culturally disadvantaged persons are often egocentric, and the incidence among people in prison is extremely high.

Often carrying an impressive looking bankroll (a $100 bill on the outside of the roll), a person in this group is usually physically strong, but not necessarily aggressive, is likely to become a union organizer, has no conception of company loyalty, and is likely to walk out on the job or fail to show up.

And he or she is usually a malcontent and extremely suspicious. He interprets good working conditions as a trick by management to get him to work harder. To this person, pay is never enough, only what the company has been forced to pay him.

However, straight pay is the only compensation he understands. He needs hard rules and will respond to firmness and threats of demotion or loss of pay. He will take full advantage of an easy-going boss.

3. *Conformist.* Surveys indicate that this type had become less common during the last ten years, but 40 percent of hourly workers still get this label.

Conformists believe that all employees should do their jobs as the company asks. They appreciate good working conditions but will not complain about bad ones. They will usually rebel when they are asked to bend or break a rule.

Effective management of conformists is keyed to a clear set of rules. By nature, they will obey rules without question and will point them out to others. They are comfortable with time clocks, because the time cards record that they get to work on time.

4. *Manipulative.* These are the self-achievers, the "wheeler dealers" who play all the angles and reap the rewards. Sometimes aggressive and overbearing, the manipulative person earns big money in sales and leadership positions. But his ethics are flexible; for example, he is likely to take orders he knows the factory can't fill.

Motivation is no problem—show him or her where the cheese is, and the person will find his or her way through the maze. The need for performance review and other analysis decreases as achievement realization increases. But money and the status symbols that go with success are important.

A manipulator's motivation can be destroyed, however, by putting in career path courses or other internal guidance and counseling situations that aim for conformity. This tends to negate his potential.

One problem: He or she can be abrasive, especially when managing almost all other psychological types. One strategy to overcome this is to point out his or her "personal barriers to success in this company" and offer to pay his or her expenses for management development courses or any other approach this employee thinks will help to solve his or her problem.

"Don't expect to change things" is one of the worst things you can tell a manipulator, because "changing things" is probably one of his or her prime goals.

Reprimands usually don't bother this employee, because he or she will react by showing that he or she is producing and merely has to cut a few corners to get results.

5. *Sociocentric.* This type is concerned primarily with the welfare of mankind, preventing stress and strife, and generally keeping the peace. This group is growing, especially among the young. Ralph Nader is their ideal and model.

Low wages don't bother them if they believe that their company is helping humanity and that the work is socially acceptable. But they will form a union and oppose the company if they think that it is persecuting the workers or others.

They can be motivated by being shown how their work benefits fellow employees and other groups. They respond best to a boss who is agreeable and gets people working together in a spirit of friendship without many orders being issued.

Sociocentric workers are the ones most likely to be motivated by group job enrichment programs, as long as they don't have to make too many individual decisions. They have little desire to move into management, because they are too tolerant of others and dislike pigeonholing people.

Most effective among the various forms of compensation are hospital and medical insurance, pension plans, and other elements of paternalism, areas that sociocentric workers like for their social, not their economic, value.

6. *Existential.* Traditionally found in areas such as research, members of this group now are part of the "new breed" of managers. Great creativity is the existential employee's major contribution to the company.

Strictly a lone wolf, the existential worker is indifferent to physical working conditions but chafes under restrictions and rebels against regimentation. Although he or she performs better when left on a loose leash, this employee also has a tendency to wander off on tangents unrelated to company objectives and must be checked periodically.

He or she is motivated by doing work of his own choosing that is challenging and requires imagination. Programs on career development, management by objective, and communications must be extremely flexible. The teamwork aspects of job enrichment hold no appeal, but the greater responsibility does.

Money is important, but primarily because of the freedom it permits. The existential employee dislikes being financially dependent on a company. Flextime, portable pensions, and other plans that contribute a measure of freedom are appealing to him.

Table 14-1 summarizes each of these six types, along with some comments about how each type might be motivated and how managers should respond in developing a positive work climate. You might also note that the "socio-centric" and "existential" types, though only a small percentage of hourly workers in the 1975 survey, are typical of the so-called "new generation employee."

Now that we've examined each of these six types, a logical question might be, What should managers do to effectively manage and communicate with employees in each of these groups?

SOME MANAGER DO'S AND DON'TS

Clearly, it's not possible for a manager to respond to all employees in a way that will automatically ensure accurate and motivating communication. Still, here are some general comments about your communications that can help you relate to your employees.

The Tribalistic Employee

This group works best in an environment of precise rules that everyone understands. The tribalistic person wants a manager whose behavior is that of a benevolent autocrat. Maintain a firm, friendly attitude toward the tribalistic employee. Communication should be simple, clear, and direct, with as little "intellectualizing" as possible. This individual is a prime target for the "re-assurance messages" we discussed in earlier chapters. The reassurance you offer should stress the stability of the environment and the employee's place in that stable environment. The tribalistic employee appreciates a manager who will make decisions and who will relate to him or her in clear, nontechnical language.

The Egocentric Employee

In many ways, the egocentric employee is similar to the tribalistic, although he or she may not need as much protective reassurance from you. An ego-centric employee is tough and aggressive. Assume (or at least give the impression that you assume) that this employee doesn't want to work. Your communications should be brief and to the point, with no hint of softness or hesitation.

A new supervisor in an air-conditioning plant assessed his employees as "predominantly egocentric." To deal with them, he always talked quickly and directly and moved briskly throughout his department looking straight ahead. This show of bravado, he felt, would help his tough, give 'em hell message. It worked well too, until one day he breezed across the department looking dead ahead, strode up to a door, briskly threw it open, and went inside—the broom closet. His red face when he came out—and the grins and cheers from his employees in the shop—suggested that perhaps a little less aggressiveness might be in order.

The Conformist Employee

This individual seems to work best in an atmosphere with structure and some semblance of goal-directed management. Managers with conformist employees should be well organized. Give the impression that you know where they're going and what you expect from them. Because the conformist is loyal, he or she expects loyalty in return from both the organization and the supervisor. With this type employee, be careful to avoid comments and statements that suggest disrespect for tradition or for the company "policies." Slick, or avant-garde, management techniques should be avoided in favor of traditional methods.

The Manipulative Employee

This individual demands treatment as an individual. He or she wants to be included in any process involving his or her personal goals. With this person, you must appear to have carefully thought-out strategies for managing. As a "game player," the manipulative employee expects you to constantly be one up. The best approach is to stress status and tie motivational *and* instructional messages to the individual's career, goals, and aspirations. On the other hand, the manipulative individual is likely to reject orders or instructions that are based solely on company policies and procedures. The manipulative employee wants to be persuaded or convinced. Given rational and personally meaningful answers and information, the manipulative employee is likely to respond in a positive way.

The Sociocentric Employee

The sociocentric values group identification. He or she wants and needs to be considered as part of a group—and not necessarily the same groups that the supervisor might identify with. The sociocentric will likely respond best to opportunities for group participation in problem solving and in job enrichment strategies that stress group rather than individual activity. You should communicate in a friendly, open way designed to create a personal bond of employee acceptance. However, if the sociocentric feels that you are using friendly

Table 14-1 Six Employee Types and What Makes Them Tick

	Tribalistic	Egocentric	Conformist	Manipulative	Sociocentric	Existential
As a % of						
managers	10%	10%	20%	20%	15%	25%
hourly personnel	40%	10%	40%	5%	5%	Almost none
general population	25%	10%	35%	10%	10%	10%
Key identifying attitude on reasons for importance of money today	Buys groceries, pays for rent and other things I need to keep going.	Buys things I want and makes me feel like somebody.	Allows me to save for rainy day, have decent standard of living, and aid the unfortunate.	Is a measure of success in my job, my company, and my community.	Enables me to enjoy many friendships and support worthwhile causes.	By itself, not as important as how it is used. It gives me freedom and chance to be myself.
Most effective management climate	Good boss, no decisionmaking, rules to follow, plenty of security, pensions. Regular pay, no piecework. Work groups of ten maximum. Short-cycle work.	Freedom of action to a point, but clear line of authority. Piecework pay. No intangibles or deferred compensation.	Rewards for seniority and loyal service. Rules and procedures for everything. Organization charts and career planning.	Keep light rein. Allow innovation. Gives status symbols, decision-making authority.	Group meetings and participation. No stress or conflict. Highlights socially useful purpose of operation. Friendly supervisors.	Loose structure. Stimulate creativity. Spell out long-range goals. Deemphasize retirement plans and other "golden-handcuffs."

Table 14-1 (con't)

	Tribalistic	Egocentric	Conformist	Manipulative	Sociocentric	Existential
As a % of						
managers	10%	10%	20%	20%	15%	25%
hourly personnel	40%	10%	40%	5%	5%	Almost none
general population	25%	10%	35%	10%	10%	10%
Most effective motivators	Good boss, steady pay. Job content irrelevant.	Hard cash; leave him or her alone.	Regular advancement by seniority. Clear procedures. Efficient management system, appraisal reviews.	Opportunity to wheel and deal. Options in pension and retirement. Money. Status symbols.	Harmonious working environment. Deemphasize merit pay and "climbing the corporate ladder."	Continuously challenging work. Freedom of choice. Job-enrichment programs.
Comment	Little desire for advancement. Will resist transfer. Recession brings converts.	High turnover. Always discontented. Recession brings converts from other groups. Highly suspicious.	Size dwindling rapidly due to broadening horizons of mass media, but reinforced by tradition. Found in bureaucracies.	Sex, poker, religion are all games. Flexible ethics. Best as salesmen.	If they see the company is hurting people, they will organize and rebel.	Increasingly found in management. Incompatible with tribalistic, egocentric, or conformist boss.

Based on studies of 1,707 supervisors.

SOURCE: This chart is reprinted from Thomas M. Rohan, "Should a Worker's Personality Affect Your Managing?" *Industry Week*, May 5, 1975. Copyright © 1975 Penton/IPC, Inc. Reprinted with permission.

communications as part of a "power politics" strategy, such messages will likely be rejected.

The Existential Employee

This is perhaps the ultimate individual. He or she responds best to individual forms of job enrichment and demands that management accept his or her individuality. Appeals to the "common good" or "what's best for the entire department" won't work with the existential. Neither will instruction from the supervisor stating that "this is what you *should* do." As a free and independent thinker, the existential wants you to provide access to information, while letting him or her make the actual decision. To the extent that this is possible, leave the existential alone — assuming that there is enough information available for the existential to make good decisions.

Clearly, we've opened some possible areas for conflict, as most managers fall into the existential, manipulative, or conformist categories, whereas the bulk of their employees are in the tribalistic or conformist categories. When a manager of one type is communicating with an employee of another type, there are bound to be distortions and misunderstandings. By testing your own motivations (see the box and questionnaire at the end of this chapter), you should have a better grasp of your frame of reference. With a little of the same kind of analysis applied to your employees, it's possible to overcome many of the communication barriers that put certain employees into the "unmanageable" category.

ESTABLISH RAPPORT

Another useful approach to the challenge of communicating with and managing the "problem employee" is to establish a management-worker rapport that sweeps away that "we and they" barrier.[8]

If workers know exactly what is expected of them, they'll do the right thing. People want and look for authority and discipline of a kind that means mutual benefit. They crave recognition. They want the assurance and tangible proof that management is working as hard and as well as they are. They want to know what's going on in the company and on the shop floor, and why. They want their ideas to be heard and to have a voice in changes which affect their jobs.

People power is apparent to all those who use it. There are key situations that we all recognize and respond to, things that turn people on. And, no matter how trite it sounds, the most important asset in any shop is dedicated people. They make your money out there in that work area.

The experience of one manager with a "typical" employee problem is very interesting. When he took over, he found a don't give-a-damn attitude, shoddy housekeeping, poor supervision, and a terrible record on work rejected. "It was so bad I had to have a form letter made so I could keep up with apologies to customers." He also realized that people want identity. They want to like the place they work in, they want it clean, they want pride and appreciation. It's management's job not to overlook the little things that count so much and add up to pride. So, in those early days workers found cigarette butt cans appearing which bore the printed invitation: "Come as close as you can."

That at least got the butts into a small area for the sweepers. Soon, they were all in the cans. Today, this manager's standard offer to every visitor is a dime for every butt found on the floor. You pay a quarter if you don't find any. And you don't find any because, for one thing, the workers know that the quarter goes to the shop fund for retarded children.

The workers had gotten in the habit of scrawling obscenities, mostly management directed, on the washroom walls. Then, one day they were confronted with blackboards over the wash basins and in the stalls (one positioned especially for left-handed writers). What's more, what they wrote on the blackboards got written replies from the superintendent, sometimes with asides such as "and at least I have the guts to sign my name." Shortly, the necessity for the blackboards vanished and the refitted washrooms remain sparkling.

This solution to a common management communication problem may seem trite or "time worn" to you, but it does work. It's also in line with the more impressive motivation theories being used by managers and academics these days. In the contemporary view of motivation, the problem employee is often "demotivated" by a job or work surroundings that do not communicate to him or her anything about personal worth or contribution. Once employees receive the message from their management that they (the employees) are important and that they can take justifiable pride in their work and their surroundings and their contribution to the overall objectives of the organization, many management problems have a way of disappearing.

Don't be misled, however, into thinking that this Pollyanna approach will work every time. It can't and it won't. Some "problem" employees are problems for management for reasons that have nothing whatsoever to do with the company, the work, or you as the manager. In some cases, the individual has personal problems. In other cases, there are important cultural or social reasons that cause you to perceive an employee as a "problem," when in fact it's really a clashing of different cultural values that's at fault.

CROSS-CULTURAL COMMUNICATION

For several years, we've been exposed to the problems of the "ugly American" — the tourist who visits other countries and makes a fool of himself or herself by violating local customs and traditions. When such miscommunications occur, it's usually because we assume that everyone thinks, acts, or behaves the same as "me." Although we've become (hopefully) a bit more sensitive to cultural differences, many managers find that their employees from other cultures pose problems of "unmanageability." Let's briefly look at some communication ideas for dealing with such employees.

There's no sense elaborating on the simple statement that "people are different." Throughout this book, we've continually made this point as we examined listening, writing, speaking, and managing in general. Often, our assumptions get in the way of our communications with employees with different cultural backgrounds. Carlos Gonzales of Eastern Airlines observed in a seminar on marketing in Latin America how important such assumptions are, either for managers or for airline personnel.

"Stewardesses used to think that Latin-American passengers were easy to serve because they were quiet, polite, and never asked for anything. And as a result, many airlines, Eastern included, lost either goodwill or passengers. We have now come to realize that the behavior pattern that Anglo stewardesses took to mean satisfaction was actually something quite different. The Latins never asked for anything because they expected to have it offered. The politeness and silence were an indication of reserve and dissatisfaction, not contentment as the stewardesses had thought. The more formal courtesy of Latin passengers makes it very unlikely they would complain. They just took their patronage elsewhere.[9]"

Although a complete summary of the perceptions, attitudes, customs, and beliefs of employees with cultures different from your own is beyond the scope of this chapter, there are several things you can do to improve your ability to work effectively with such employees:

1. *Examine Your Prejudices.* Often, the stereotypes that we hold about persons who belong to certain racial, cultural, ethnic, or social groups are buried in our unconscious mind. Thus, the manager who tries to be fair and even handed with all employees may possess some deep-down prejudices that influence his or her communications with those employees. Look closely at your actions, and your motives for signs of prejudice. The self-analysis will help point out areas for improvement.

2. *Open Contact.* Develop a habit of encouraging meaningful communication between yourself and your employees or other managers whose backgrounds differ from your own. Just as "consciousness raising" has been useful in giving women, blacks, and others a better sense of themselves, their heritage, and their strengths, such open dialogue can help you break down barriers.

3. *When in Doubt, WAIT—or Ask.* Obviously, you can't avoid *all* misunderstandings. When miscommunication does occur, or when you think it *might* occur, delay your reaction. If possible, ask others who might be better informed about another group's customs for an interpretation of what behavior is appropriate.

4. *Be Tolerant.* Above all, keep in mind the tendency we all have to assume that "different is wrong," or bad, whereas "similar is good." We all tend to assume that people in Mississippi, or Chicago, or Boston, or El Paso "talk funny"—just because their speech patterns differ from our own. After the 1976 Presidential election, an Atlanta woman remarked that "It'll be wonderful to finally have a President (Jimmy Carter) who doesn't have an accent!" The essential point in dealing with employees who differ from ourselves is that they are different—not wrong. This perspective requires a certain humility in our outlook. It can also contribute to better communication between all individuals including those whose backgrounds and beliefs are the same as yours.

WHAT ABOUT THE REAL TROUBLEMAKER?

There are several communication strategies for dealing with a troublemaker. Some have been covered in other chapters. All involve developing a positive approach to good discipline in any supervisory situation.

When dealing with a troublemaker, try to get his side of the story as soon as possible. This doesn't mean that you should accept everything he has to say, only that you listen. Often, troublemakers do what they do to get a sympathetic listener or to mask a problem off the job. The troublemaker may be wrestling with marriage problems, financial difficulties, excessive drinking, or other serious problems. When you provide him or her with an opportunity to "unload," you may be helping the individual come to grips with his or her problem.

Keep your eye on the issue. Don't let the troublemaking employee bring into the discipline discussion a variety of side issues that take attention away from the issue at hand. At the same time, don't you bring up other issues to strengthen *your* case. Keep the discipline discussion on track and away from diversion.

Remain calm and in control of yourself. In the listening chapter (Chapter 5), we spoke of the supervisor who exploded whenever one of his employees used a certain ethnic slur. He "blew his cool" and, in the process, lost control of whatever conversation was underway. In a discipline situation, you can't afford any emotional side trips. Don't accuse, threaten, or get mad at what the employee says or does. Try also to avoid the temptation in the advice "Don't get mad, get even."

Get *all* the facts. This is perhaps an impossible task, as facts are subject to individual perceptions. A grievance filed by anyone who feels wronged may not be seen in the same way by the manager involved or by outside third parties. Get as much information as possible about the troublemaker *as it relates* to a *specific incident*. Bringing up past offenses, especially if they went unresolved, will seriously weaken a discipline case, especially if it goes up for resolution at a higher level.

Remain firm, but flexible. Keep in mind that, with employee discipline, there are few absolutes. Instead, there are shadings and nuances. Although a rigid stand on a matter of discipline might be understood or applauded by a tribalistic or egocentric employee, it doesn't always solve serious problems when dealing with other employee types.

DON'T PERSONALIZE DIFFICULTIES

In a recent seminar on handling grievances under a negotiated labor contract, a group of managers repeatedly expressed feelings of personal threat whenever their employees created a disturbance or filed a grievance. Such personalizing is unwise and unhealthy. It can lead to supervisors' reacting by doing things that preserve their sense of self-image rather than resolving the problem itself. One supervisor in the seminar gave an example from his experience. Some time before the seminar, one of his employees filed a grievance over a ruling that the supervisor had made in a dispute between two employees. In making his ruling, the supervisor felt that he had been fair and impartial. Obviously, one of the employees involved didn't agree. Think about how the supervisor described his reaction when he heard about the grievance:

"I got really mad. After all, those guys both deserved a discipline layoff for what they did. I worked my tail off to keep 'em out of trouble with the unit manager, and then one of the _____'s has the nerve to file on me to the union. It's on *my* record, and, believe me, it'll never happen again. They can't do that to me, man, and, if they haven't found that out by now, they sure will soon!" A common practice (filing a grievance) has been turned into a personal vendetta and a call for revenge. The manager really gains nothing from his personalized hostility, except perhaps an ulcer, and the example set by such personalization may only serve to influence other employees to misbehave, creating more problems.

A SELF-TEST OF EMPLOYEE TYPES: WHICH TYPE ARE YOU?

To find out which type you are, answer the following questions. There are six choices for each question. There are no right or wrong answers; simply circle the statement you like best. If you have a second choice, place a check by it also.

1. A family should
   a. Stay close together and take care of one another
   b. Let each person go his own way without interference
   c. Provide guidance to the younger members on what is right and wrong
   d. Help each other succeed in a career and see that the children get ahead in the world

e. Provide warmth and harmony among all the members and their friends
   f. Permit family life to be like real life, with all of its good and bad points
2. Freedom is
   a. Not having to worry about money and other problems
   b. Not being pushed around by people who have more power or money
   c. The chance to work and live where you want and be a good citizen of the community
   d. The opportunity to do and to pursue success
   e. The right of people to be themselves without prejudice and social differences
   f. Doing what you like to do without denying others their freedom
3. A good job is
   a. Having a good boss regardless of the work
   b. One that pays enough money
   c. Knowing exactly what should be done
   d. Where good work leads to promotion
   e. Working with a good group of people
   f. Solving interesting problems
4. Laws are
   a. To tell us what to do and protect us from people
   b. Not important unless you get caught breaking them
   c. Necessary to keep order in society and should be obeyed by everyone
   d. Sometimes unnecessarily restrictive in getting things done
   e. Useful if they promote social causes
   f. Necessary to make any society function
5. Money means
   a. Paying for the things you need to keep going
   b. Buying things that make you feel important
   c. Security for the present and future and a good standard of living
   d. Power and status and belongings that you have earned
   e. Social distance and barriers in society
   f. Freedom and opportunity to be myself
6. Personal possessions
   a. Are necessary for living
   b. Make you feel like someone important
   c. Come from hard work and should go only to people who deserve them
   d. Are a sign of success and a source of pride
   e. Are not as important as personal friendships
   f. Are important only for what they mean to the individual
7. A good boss
   a. Tells you what he wants done and helps you do it
   b. Is tough but lets you be tough also
   c. Sets clear policies and sees that people follow them
   d. Helps you understand the objectives and rewards you when you achieve them
   e. Is more of a friend than a boss
   f. Sets goals with you, then trusts you to do the job the best way

SCORESHEET: WHICH TYPE ARE YOU?

This is a demonstration test only and is intended to give participants a "feel" for the way the system operates. It is based on attitudes in personal life, not in work, which in 80 percent of all cases are different.

To score the test, count the number of statements circled behind each letter and enter the total for each below. Do the same for the second choice. The totals for the number of circles and checks will give you a general indication of your primary and secondary patterns.

		TOTALS	
Response	*Represents*	*First Choice*	*Second Choice*
a	Tribalistic	_____	_____
b	Egocentric	_____	_____
c	Conformist	_____	_____
d	Manipulative	_____	_____
e	Sociocentric	_____	_____
f	Existential	_____	_____

Ways to Improve Your Communication Skills

1. Recognize the importance of labels. Often, the employee we label "unmanageable" is, in fact, "different." Thus, our labels can change the reality of a situation and make problems appear greater than they are.

2. Motivation means paying attention to both the job and the work place. The quality of management that an employee receives will be a major factor in determining whether he or she feels the job is worthwhile and motivating, or "dead-end" position.

3. Employees and managers have different personalities. Each personality type has its own problems, and managers who are interested in effective communication and management should make every effort to analyze employees and themselves in terms of these and other "models," to learn which approach to motivation and communication is best.

4. With the tribalistic employee, be a friendly decision maker; give reassurance all is O.K. Don't be "iffy," intellectual, or use technical terms.

5. With the egocentric employee, be tough and aggressive and assume that he doesn't want to work. Don't be soft, indecisive, or cause suspicion.

6. With the conformist employee, be straight, businesslike, respectful, and well organized. Don't be slick, profane, or disrespectful of tradition.

7. With the manipulative employee, stress strategies and status and tie these to employee career goals. Don't force him or her to follow company policy and procedure.

8. With the sociocentric employee, be friendly and gain personal acceptance. Don't use power, influence, or politics.

9. With the existential employee, give him access to information and let him make the decisions. Don't tell him what he "should" do.

10. Test your own personality against some of these personality types and see if your motivators are the ones indicated for your type. Also, keep in mind that neither you nor your employees will fit neatly into just one category. Instead, use the self-test and your employee analysis to determine the one or two dominant personality factors, and use these as clues for better communication.

11. Develop a "we" approach to communication by including employees in the decision making and, in turn, impressing on them the importance of their taking responsibility for their actions and contributions to the workplace.

12. When dealing with employees with cultural backgrounds that differ from your own, examine your prejudices and strive to maintain an open mind and an open spirit of contact and communication with your employees in these cultural groups.

13. Don't personalize difficulties with troublesome employees. In virtually all cases, their hostility and deviant behavior on the job is not a direct reflection of their feelings about you. Instead, they are likely using you as a focal point for their frustrations, anger, or general hostility with their jobs or the organization.

14. Get involved in attempts to settle problems, and, when they go beyond "troublesome" to "discipline" problems, take a firm stand. In our next chapter, we'll take a closer look at the "problem" employee, particularly when real discipline problems are involved.

Further Reading

To follow up on the material in this chapter, you may also want to read:

LAWRENCE L. STEINMETZ, MANAGING THE MARGINAL AND UNSATISFACTORY PERFORMER (Addison-Wesley)

This book presents theories and practical strategies for realistically dealing with the fact that not all managers or employees work up to the limits of their capabilities. Some employees fail to perform satisfactorily and to meet the requirements and desires of their employer or their supervisor, even when the supervisor applies good managerial theory. In this book, the author develops techniques and strategies for dealing with unsatisfactory employees along with some strategies on dealing with the problems of firing those employees who can't measure up.

15

Communication Strategies for Effective Discipline

"In all human organizations there will be kinds of behavior which cannot be permitted, for they keep the organization from going toward its objectives, bar individual members from being free to do their own work, or interfere with the personal rights of others."

George Odiorne

In most management books, there has been little really useful information available on the subject of employee discipline, at least not in recent years. Most information available seems to focus on disciplinary actions rather than on employee discipline as part of an overall communication strategy.

As such, discipline should be approached from the point of view of prevention rather than from the point of view of applying principles or rules to problems that arise in an organization wherever employee performance does not measure up to management's expectations.

To do this, it is necessary to define discipline. Discipline is a condition in a department or organization that produces orderliness, sensible behavior, and employee conduct that is in keeping with the goals of the organization. It is also a state of personal self-regulation that results when an employee or manager has a commitment to and a motive for working within a work group. These views of discipline focus on employees themselves and the process involved in getting the desired behavior. The idea of committed self-regulation and its relationship to communication, are very important.

We should also define two other terms. A *disciplinary problem* is a situation that exists when a person fails to perform up to his or her capability or our expectations and standards; it can also be behavior that prevents other employees from reaching their goals. In contrast, a *disciplinary action* involves the steps taken to correct a disciplinary problem.

Disciplinary *problems* and disciplinary *actions* occur after an employee behaves in a certain way. Although all managers must act "after the fact" from time to time, a more productive approach for dealing with problems is one in which *prevention* is the primary goal. If employees aren't committed to their jobs and are unwilling or unable to regulate themselves, managers can't. expect to fully reach their objectives.

When faced with a discipline problem in the plant, most managers generally think of *what* and *how much*. What should the penalty be? And how severely should the employee be punished?

This is a superficial attitude toward industrial justice, and it loses sight of one thing: discipline is not an end in itself, but a tool designed to improve productivity and human relations in the workplace. A better approach is to decide *why* we punish employees before we decide anything else. A poorly conceived discipline policy can not only produce a hellish labor-management atmosphere in the plant, but it may also result in a string of adverse rulings for the company if and when grievances come before an arbitrator. Using this view, punishment should be meted out to improve productivity and should be viewed as a learning situation for the employee.[1]

WHY DO WE HAVE DISCIPLINE PROBLEMS?

Obviously, discipline problems are important to any organization, as they involve time, money, morale, public relations, and public image. To prevent such problems, it's necessary to understand how they are caused. In general, there are three causes of ineffective employee performance: organizational or managerial failures, employee failures, and outside influences.

Organizational and managerial failures may include a lack of proper motivators in the organization. If the organization or the management isn't aware of the needs that motivate employees and the fact that these needs differ from one person to another, there will be difficulty maintaining a committed, self-regulated, work force. Poor job assignments also fit here, as people work best and produce most when they are doing jobs suited to their abilities and interests. Another organizational shortcoming that contributes to poor employee performance is improper supervision. In fact, some experts suggest that this is the *only* cause of discipline problems, because supervisors should have the skills necessary to get the most out of their employees in any situation. However, improper supervision may be related to supervisors being overworked and not having the time needed to develop their management skills better.

Individual employee failures also contribute to behavior problems. Most employees have some desire to do a good job; satisfactory performance is a matter of channeling that desire in the right direction. Still there *are* some employees who simply lack the desire to produce. They feel this way because of their "position in life," such as waiting for retirement or being passed over for promotion, or because of personality clashes, laziness, mental instability, alcoholism, and similar problems.

Finally, *influences outside the organization* can have a big impact on morale, productivity, and the need for discipline. For example, conditions of the labor market, the availability of alternative jobs, and the protective actions demanded by labor unions influence an individual's on the job performance.

RESPONSIBILITIES

Of course, many other influences can affect employee behavior, as each individual is different and interacts with his environment in a different way. Therefore, it's not possible for a manager to control all these variables. However, managers *can* establish areas of responsibility for keeping good employee discipline. When an employee first joins the work team, he or she should have some self-controlling ability. Most mature persons accept the idea that following instructions and rules is an individual responsibility, something they'll do most of these lives. The majority of employees want to do the right thing, for they recognize that conformity calls for a reasonable degree of subordination of personal interests to the needs of the organization.

A PREVENTIVE APPROACH

Because the most practical approach to discipline is that of preventing problems, not treating them, a preventive approach must start with the selection of individuals for all positions within the organization. Once an individual is accepted for employment, his or her problems become the problems of the organization. Therefore, the selection procedures for hiring new employees must be sensitive to this issue.

To make that important second step toward preventive discipline, managers should keep some of the following factors in mind. These involve everyday aspects of interaction between employees and managers and are the greatest influence on employee behavior.

1. Morale is *always present* in some form; it affects employees' performance and their will to work.

2. High morale is not the cause of good human relations—it is the result.
3. People tend to live up to the expectations that others have of·them.
4. Without self-regulated discipline, it is difficult to harness and direct the resources of members to a common organizational goal.
5. The most effective discipline comes from within an individual.
6. Violations of company rules are usually a symptom of more basic employee or management problems.

In all organizations, good human relations begin with proper climate. This climate should focus on employee needs and should help employees to develop a commitment to the organizational goals. Most employees need to work in a predictable environment and to be given some recognition for jobs well done. If managers establish good communication lines to their employees, it is possible to create this environment that encourages positive discipline. In addition to a general strategy, here are some specific steps for preventive discipline:

1. Every employee should be given a well-structured job, with clear responsibilities.
2. Employees should be given continuous feedback about their progress and should be told *in advance* about any changes in their jobs that will directly affect them.
3. Each individual employee should be encouraged to "get involved" with his or her fellow employees and should be given opportunites for participation in programs of professional training and personal growth.
4. Set a good example, as much employee behavior (and mischief) is a reflection of their boss's example.
5. Establish and maintain a "helping" relationship with employees. When this can't be done (or isn't done), employees facing problems will likely become frustrated. This makes the manager and supervisor dissatisfied, the organization is shortchanged, and the stage set for discipline and behavior problems.
6. Avoid becoming overworked and preoccupied with administrative tasks and miss out on your best communication tool: simple observation. Much information can be gained about individual employees by observing their work habits and their interactions with other employees. Such observations can be the first clue to the potential problems later on. The sooner these problems can be spotted, the sooner some step can be taken to prevent possible disruptions and discipline problems.
7. Managers should hold periodic conferences with all employees, to be sure that they are mastering their jobs and to determine if they feel satisfied with their work environment. If the proper helping relationship has been created by the manager, employees will be more likely to express their true feelings about their jobs. Likewise, managers have an

FIGURE 15-1

obligation to give their employees prompt feedback about their performance, both satisfactory and unsatisfactory.

Every organization and every manager will have occasional disciplinary problems. The number and seriousness of such discipline problems will depend on how effectively you have used prevention rather than enforcement as your guide to personal actions. Clearly, you can't solve all the discipline problems using a preventative approach. However, it *is* an important first step to effective discipline, because it sets the stage for positive communication and work relationships. Further, when disciplinary action does become necessary despite your best preventive efforts, you can be more confident that your discipline is fair and effective.

LAYING DOWN THE LAW—PRODUCTIVELY

Let's assume that you've followed all the rules, you've set up lines of communication between you and your employees, you've done everything you can think of to foster a productive atmosphere that will make discipline problems a thing of the past. Yet, you are faced with a thorny discipline problem. How do you handle it and still keep the productivity and good communication you've spent so long developing? Let's examine some realistic suggestions.

Reprimand Constructively

Occasionally, it is apparent that some member of the group is not doing his part or is deporting himself in a way that is contrary to the best interests of the company or the group with which he works. If such a situation persists, it becomes necessary for his immediate supervisor to do something about it. Disciplinary action in some measure is usually in order.[2]

The word discipline is not intended here to suggest negative or punitive action. Rather, it means close supervision with sympathetic understanding, backed by a thorough knowledge of the worker's personality, potentialities, and character.

For constructive results, it's obvious that the administration of discipline must always be impartial. A manager is treading on dangerous ground if he or she reprimands one worker for a misdeed but says nothing to another for a similar infraction.

These are many common violations, and some, obviously, are more serious than others. In the case of such infractions as stealing or intoxication, strong and immediate disciplinary action is clearly needed. However, by far the largest percentage of violations of good practices may be handled by the intelligent use of the reprimand.

Be Sure It's Deserved!

Fairness, it must be repeated, is the first consideration in deciding whether or not to reprimand an employee. It should be borne in mind, too, that the worker is being reprimanded because he or she made a mistake but is a sufficiently promising member of the organization to correct, work with, and try to steer on a straight course. If the reprimand is used wisely, the manager may develop and acquire a friendly and loyal supporter in one who might otherwise have been a disgruntled and indifferent employee.

There is nothing more demoralizing to a worker than a false accusation. If a man is reprimanded unjustly, it is difficult — if not impossible — for his supervisor to counterbalance the effects of that reprimand and to restore his confidence, respect, and loyalty. Consequently, supervisors can hardly overestimate the importance of being sure of themselves before reprimanding.

Each worker needs to be disciplined differently. For a reprimand to be effective, the supervisor must know and understand the employee concerned, be able to evaluate his or her character, work habits, outlook on his or her job, past record, and present attitudes. The exact nature of the reprimand should be dictated by the supervisor's knowledge of the person and of the situation that necessitates it.

Remember This Basic Premise

Employees are usually conscientious and want to be fair. They want to be able to take pride in their jobs and the company with which they are associated. In the final analysis, there is little real satisfaction in lying down on the job or finding fault with one's associates, boss, job, or company. A supervisor should proceed on this premise. If he maintains two-way communication between himself and the members of the group and his company and keeps his eyes and ears open, he should be able to detect, in its early stages, the development of any practice or behavior that is contrary to the accepted and approved way of doing things. It's always far better to eliminate the need for a reprimand than to have to invoke it.

Sometimes, however, no amount of "understanding" on the part of the supervisor or efforts to eliminate the necessity for a direct reprimand seem to work. Then, it's time to get down to cases.

Keep Your Feet on the Ground

Under no circumstances should a supervisor lose his temper and "bawl the hell" out of a worker. This basic "rule" would seem too obvious to mention were it not for the fact that it is so often violated. The supervisor must keep his composure if he is to discuss in a logical way the problems and actions that made the reprimand necessary. If he loses his temper and reprimands while he is in a state of agitation, he stands to lose the respect and confidence of the members of the group.

Make It Private

Reprimands should always be delivered in private. The surest way to make enemies and lose friends is to reprimand a man with his fellow workers listening and looking on. Not only does this engender resentment, but it negates the value of the reprimand itself, and the supervisor can usually look for a recurrence of the same or a similar offense in the near future.

It is always desirable and important to talk straight when reprimanding. The supervisor should not shilly-shally. Nothing should be said or done that will give rise to doubts, misgivings, or misunderstanding. The employee should understand why he is being reprimanded, what he did to bring it about. He should know the consequences of what he has done; he should know also what to expect if the infraction is repeated.

Get at Causes

The supervisor should look for reasons why. Hidden causes underly many misdeeds or mistakes, ill health, family troubles, or other worries or pressures—and the likely causes of the situation—be they worry, indifference, resentment, whatever—should be considered with care.

Be sympathetic. If the approach is hard-boiled and the supervisor proceeds to "bawl out" the offender, immediate resentment and opposition is aroused. Using a sympathetic approach, the supervisor can gain the worker's confidence, learn his or her side of the story, and make him or her receptive to advice and suggestions.

The worker should understand the implications of the offense. This is important in gaining his or her cooperation. The worker should know what the effects may be on his or her company, supervisor, fellow workers, and himself or herself.

"Complete the Sale"

The offender should be told what is expected of him or her, how he or she should have acted in the circumstances in question, and why. It is necessary to be specific in this explanation and in telling the employee what will be expected of him or her in the future. At all costs, avoid threats or intimidation. Be constructive and show the employee how to improve the situation.

To complete the sale, the manager should get agreement from the employee —a sort of meeting of minds in which the employee takes on the responsibility himself to improve his future conduct on the job. This is the final objective of every reprimand. If you can gain his genuine and willing cooperation on this point, you have a good change of acquiring a loyal, enthusiastic, and dependable player on the team.

Use Restraint

The wise manager institutes a system of graduated penalties intended to be corrective and to discourage future infractions, a system that is neither too permissive nor overly oppressive.[3] Use restraint when dealing with a discipline problem, but, by the same token, too much restraint will come back to haunt you.

Be Consistent

A fundamental building block for a successful discipline program is consistency. Most managers are too lenient in early disciplinary situations and too tough in the later stages. They tend to overlook the little things, and, then, after the situation builds to where it can't be ignored, they explode. When you overlook first-time offenses, you condone such actions and encourage repeat performances, whereas overreaction later can breed contempt among workers and irreparably damage the employer-employee relationship. However, don't just tell someone when he or she is out of line, if you want the message to stick. Put it in writing to the employee and send a copy to the personnel office, giving the company ammunition for future grievance hearings.

Be Reasonable

Many managers believe that companies whose inflexible policy is to discharge employees for any degree of theft are not being fair or even reasonable. There is a lot of piety about this on the part of management; for example, if a guy goes home with a pair of company gloves, he's fired. "But how about someone who takes an extra few minutes at the coffee machine, or a long lunch hour, or heads home early on Friday? Even managers do this; this is stealing, too, especially when you figure how much that person's time is worth? Here's a suggestion: Don't dock the entire crew because somebody threw a wrench in the works and stopped the line for a day and a half. Guilt is a personal commodity, and, unless you can prove who did it, you better not discipline an entire group when the evidence indicated that less than the entire group was involved.

Be Fair

Don't make exceptions when issuing penalties. Many grievance decisions turn on this point of uniformly applied punishment. Fair and equal treatment of all employees will help you earn the respect you need, to be effective over the haul. Be fair, too, when you deal with unforeseen consequences of "horseplay" or other misbehaviors. They should not be the major consideration in setting the punishment. We all experience lapses of concentration, and, when that happens in the shop, the damage can be extensive. You must evaluate the entire act and the records of those involved.

THE LAST RESORT?

Many experts believe strongly that the employer's power to discharge an employee should be exercised only when all penalty provisions of the progressive disciplinary procedure have been exhausted. The exception: an extreme breach of conduct, such as the use or threatened use of a weapon in the plant.

You don't reform an employee, or teach him anything, by discharging him. Discharge should be used only when the effects of a discipline problem are so devasting to the employer-employee relationship that it cannot be repaired.

If a discipline problem goes to the stage of a formal grievance, there has likely been a communication failure on the part of someone. However, a grievance need not end the process of effective communication. When grievances do occur, there are four important areas to watch for. We must be sure to handle each of them with care if grievances are to be resolved properly and without delay. Let's take a look at them.

1. Receive the Grievance Properly

The way to receive a grievance is important, because the way you treat the person who comes in to make a complaint may have a lot to do with the ease or difficulty of settling the problem.[4] Here are the things you should do when you receive the grievance:

Give the employee a good hearing. When someone comes in to talk to you about a grievance, give him or her your entire attention. Even if your employee is boiling mad, keep your temper. Remain calm. Let the employee tell his or her full story without interruption. Let the worker get it all off his or her chest.

Now, in a calm voice, ask the employee to repeat the story. While the person is speaking, take a few notes, both to get the story accurately and to impress on the employee that you are taking his or her complaint seriously and intend to give it the consideration it deserves.

Repeat the essentials in your own words. After you have heard the employee out, repeat the complaint in your own words. Pick out the two or three essential points of the story. Ask the employee if these are the facts and if you have put them straight.

Tell the worker when he or she can expect an answer. When you have the facts and everything is straight in your own mind, your course of action should be clear. If the answer to the complaint is obvious, you can very likely give him the answer right there. But, if you are not 100 percent sure, give yourself time to check further. Ask the employee to come back at an appointed time. But, above all, assure that worker of prompt action, tell the employee when he or she can expect an answer, and then make sure you have it.

2. Get the Facts

Remember to handle the case from the beginning as if you expected to defend your case before an arbitrator. After you have received the grievance, you will find that you have a little time get the facts collected. And here is the heart of the whole business—get the facts. Here's how you should go about doing so.

Check every angle of complaint. First, go out in the plant and get every detail bearing on the complaint. Go over every angle of the story. Talk to the people concerned. Take careful notes of your findings.

Check the relevant sections of the current union contract. Make sure that the settling of a recent case hasn't placed a different interpretation on a particular clause from the one that you understand. You can't know your union contract too well. Even though you feel you know every clause, check it again.

Check company policy. Go as high as possible to get information on previous practices, current interpretation, and present company policy. This is the best insurance against getting reversed if the grievance passes your level. Be sure, when you ask for the opinion of your boss or someone else in higher management, that you tell the whole story, uncolored, including the part that reflects unfavorably on you.

Before making your decision, examine the employee's record. What is his or her production record? What is his or her absentee, safety, and discipline record? Is the employee constantly complaining? You should have a simple record system from which you can tell whether a person is dependable, stable, and productive. Your decision should be made on the facts of this particular grievance. The record will help you interpret these facts.

3. Take Action

Now that you have received the grievance and learned the facts of the case, you are ready to take action. These are steps you should follow when you do.

Make a correction if the company is wrong. If the company is shown to be in the wrong, make the correction promptly. If the employee is mistaken, be sure to make a full and considerate explanation of how and why he is mistaken.

If you are right, maintain you decision, but explain your decision to the employee. If you are sure you are right and have made the right decision, stick to it. Don't be bulldozed by threats to carry it higher. Remain calm. Say nothing that can place you in a bad position. In fact, even tell the employee the exact steps to take to get consideration at the next step in the grievance procedure. This will show him or her that you have confididence in your decision and would be willing to have it reviewed.

Pass on all the facts to the next level. Now, prepare the best case possible for the next step in the grievance procedure. Tell the complete story, particularly the part, if any, that may be critical of you. Back up your case with whatever factual record is available. If the case should go to arbitration, it is remarkable what value will be found in a dated, written memorandum.

4. Follow Up

Be sure to follow up. This last point is most important. The success of your grievance handling often depends on your followup. Here's how to carry out your followup:

Make sure that your plan of action was carried out. Be sure that your decision and course of action have been carried out. In doing this, be certain that you go to the heart of the matter so that another grievance will not come from the same source.

Maintain an atmosphere promoting the highest morale. Check throughout your department to find out whether potential irritations may become grievances. Study your entire organization to see if you can improve morale and develop an atmosphere in which employees and management will gain the greatest satisfaction while keeping production high.

All of us should know how to handle grievances. All of us can do something about preventing grievances. There are very few things around the plant that we can't have a saying about, either directly or indirectly.

Don't try to pass the buck to somebody else. When you have sized up a situation that may lead to grievances, if you can't do anything about it yourself, bring it to the attention of your superior. Outline all the facts. Then, when you feel that your superior has the right story, come back and check up again, so that you can be sure that something will be done about it. Report back to your people if a complaint has been made to you about the situation. This will show them that they aren't getting the brush-off, that something is being done about it. That is good business—your business. That is good management—your management.

Ways to Improve Your Communication Skill

In your role as a human trouble shooter, you have three parts to play.[5] You must diagnose difficulties, you must apply or recommend remedies, and you must try to prevent grievances from developing.

1. *Your task of diagnosis* is to find out what is wrong, to determine the nature of the grievance or disturbance. It includes weighing the employee's complaints and their other reactions as symptoms, observing conditions both within and without the job to discover the particular demands the employees are making in their job, how their total situation is failing to meet these demands, and which of these failures are disturbing them most.
2. *Your task of adjustment* is to bridge the gap between the employee's demands and the satisfactions that they get as far as is necessary to get those employees back into a satisfactory working relationship with

239

the job. Accurate diagnosis frequently shows you what you can do to help. Sometimes, it is changing the work situation itself. Often, it is helping an employee to modify the demands that he or she is making on the job, that is, to adjust the employee to the necessary conditions of his or her work situation.

3. *Your task of prevention* is to arrange the work situation and to supervise your people in it so the satisfactions they are getting will not fall so short of the demands they are making that they cannot adjust themselves. This is not saying that the organization exists to give employees everything they want. It is simply saying that insofar as supervisors can conduct the company's business in harmony with the human demands of employees and assist employees to adapt their demands to the conditions of business, grievances can be minimized.

Some managers are known for their soundness of judgment, others for their lack of it. How do they differ in their thinking and acting processes? Both good and poor thinkers, when they attempt to solve a problem, take what facts they have and draw inferences or form opinions almost at once, but the poor thinker stops here. "Snap judgment," someone has said, "means closing one's mind with a snap, never to open it on the problem again." The good thinker, on the other hand, goes on to test his or her inferences by observing and investigating. He or she gets as many useful facts as possible and weights each carefully in relation to the problem, tossing aside any that have no bearing on it. Then, he or she revises conclusions with rigid honesty to fit the facts wherever they may lead. In deciding what to do and planning how to do it, the person of good judgment continues to draw his decisions from the facts fearlessly and to select plans of action that are in harmony with the total situation, not just a part of it.

ADVICE FROM AN ARBITRATOR

Ever wonder what a professional arbitrator looks for when deciding a grievance case? Clair V. Duff, who has been handing down such judgments for nearly 30 years, offers these tips:[6]

Present your case naturally and make it plausible — but not necessarily airtight. Nothing looks more suspicious than a string of "witnessess" all repeating an obviously rehearsed story that has them "recalling" details that nobody would ever remember.

Don't introduce unrelated or "ancient" incidents that can make the case look like a vendetta. For example, a shouting match between an employee and a foreman six years ago that resulted in no disciplinary action being taken "is a waste of everyone's time at a discharge hearing today," says Mr. Duff. Reporting several disciplinary actions that took place in the last two years shows a pattern and is more convincing than dredging up a long list of fossilized complaints.

Keep written records of all disciplinary actions, including warnings. The pertinent ones will help substantiate your claims at the hearing.

4. The subject of discipline has too often been associated solely with reaction to disciplinary problems and actions that happen after some employee failure exists. Clearly, there are reasons for disciplinary actions, and, yet, the more positive approach is to prevent discipline problems by working to develop an open atmosphere of communication and cooperation in your organization or department.

5. People tend to live up to the expectations that others have of them. If you assume that certain employees are going to be behavior problems, it is very likely that they will live up to these expectations, just as they will live up to expectations that they can produce without behavior or discipline problems.

6. Whenever possible, employees should be given jobs with as much structure as they can handle. This does not mean that every employee should have a highly structured job with no opportunity for self-expression, only that employees have varying degrees of tolerance for uncertainty If that tolerance is exceeded, they are much more likely to become behavior problems.

7. Set a good example for your employees.

8. Establish and maintain a "helping relationship" with employees, although take care that you do not appear to be "treating them like children."

9. Avoid becoming preoccupied and overburdened with administrative tasks. This takes you away from the workplace and contributes to an atmosphere of potential trouble.

10. Hold periodic meetings or conferences with your employees. The conferences can be formal meetings with agendas or they can be informal affairs with everyone simply taking a few moments off the job to relax and share ideas. Either way, they are opportunities to communicate and, thus, head off problems before they get out of hand.

11. When disciplining an employee, be sure that it's deserved.

12. Keep your temper under control at all times.

13. Make reprimands private.

14. Get at the causes of the trouble. Don't settle for some of the symptoms. If you treat symptoms without getting to the heart of the problem, you'll find yourself with future problems of the same kind you just handled.

15. Be consistent in your discipline efforts; be reasonable in your interpretation of policies.

16

Performance Appraisal: Two Communication Problems

"Managing requires special efforts not only to establish common directions, but to eliminate misdirection. Mutual understanding can never be attained by 'communications down,' solely by talking. It results too from 'communications up.' It requires both the superior's willingness to listen and a tool designed to make employees heard."

Peter Drucker

Performance appraisal is a tool for developing and improving communication in an organization. Properly done, it can be a significant factor in improved communications between managers and employees at any level in an organization. However, in even the best performance appraisal systems, there are two basic communication problems. One is the actual operation of a performance appraisal—the giving of evaluations. The second is successfully "selling" a new or revised performance appraisal system to one's employees.

SUPERIOR-SUBORDINATE INTERACTION

Performance appraisal has for a long time been studied by managers concerned about effective management and the implementation of effective motivational programs. In your performance appraisals, you may have asked

242

such questions as, "am I measuring the right things?" "Are the measurements being used objective?" "Do the measurements being used include all relevant work activities?" The answers to these questions are, of course, extremely important. However, there is another important dimension of the performance appraisal process that has received much less attention. It is the communication between you and your subordinate during the course of the evaluation.[1]

What should be measured and how it should be measured is critical, but perhaps of greater significance is the way you present the evaluations of the performance measures to your employees. This process directly affects the subordinate, either modifying his or her behavior or ignoring these suggestions. This interaction between superior and subordinate can be extremely difficult. It is easy to tell a subordinate that he or she is performing beautifully or that you are going to give a raise. Unfortunately, there is another side to that coin. It is unpleasant to criticize an employee, to inform the person that he will not be promoted, or to try to "persuade" someone that they should come to work on time . . . or else!

It is exactly this unpleasantness that Douglas McGregor had in mind when he noted that[2]

> managers are uncomfortable when they are put in the position of playing God. The respect we hold for the inherent value of the individual leaves us distressed when we take responsibility for judging the personal worth of a fellow man. Yet the conventional approach to performance appraisal forces us not only to make such judgments and to see them acted upon but also to communicate them to those we have judged. Small wonder we resist.

Superiors dislike giving "bad news" almost as much as subordinates dislike getting it. For this reason, employee appraisals are often avoided completely. This problem of "vanishing appraisals" is important to managers because the absence of feedback undermines the effectiveness of any motivation program.

One way that managers avoid giving negative criticism is to tell all employees that they are performing well. Although this is how we measure performance, not how it is communicated, these issues are related. If a manager rates 80 percent of his or her employees as "good" or "outstanding," but only gives raises to 20 percent, there appears to be an enormous communication breakdown, at least from a subordinate's viewpoint. The subordinate has every reason to believe that he will be rewarded, because he was told that he was performing well. When the reward doesn't come, distrust and bad feelings are sure to emerge. Even if this animosity doesn't occur, the employee has no way of knowing how to improve, as the manager abdicated his responsibility in giving accurate feedback. Attempting to minimize the discomfort of both subordinate and superior, the superior may have created an even bigger problem of employee dissatisfaction, because a main reason for poor performance evaluations is a lack of supervisor skill in handling these difficult interview situations.

Another way to avoid these unpleasant sessions is called *dehiring*. If a manager doesn't want to tell the person that he or she is not performing up to standard, dehiring helps avoid the problem. Dehiring the employee doesn't *solve* the problem, but it may make the problem go away. Using this strategy, the manager attempts to make life on the job as miserable as possible for the employee hoping that he or she will "read" the signals and leave "voluntarily." If dehiring is effective, the supervisor never has to give the "bad news." Although this managerial unwillingness to assume responsibility can hurt both the employee and the company, dehiring is very widely used.[3]

Performance appraisals serve two purposes: planning for, monitoring of, and training of the subordinate and administration of salaries and rewards. Both are extremely important, and both put the manager in a classic role conflict. Can a manager be a friend, confidant, counselor, and trainer, but still be the coach and the keeper of the purse strings? It's a difficult position, because the manager can't really be sure which of these roles should get more attention — and commitment. This is obviously a choice that each manager must make. From a communication standpoint, the critical issue is which of these roles do employees perceive the manager to be emphasizing. This conflict between being a coach and being a counselor adds to the discomfort and conflict during the performance appraisal.

COMMUNICATION STRATEGIES

Let's turn our attention to strategies for reducing the role conflict experienced by managers, to communicating performance information to subordinates in a nondefense provoking manner to achieve the desired results and outcomes in employee behavior. Prescriptions for managerial behavior are often viewed suspiciously by supervisors and managers who realize that there isn't *AN ANSWER* for all situations. Because many contingencies are involved, the following suggestions must be interpreted in light of one's own managerial setting. Although there's no "definitive" technique, think of these suggestions as guidelines and begin to merge them with your own managerial style, skills, and organizational constraints.

1. Identify the Behaviors

To achieve the desired performance from an employee, the employee must know *exactly* what is expected of him. The manager's responsibility is to provide the employee with a complete, precise, and clear understanding of the behaviors that are desired. This provides the subordinate with a greater appreciation of what he or she is to do and forces the manager to be more specific in his expectations and, therefore, more objective in his evaluations. Properly done, it can create a less defensive atmosphere between the superior and the subordinate.

If a manager tells a subordinate to "take care of that problem," there is a good chance that the subordinate may not completely understand how he is to proceed, as many alternatives are available to him. On the other hand, if the manager tells the subordinate to perform three specific tasks, the subordinate experiences less uncertainty as to what he is to do. Defining expected behaviors provides direction and focus needed by many employees, even though it presents a risk of restricting employee creativity and initiative.

Once a manager has identified specific behaviors, subordinates can be evaluated in terms of how well these goals were reached. Because the standards are established ahead of time, the manager can be more objective in evaluation.

Finally (and most important), a focus on behaviors can minimize defensiveness in an evaluation interaction. Consider the difference between the following statements:

1. "Jim, you really didn't do a very good job on the report."
2. "Jim, the data collection and writing style in the report were fine, but the punctuation was inappropriate in the spots I have indicated."

In our first example, the manager evaluated Jim's performance, but this kind of feedback doesn't give Jim any idea as to how to correct his failures. In the second example, the manager told Jim what behaviors were acceptable and identified the sources of difficulty in a way that could be corrected. This description, rather than evaluation, creates a more supportive communication climate. It is important to make the distinction between person and behavior. When a manager has to give negative feedback, resentment is minimized when he can say "I like *you*, but I don't like these *behaviors*."

2. Identify the Criteria

You can make evaluating employee behavior much easier and much less subjective if you define clear and precise criteria for "comparing" employee performance. These criteria should include all relevant job activities, and they should be weighted as to their relative importance.[4] This gives the manager a "yardstick" with which to more objectively evaluate an employee. Note that we say "*more* objectively." Complete objectivity, although desirable, is an unattainable goal, as the manager is always perceiving employee behavior with his own biases, prejudices, blind spots, and unique frames of reference. These perceptual influences can never be eliminated, but their influence can be reduced as additional criteria are used in performance appraisal.

If criteria for employee behavior are not clearly established, the manager takes the risk of falling into the trap of giving some employees the benefit of the doubt, to the point where favoritism emerges. This "halo effect" is a real danger and can create dissension among other employees. If all employees know the criteria and feel that the manager is using these criteria, they will know what to expect. Because their doubt and uncertainty has been removed, they know better what must be done to earn rewards. If the criteria are well established, employees can feel that changing their behavior and "shaping up" will produce personal benefits. This potential for increased motivation won't appear until the relationship between behaviors and rewards is clearly spelled out and the employee sees what it is that the manager is going to reward.

3. Don't Just Focus on the Negative

It is often very difficult to get employees to "hear" what we are saying and to appreciate the implications of our messages. All too often, employees may sit and listen, but not really hear the message we intended. To achieve the results we want, the message must be presented so it is at least minimally acceptable to the employee.

When people find themselves in a threatening situation, their natural response is to seek protection. If someone throws something at you, it's only natural to duck and try to avoid the object. The same is true of an employee being criticized. As soon as the inevitable "or else" is heard, defensiveness commences. This defensiveness in appraisal sessions can later result in inferior employee performance, leading to a cycle of "poor evaluations-poor performance" that is very hard to break.

Managers must develop communication strategies to minimize defensiveness in performance appraisal. One strategy is to use an indirect approach that "sandwiches" the negatives between positive evaluation and praise. Although some managers suggest that praise doesn't affect this process one way or another, they fail to consider the "positioning" of bad news in relation to praise. When being criticized, a subordinate's first reaction may well be "... and I suppose I never do anything right." When the manager recognizes and praises positive behaviors of the subordinate at the beginning of the interview, this counterargument cannot be used. The criticism can be put in perspective and perceived as being more "fair."

"Sandwiching" negatives is really just the use of empathy. By putting yourself in another person's shoes, you can make better predictions about how a subordinate may react. In advance, you may decide to avoid a particular approach. Empathy tells us to look at an employee's particular set of circumstances rather than operate from some neutral stance or from an arbitrary set of rules. Empathy can reduce defensiveness, and thus help subordinates really "hear" what you want them to hear.

4. Minimize the Differences

When giving feedback, another way to reduce defensiveness is to minimize the differences in role status. Instead of telling a subordinate that it is *his* problem, emphasize a joint concern that must be overcome.[5] This mutual interest allows the subordinate to feel less alone, or stuck with the problem.

Defensiveness can also be reduced if the evaluated person is not made to feel inferior or "second rate." When a manager assumes an arrogant attitude, flaunts his superiority, or just shakes his head in disbelief, a subordinate will invariable become defensive. This is *not* to suggest that a manager must denounce his role or that the manager must be "first-name buddies" to prevent a defensive attitude. Rather, we suggest that the manager treat subordinates with genuine respect, even though some employees' behavior may be far from acceptable. If a manager is concerned about improving work behavior, he or she must first demonstrate at least minimal concern for the employee.

Again, we see the conflict in the multiple roles of the manager. The manager suggests to the employee that it is "our" problem, but, because you did poorly on "our" problems, you won't get a raise. The manager is to be a counselor, hence, it is "our" problem, but he also must be an administrator of wages, which is, by definition, a "superior" role. One way to reduce this conflict is to conduct employee improvement interviews *separately* from those in which salary matters are discussed.[6] This won't eliminate role conflict, but it does help to minimize the negative consequences.

5. Don't Gunnysack

When giving negative feedback, the manager may want to "correct" one or two things in the employee's behavior; yet, many times, these objectives get lost once the discussion begins. Have you ever been in an argument and, when it started to get tough, someone threw out in phrase, "Well not only that, but ..."? Saving up things that annoy us can get us into trouble. When the battle starts to get really rough, we start digging out all of the ammunition we can find. All those little things that have been "under our skin" finally have a way to get out. All of us have been guilty of this kind of argument, but let's look at the results of this approach.

As a manager you come into the session with one or two things that you wants to correct. When the employee puts up a fight or gets defensive about some of these things, you may feel backed against a wall and strike out with whatever is at hand. We've saved all those little gripes and put them in our gunnysack, for use at the right time. "Gunnysacking" detracts from efforts to correct real problems. The subordinate can now justify his or her behavior because "obviously you're just nit picking." You dilute your message to the employee if you add too many additional issues. A better strategy is to confront these minor issues as they arise. If the issues aren't important enough for you to bring up as they occur, forget about them. Don't save gripes and then let them get in your way when something really important arises.

The effectiveness of feedback often depends on *when* that feedback is given. When feedback is given immediately following a behavior, the feedback is more likely to be effective. It doesn't make sense to reprimand a child several hours after he has misbehaved. Similarly, it doesn't make sense to withold evaluative information from an employee until the next six-month evaluation. Feedback, both positive and negative, should be given continuously. Regular feedback allows the subordinates to correct their behavior when necessary, while reinforcing desirable behaviors now present.

6. Recognize the Difference Between Can't and Won't!

Too often, managers fail to identify the cause of poor performance. Performance has at least two major elements: motivation and ability. If performance is poor, a common managerial response is to assume that the employee *won't* perform (a motivational problem). Although this may be the case, there are many times when lack of performance is due to the employee's low ability or lack of training. These two elements of poor performance demand very different correcting strategies.

If an employee *won't* perform, the manager must evaluate the motivation strategies being used. However, if the employee *can't* perform, the manager's responsibility is to train the employee (if possible) or find an alternative solution such as transfer or termination. Don't simply shift the burden to the employee, assuming that he or she won't perform. Make this important distinction. One way to do so is to directly involve the employee in the performance appraisal process. A joint evaluation procedure not only helps managers to more accurately perceive problems. It also provides employees with a better understanding of evaluation. It leads to greater employee satisfaction with the entire evaluation process. [7]

7. Split the Conflicting Roles

Some managers have little or no real control over the details of their firm's performance appraisal system. The timing of the supervisor-subordinate "joint review session" is given, as is the general format of the meeting and the "suggested" method for presenting bad or negative information. For these managers, this strategy will not be possible. However, for those with a flexible performance review system, a productive approach is to hold two face-to-face sessions with each employee, one dealing with the administration of salaries or rewards (or punishments) and a second dealing only with the counseling/planning/training function.

Although such an arrangement clearly takes more time (in effect, it can double the actual amount of supervisor-subordinate contact time on each review cycle), the benefits of this split strategy are many. Above all, it permits the supervisor to wear one hat at a time and, thus, concentrate on a single task without having to shift from one role to another. Assuming that the first of the two meetings is devoted to the salary/reward phase, the employee has some period of time to digest the feedback given him or her. Even if the feedback in the first session is negative, both the news itself and the employee's offhand reaction are isolated. The counseling phase (meeting 2) can be held in a more open or productive setting, one relatively uncharged by an emotional response. Also, the employee has the benefit of reflection on his or her evaluation. With this reflection, the counseling can usually be directed toward more clearly defined and agreed-on goals. The employee's mind is reasonably clear of evaluative information and is better able to focus clearly on the planning/training session objectives.

Managers using a split session must exercise extra caution in the second-phase session. Some employees (usually those given low ratings or negative feedback in the first session) will try to resurrect the subject of their rating in the second counseling session. It is here that the manager must exert discreet but firm control, if the benefits of the split appraisal approach are to be realized.

8. Watch for Manager Defensiveness

A new and interesting (and potentially damaging) phenomenon in performance appraisal is the problem of managers' perceiving negative employee ratings as reflections on their own abilities. Recently, several people in management seminars conducted by the author have suggested this new barrier to the communications in performance appraisal. In this situation, the manager feels that an employee's poor performance directly reflects his or her performance as a manager. With this perception, the manager is reluctant to criticize and becomes highly defensive whenever a low-rated employee's defensiveness seems to backfire. In some instances, your attitude results in the employee's gaining practical control over the performance appraisal process. The minimum cost of this occurring is a higher than deserved rating. At worst, the entire appraisal process for all employees can be seriously compromised.

There are no simple remedies to this final communication problem. However, should such defensiveness occur, it may indicate a performance appraisal failure of another sort at the next highest organizational level. The defensive manager's immediate superior has perhaps failed to properly communicate or to conduct meaningful counseling activities with the individual. Thus, "rater-defensiveness" may well be a symptom of problems higher up the chain of command.

Thus far, we've looked at communication strategies for running a performance appraisal system that's already in place. However, what communication strategies are available to managers when they are responsible either for installing a new performance appraisal system in a department or division when there has not been such a system before or when major changes are being proposed to an existing system? In the latter part of this chapter, we'll explore this side of performance appraisal.

SELLING PERFORMANCE APPRAISAL
TO THE EMPLOYEES

Too often, managers have been criticized for plying their trade behind the backs of their employees. Their plans for organizational improvement are often rejected because employees don't get involved in the performance appraisal program.

For an effective performance appraisal program, managers must put into practice many of the behavioral principles to which they've often given lip service in the past few years. They can "sell" performance appraisal in some of the following ways. [8]

1. Don't Dictate—Participate

Participation is one means by which management can encourage organizational members to take an active role in the decision-making process in which they will be affected by the outcome. It is hoped that such participation will enlist individual creativity and enthusiasm. All managers and, for that matter, employees, are vitally involved with the performance appraisal system in use. But how many have ever had a say in its existence. Participation builds commitment to results. What commitment do your employees now have in the existing performance appraisal system?

The participative approach builds both the power of the group and emphasizes the dual role of the manager as a group member and a representative of management. The participant is being asked to play an additional role within the established organization structure. His self-esteem is increased by his selection, and, consequently, the perceived value of his contribution will be increased. Employees should be allowed to affect the instrument they will be using. Put simply, "Skills follow values, values rarely follow skills." You cannot expect effective use of your performance appraisal system if the managers doing the rating don't believe that the system reflects their values. Participation allows employees the opportunity to incorporate their ideas (values) into a system that, as creators, they will support.

2. Create Honest, Open Meetings

Publicize the creation of a performance appraisal project and invite to this informal meeting any employee who's interested. The purpose of this meeting should be to create and measure interest in performance appraisal and to informally present the purpose of the evolution that is planned. Review the present system. Point out some common complaints that you have received. Be honest about why the performance appraisal review committees are being formed and delineate how much authority they will have to change the system.

Realistic boundaries or limitations will clarify for the participants the realm in which they can effectively operate and clarify the goals they wish to accomplish. Lack of clarification may result in confusion, misdirection, and often useless results. Few mistakes are more serious than allowing the group to pursue blind alleys with the result that the members lose interest and drop out. Also, if the results are misdirected and prove to be unusable, some members will see the venture as lacking genuine participation and refuse to contribute further. Any subsequent appraisal system will likely fail to meet with their approval, and its acceptance by them will suffer.

3. Establish Workshops Within the Committee

Ideas and suggestions may seem fine at first. However, workability in practice is the primary goal of the performance appraisal system. To iron out suggestions, the performance appraisal review should break into groups and role play the suggested instrument. Role playing is an excellent technique to point out operational flaws which might exist. Often, one group will find that the suggested appraisal system works fine, whereas another may discover many stumbling blocks to effective use. Such "testing" allows those involved an opportunity to deal with potential problems before the appraisal system is put into use. It also helps to avoid major and costly changes later.

4. Develop a Posture of Communication

All too frequently, the old communications workhorse is dusted off by managers and trotted out to help implement a new program. When failures, and worse, marginal successes, occur, they can be blamed on a "failure of communications."

Certainly, good communication is essential to the successful implementation of any appraisal system, particularly because the system is only as good as the way it's used by managers and employees. If the employees don't see themselves and their objectives in the performance appraisal system, it will not work.

One major hurdle in developing a positive mental attitude toward the new (or revised) performance appraisal system is individual manager involvement in the system. To accomplish some measure of real involvement, meetings and other participation activities are usually conducted in a manner that forces maximum participation. Each manager in the meeting is encouraged to share with his peers whatever feelings, reservations, modifications, and the like that he may have about the new system. But this is not enough.

Many studies of human communication, particularly in participative activities, have demonstrated a clear difference between *vocal participation* in an idea or program and actual personal involvement with the program. Employees who speak out frequently and appear, at least on the surface, to be actively participating in hammering out a performance appraisal system, may in fact, be the least satisfied with the eventual outcome and shape of the program. Conversely, we have seen a high correlation between group participant satisfaction with a program and the "perceived opportunity" for participation.

Encouraging all employees to be vocal in their feelings about a new system is not in itself open communications. In dealing with employees who are actually wrestling with a new system, management people should focus on the *process* of communication within the work group. Do individual members feel that they will be given a full hearing on their ideas? Does the group of employees assembled to explore the new system actually seem to be exploring? Are they merely ratifying an agreed-on plan over the real but unstated objections of some of their colleagues?

Good communications in any group participation effort, and particularly in the important activity of accepting a performance appraisal system, is based on a posture of communications. This posture, which develops over time and out of a feeling between the managers and their employees that there is mutual honesty and trust between them, will be far more valuable than a mere facade of manager-employee meetings.

5. Give Full Information

It seems almost unnecessary to say that effectively selling a performance appraisal system requires that the employees "buying" the system be given all relevant information.

Unfortunately, in too many situations, managers have given employees only a capsule summary of the relevant information about the new performance appraisal system. The rationale was simply that the employees should concern themselves only with those parts of the program relevant to their specific evaluation. Using this line of thought, employees do not need to be aware of the intricacies of the entire system. This is absurd.

A maxim of selling is that the customer must be shown (or allowed to find for himself) the relevance of a particular product or service to his own needs. What will this product *do for me?* This is no less true in selling a performance appraisal system. The employees have to see relevance to the new system to their problems and performance, and this point of view can only be cultivated by giving them as much information on the plan as there is available. Human nature abhors a vacuum of information. When information is missing (its relevance to the task at hand is unimportant), we all try to fill in with assumptions, opinions, and inferences. Insights based on assumptions can often lead to faulty and dangerous conclusions that could render a well-designed plan quite unworkable. In the delicate business of selling a performance appraisal system, information "overkill" is preferred to information "drought."

6. It is Better to be Clear and Human than Precise

Precision is admirable. Ultimately, a performance appraisal system will succeed or fail on the basis of the precision with which it is implemented. However, at the selling stage, where employees are actively participating in planning, precision can create an unnecessary barrier to successful implementation. What does the system mean to the individual? Can the advantages of the proposed system be expressed in human terms, rather than in some vague sort of quantitative-sounding set of parameters? Selling a program requires that the human aspects be stressed over the less involving aspects of the technical detail.

7. Feedback

A final, and critical consideration is what the manager does with the inputs from the employees about changes and ideas for the new system. All the participation in the world will be worthless unless every participant can see tangible results from his or her efforts. Simply calling for participation and then following the original, preparticipation plan will negate all the positive mental attitudes of the employees.

Responses (feedback) must be given to all worthwhile inputs. Reinforcing the importance of employee participation as well as the importance of a performance appraisal system is essential for effectively installing any new system.

SUMMARY

All motivation strategies depend on the efficiency of the evaluation process. Efficiency requires clear appraisal procedures and effective managerial communication skills. Despite the incentives used and the "objectivity" of appraisal mechanisms, evaluation efficiency ultimately depends on the way in which the manager communicates with the subordinate. It is your responsibility to be aware of the pitfalls of the evaluation process and the communication strategies available.

When a performance review for your employees is coming up, carefully consider some of the ideas and suggestions presented in this chapter. Watch for signs of resentment, gunnysacking, defensiveness, and "fuzzy" criteria. Develop with each employee an acceptable, understandable relationship between the suggestions and standards that the employee is being asked to follow and the employee's personal interests. Recognizing the difference between the employee's interests and the standards being set and minimizing those differences is a positive first step to take toward effective performance appraisal.

Ways to Improve Your Communication Skills

1. Identify the positive behavior that you want your subordinates to use as goals. It does little good to be subjective and suggest that "you're doing fine, but could do better." Be as specific as possible.

2. Identify the criteria you'll use to evaluate an employee and compare his or her performance with that of others.

3. Maintain a balance between positive and negative performance appraisal. Don't just focus on the negative.

4. Don't make mountains out of molehills by accentuating the differences between ideal and actual performance.

5. Don't "gunnysack" problems, saving them up for the periodic review. Bring up your concerns as problems develop with an employee's performance.

6. Distinguish between an employee who won't work and an employee who can't work. It's the difference between *ability* and *motivation,* and it is vitally important to communication.

7. Whenever possible, separate the performance and salary part of the review from the counseling part. The counseling messages are less likely to be met with a defensive reaction.

8. Watch for and control your own defensiveness, especially when employees react to poor performance appraisals by striking out in frustration at you.

9. When a new performance appraisal system is being installed, encourage your employees to participate in as many phases of the operation as possible. Simply dictating to them won't create a positive climate for the system.

10. In the early stages of a performance appraisal system, keep meetings honest, open, and informal. Also, set up working groups to handle thorny problems.

11. Develop a posture of communication within your department. Effective performance appraisal operates in such an atmosphere.

12. As much as possible, give your employees full, factual, and complete information. In effect, they are in a position to "buy," or not buy, the system. Like customers in other buyer-seller situations, they need as much information as possible.

17

Overcoming Resistance
to Change

"There are two kinds of fools. One says, 'This is old, therefore it is good.' The other says, 'This is new, therefore it is better.'"

Dean Inge

Change is a condition that constantly influences the actions of all managers. In fact, dealing with change is a basic responsibility of management, which can be defined as the ability to state a goal and to reach it, through the efforts of other people, to satisfy those whose judgment must be respected, under conditions of stress, in an environment of accelerating change.

In predictable or certain conditions, little real leadership is required of most managers. Their work communications are quite routine, following well-defined patterns. When changing conditions or stress is involved, however, the real ability of the manager becomes important. Recognizing this, many organizations use "stress testing" to evaluate potential managers and supervisors during the employment interview process. These organizations recognize, as do many supervisors, that a manager's real value to an organization or a department shows best when uncertainty prevails.[1]

255

CHANGE THREATENS

Managers and employees often view any kind of change as unnecessary and distasteful, to be resisted or avoided at all costs. Some individuals have a high "tolerance" for ambiguity—they are able to function effectively in changing situations. Other managers and employees feel more comfortable with the status quo. However, change is a fact of life for all managers, those in very routine-oriented organizations as well as those in dynamic, high-technology organizations. To be effective, a managers must not only adapt to change personally. He or she must also be able to communicate the importance of developing positive personal attitudes toward change.

IS CHANGE ALWAYS BEST?

Certainly not. Change solely for the sake of change is just as foolish as refusing to change when change is clearly warranted. Developing a positive attitude toward change does not automatically mean that one must greet all changes with unquestioned enthusiasm. It does require an open mind, a willingness and ability to see "reality" wherever possible.

RESISTERS OF CHANGE

It is impossible to generalize accurately about any particular group of people. However, it is possible to identify some characteristics of persons inclined to support organization change and some attributes of those who resist change.

Resisters of change are generally the following types.

1. *People Who Rely Heavily on Personal Experience in Making Decisions.* This individual views change as a force that will render valuable information obsolete. For example, consider the plight of an executive whose 27 years of management experience in his industry is suddenly made obsolete by the introduction of advanced and sophisticated technology in that industry —technology that drastically changes not only the work done in his company but also the relationship among companies in the industry. This change poses a direct personal threat to the executive by changing his way of managing. This person's resistance to any kind of further change is now frequently expressed by after-the-fact comments such as "I told you so," or "Don't tell me you troubles—I was against this thing right from the start." Often, even subtle changes (such as changes in staff hiring procedures) come to be viewed

256

as personal attacks on the managers who earned their expertise in the "school of hard knocks."

2. ***People Who Prefer "One Best Way" of Doing Things.*** For resisters of change, a single, obvious solution is preferable to a range of options. It's more comfortable, more reassuring when there's little or no change taking plac₃ and we can find a "best way" of doing things. But, with change, the situation is so unique each day that no one approach or alternative will always work. New solutions are needed. Because change removes the comfort and security of one best solution, those supervisors who look for a single, constant answer reject change.

3. ***People Who Have Little Propensity to Take Risks.*** Because change of any sort involves the unknown or unpredicted, change brings risk. Those who prefer a sure thing or who don't like to "rock the boat" will resist any change that presents even the possibility of more risk. These executives can often be spotted by such reactions as "Why should we make that change? I've already got enough problems."

Tolerance or acceptance of risk is largely a psychological characteristic. Yet, it can be controlled by managers who are genuinely interested in improving their ability to deal effectively with change. Managers with change-resistant employees can improve their risk propensity by showing a good example in the face of change. Because risk *can* mean failure, be tolerant in your reaction to employees who accept risk and occasionally fail. By communicating an attitude of tolerance for change-induced risk, managers can add measurably to their employees' willingness to accept change when it does occur.

SUPPORTERS OF CHANGE

Generally, persons who support continuing change are those who have personal characteristics opposite to those of the change resisters. Supporters of change are interested in continued personal growth, which occurs only when challenges continue to apprear. A Colorado manager of a swimming pool company observed recently that she has 16 years of experience in the pool business. However, she realistically added that what she *really* has is one year's experience repeated 16 times. Doing the same job in the same way does not bring personal growth or experience in the positive sense. Reducing resistance to change in your department or organizations begins with developing an attitude that change is personally beneficial to all employees. With this attitude, introducing change is made far easier and more productive for all.

SOURCES OF CHANGE

Some change in organizations comes from decisions of managers higher up. New administrative processes, customer services, policies, or financial arrangement all involve some sort of change. Many times, these changes are subtle and require little adaptation or acceptance from employees. Other changes appear (and often are) massive in scope, profoundly altering the basic personal and working relationships in the organization. A change in a machine process or a sales policy may have only a passing effect on a few employees. Yet, another "simple" change in the timing or scheduling of a supervisor's meeting or a payday can alter social relationships, employee attendance and motivation, and supervisor participation. The "simple" change can even affect the harmony (or discord) among employees in the department.

Usually, top-down organizational change cannot occur without the consent of the top manager. Resistance to this kind of change usually intensifies when the top manager fails to adequately and fully explain the reasons for the changes and how the proposed changes affect individual employees, departments, or activities.

Change is also imposed on all organizations from outside. Technology causes change by altering the way that information travels within the organization. For example, computer technology has contributed to the problems usually associated with change. A sales manager with 12 salespeople operated a sales division covering a five-state territory and headquartered in Kansas City. Each salesperson would regularly send in sales reports to the manager. The manager summarized the division's performance and sent his report to the company's central office in Chicago. The sales manager was an important link in the communication system of the company.

With the introduction of a sophisticated computer set-up, this relationship changed. Salespeople were now able to directly contact the central office by remote computer terminal. Their daily sales reports were available to top management the following morning, yet it was two days before the sales manager in Kansas City had the same information. The change made the sales manager appear unnecessary, and he resisted the change both before and after the new technology was installed.

Even subtle changes in technology (such as a new machine or a new process) can result in resistance and behavior problems for supervisors and managers. The administrative vice president of an Oklahoma trade association discovered to his dismay that substituting a coffee service for the old office coffeemaker caused change in his office routine. It gave the staff who used to make coffee more time to do their jobs. However, the new service removed an opportunity for the staff to control money, even though the amounts involved were very small. The point of the change was lost on staff, whereas the unintended effect caused resistance.

Naturally, not all change in departments or organizations is this minor. Some changes in management policy—the power and authority of the supervisors or the job descriptions of employees—are due to combinations of technology, changes in organization product, markets, or customers, needs, and even the growth of the company, industry or agency.

Growth is a major source of change. As organizations get larger, their basic communication patterns change. This, in turn, alters the relationships between people in the organization. Growing organizations usually manage their growth by using more specialization, which also means more levels of management. These new levels of management are necessary to keep the span of control and the responsibilities of any one person within reasonable limits. An individual can effectively supervise the work of a limited number of employees or projects. The exact number of employees or duties under one person's "span of control" will, of course, vary from one individual to another. Nevertheless, growth means more management levels, and this in turn leads to longer lines of communication.

The cover of *Association Management* magazine in November 1976 suggested that the manager "hire two new staff members; redistribute workload and everyone's happy." They (meaning the old staff) may be happy with a reduced work load, but this simple, supposedly beneficial, change, may cause some hidden resistance. In some organizations, very simple changes are resisted more than broad sweeping changes because smaller changes often have a more direct, personal impact on the individual manager or employee.

For example, suppose that your present department has 12 paid employees under your direct supervision. As the organization grows, the number of regular employees rises to 37. Assuming that this is too many people doing too many things for you to effectively supervise, a logical solution is to hire four assistants, each responsible for supervising 8 to 13 persons. You, in turn, are now directly supervising only four employees (the assistants), as well as coordinating their activities, and setting goals and policies for the department. The formal, day-to-day contacts between supervisor and employee now occur between the assistants and "their" people. The employees' direct, formal contact with you is now limited.

In Figure 17-1, we can compare the old and new structure in the organization. The old, 15-person staff had only one link of communication between employee and his or her supervisor. However, in the new, 42-person department (the 37 employees, 4 new assistants, and the manager), there are two links of communication between employee and department manager. As growth enlarges every department in an organization, the same fundamental changes

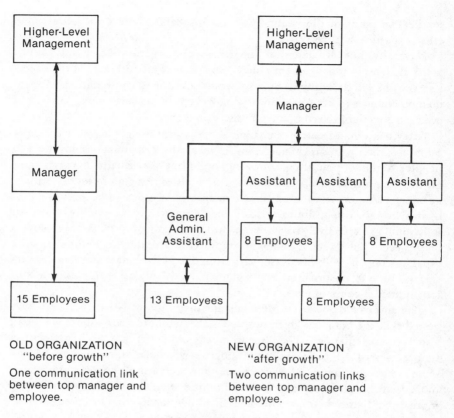

OLD ORGANIZATION
"before growth"

One communication link
between top manager and
employee.

NEW ORGANIZATION
"after growth"

Two communication links
between top manager and
employee.

FIGURE 17-1

in communication links and communication patterns result in each of the departments.

To summarize briefly, change in organizations is caused by many forces, most of which are beyond the ability of the management to control. Rather than resisting or rejecting change, supervisors and managers should take a positive role in supporting change and in selling the benefits of change to their employees.

STRATEGIES FOR SELLING CHANGE

As a manager, you face two responsibilities with regard to change. One responsibility is to maintain an open mind toward change. For reasons we've already discussed, change is a fact of organizational life. Some change is imposed on organizations, whereas other change is caused (or encouraged) by people within the organization.

Regardless of the cause or source, change can represent both hardship and opportunity for managers. Resisting change (for whatever reason) means a never-ending pattern of frustration and anxiety. Supporting change can lead to renewed opportunities for personal and professional growth. By keeping an open mind toward change, you provide your organization with the ability to respond to changing needs and, thus, operate more effectively.

Selling change and its benefits to employees is a somewhat more complicated matter. We all fear change for a variety of personal and job-related reasons. Change means a new way of doing things on the job — new relationships and the severing of old relationships and contacts. To employees, change can mean uncertainty about future job responsibilities, or even raise the spectre of having no job at all. Change may also imply loss of the familiar, the introduction of the unknown, and the uncertainty of a new future that they can't control.

Naturally, managers can appreciate these fears, as they too experience them. However, by taking a positive view of change, managers can help those affected to see the positive side of change. There are several practical ways in which this can be done. Some ideas won't apply to your situation or, perhaps, won't be right for your employees. Others will apply to you. Either way, consider these strategies carefully. Each represents an opportunity to reduce the uncertainty associated with change, and to change things in a way that is more productive.

1. *Take Stock of Yourself.* This perhaps may seem to be a strange suggestion for overcoming resistance to change, but it is a very sensible first step. Only after you feel comfortable with your response and attitude toward change can you help others deal with it. Inventory your attitudes, your strengths, and your weaknesses. Honestly appraise your ability to overcome managerial obsolescence. With the answers to simple, self-searching questions, you'll be in a better position to assess your people (and your department or work group) and facilitate change as it occurs.

2. *Cut Corners.* This, too, may sound a little strange at first, but consider the following. As managers, we base our actions on two considerations: the *factual information* we have available about processes, schedules, and people and the *assumptions* we make about requirements, needs, services, attitudes, and people. It's in the second set of considerations — the assumptions — that we can begin to cut corners. Often, we impose restrictions on ourselves that are not really necessary or even productive. These self-imposed assumptions tend to accumulate and can bog down realistic efforts to institute meaningful or useful change.

Departmental operating policies often fall into the category of self-imposed job restrictions, even if the department manager is not personally responsible for imposing them. Rules adopted years before you became the boss may still be in force, simply because "we've always done it that way" or because "it's been that way as far back as anyone can remember," or even because "that's the way *they* want it!" Nevertheless, are your current assumptions about your people and their needs correct? Are the requirements of your job and the activities for which you and staff are held accountable imposed by *you* or by "precedent"? Are the things you do for and to your employees really important to them, or do you just assume they're important?

3. ***Check Your Paperwork.*** The dipstick on your car tells you when the oil is low. Your paperwork does the same job for your department or organization. Too much paperwork is a symptom that too much effort is being spent on essentially reporting (and thereby usually nonproductive) effort. The clog of paperwork (like the clog of unnecessary self-imposed assumptions) makes an organization sluggish and unable to respond to pressures for change. Cleaning up the unnecessary paperwork is a streamlining strategy that should be continuous. It puts the organization in a much better position to respond quickly and positively to external change pressures.

4. ***Plant Seeds.*** Changes are more likely to be effective if those persons directly affected by the changes have a hand in causing them to occur. Confrontation or force, while occasionally a good means of overcoming immediate problems of change resistance, is not a good long-run strategy for implementing or overcoming resistance to change. On the other hand, dropping hints, making suggestions, and offering praise when good ideas surface are excellent ways to develop a free flow of useful ideas—including those ideas that *you* want to surface.

Although taking personal credit for innovation and change may be good for your ego or your job security, letting others take credit is more than just an ego trip. It's a way to build commitment. It's also a way to co-opt resistance to change, by making the resisters a part of the change itself.

Timing is an important aspect of seed planting. Whenever possible communicate well in advance of actual changes taking place. Last minute notice of new procedures, programs, schedules, or policies can be unsettling. Such notice seldom gives people the option to respond. They usually figure that their feelings are unimportant or are not even being considered. Naturally, not all changes are known to you well in advance. You often must implement new procedures or programs with minimal preparation and planning. However, this usually is not an everyday occurrence. Just as clearly, changes that you personally institute need not be kept secret until the last minute. Advance notice invariably puts people in a better frame of mind to receive and accept change.

Rocking the boat from time to time is another way to plant seeds for change. Ask questions of your employees. Refuse to accept the "conventional wisdom" or the "usual answers." Keep your people on their toes, ready for inquiries into what they are doing and why. The status quo is very easy to fall into, and a little periodic boat rocking (if not overdone) can keep things rolling smoothly and make change easier to accept when it occurs.

Traveling through eastern Kentucky a few years back, a motorist fell in behind an old truck loaded with crates of live chickens. He was intrigued by the truck driver, who would periodically slam the side of the truck with a long pole. This action caused a considerable noise and a commotion among the chickens, and the pattern continued as he followed the truck for several miles through the mountains. Reaching the top of a steep grade, the truck driver pulled over to let the following traffic pass. Intrigued by the trucker's behavior, the motorist pulled off the road behind the truck and walked over to ask the trucker about the pole and the chickens.

"Simple," he said. "This here truck is old and overloaded. With all these chickens, it would never make it up all these hills. Hitting the side of the truck scares the daylights out of these chickens and keeps half of 'em in the air all the time — it's the only way to lighten the load and make it to the top."

Keeping a few employees in the air from time to time can lighten your load too, especially when doing so plants the seeds of change in their minds.

5. *Don't Over Plan, or Oversell.* Too much planning, or too much selling, is as dangerous as too little. It's virtually impossible to preplan for every minor contingency, and attempting to do so can lead to frustration and anger for you and similar reactions from you employees.

Overselling is usually seen as a sign that there's something wrong with a product. When a salesperson gets too excited extolling the merits of a product, our usual reaction is to back off and begin asking some critical questions. Just as your reaction to a "soft" sell is more likely to be positive than your reactions to a "hard" sell, your employees will more likely respond favorably when your change strategy is not over sold.

6. *Don't Fall in Love with Your Own Ideas.* Just because the manager came up with the idea doesn't make it the greatest innovation since sliced bread. Naturally, we're all more comfortable with our own creations, but it's foolish to assume that others hold our ideas in the same reverence.

Subject your ideas to the same scrutiny you would to evaluate and consider ideas from your employees. You'll be less likely to be mislead by a "pet project" and more likely to identify ideas (from yourself and others) that are really meaningful.

7. *Communicate Reassurance.* Above all, change of any sort implies a threat of the unknown. Rather than a detailed technical discussion of the relative merits of the new approach, your first message should be one of reassurance. Airline people are counseled to offer reassurance when a passenger's luggage is lost. Details about tickets, luggage size, and color can come later. The first duty of the baggage claim agent is to offer reassurance.

While traveling across the open spaces of West Texas, an out-of-state tourist heard an unfamiliar noise coming from the rear axle of the car. Not wanting to risk a breakdown in the "middle of nowhere," he limped slowly into the Ford dealership in the next town (which happened to be Dimmit, Texas). The dealer's service manager came out and drove the car around the block. His first words when he returned were "Don't worry, I don't think it's too serious. We can help you." Only then did he offer any technical detail about what he though the problem might be. Reassurance.

That service manager was a good salesman for his company's products, and he would probably make a good manager too. Few of us like surprises in our job or in the activities and statements of our superiors. When changes do occur, we all want to be reassured that the interruption will be minimal, that our fears will be calmed, and that our needs will be satisfied. As with so many aspects of communications, consider the other person's point of view by looking at the way you would want to be treated.

8. *External Threat.* A threat to a department or an organization can be a powerful force for bringing about change. Changes in funding, new political, social, or market conditions, and new processes, procedures, and policies all represent real threats to the security and stability of a department or an organization. When an external threat occurs, people are often more willing to go along with changes designed to combat or deal with the threat.

When there's no external threat, some managers try to invent one. This is, of course, a very risky strategy. It can blow up into a messy situation. It should be used only under extreme conditions, or when the penalty for ignoring change is far greater than the risk of a phony threat.

FIGHTING FOREST FIRES

A useful analogy to use when looking at strategies for dealing with conflict or pressure within your department is the analogy of fighting forest fires. Few of us have direct experience with forest fires, but we can all appreciate the seriousness of a major fire. Think about your problem (perhaps a major difficulty in the past) and see if it fits the pattern of the forest fire.

Very often, a crisis develops in a department when someone challenges the supervisor's authority. When this happens, many of the "standard" lines of communication don't work in quite the same way that they do normally. Consider carefully the following.

Ten Rules for Fighting Fires

1. *Probe the Perimeter.* When a crisis (or even a problem that is not yet at the "crisis" stage) arises, the first step is to gather as much information as possible. Don't try to develop a strategy *until* you have enough information about the problem (see Figure 17-2).

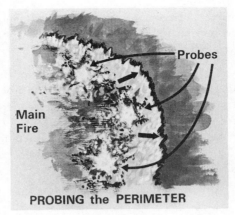

PROBING the PERIMETER

FIGURE 17-2

When a forest fire breaks out, it is likely to be in a place at some distance from the forest service headquarters. If the fire fighters don't know the fire area well, they first survey the area. They map the terrain and put probes into the fire to learn how deep it is. They learn about the potential fuel for the fire (dry fallen leaves or old timber will burn faster and hotter than green open meadowland). They identify obstacles to fighting the fire, and they catalog and assess potential natural fire-fighting tools (such as stream beds, natural water breaks, mountains, roads, etc.). Armed with this information, they are then (and only then) prepared to develop a strategy. No two forest fires are exactly alike, just as no two departmental crises are alike. The same answers won't work time after time.

Managers facing a problem need factual information. Probe the problem. Who is involved? How long has the situation been developing? Which individuals in the department are directly involved and which individuals are likely to be sympathtic to the problem instigators? What information do they have? Where is it coming from? What potential does this problem have for damaging the department and its work toward reaching its objectives? What information do you have that could be useful in dealing with the situation? If you are wrong in your assessment, what is the best way to admit your error? Are there any tactical considerations (such as timing)? Who in the department can be counted on to support your efforts to deal effectively with the problem. What support can you expect from your superiors in dealing with the problem? Does the problem go beyond the boundaries of your department and involve other parts of the organization? What are the *realistic* limits of your formal authority and your informal ability to persuade and compromise?

Important questions. They must be answered before a strategy is developed. Some answers are common sense, some have come up before, others must be found using whatever communication skills you've developed. There is a simple rule in planning: one hour of planning can save three to four hours of execution. Gathering information is a valuable investment of your time, even in the face of a crisis. Your response to the crisis (and your likelihood of success) will be far greater if you make the investment.

2. **Containment.** Once you've learned all there is to learn about the problem, your first action should be to take steps to bring the problem under control. This stage involves containing the problem, keeping it from spreading into areas so far unaffected by the problem (see Figure 17-3).

The forest service will deploy groups of fire fighters to various locations around the fire. They are to take only those actions necessary to contain the fire or to protect themselves.

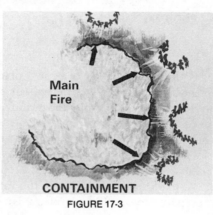

CONTAINMENT

FIGURE 17-3

In fighting a "managerial" fire, it's often possible to contain the problem by assigning small groups of employees to "study committees" responsible directly to you. This action helps hold the problem in and can result in some good additional information that might come to you in no other way. For example, if the problem involves a direct challenge to your managerial authority, the challenger may be unwilling to directly confront you or communicate with you. Using "neutral" employees can provide a means of getting information, while helping contain the problem. Like all the strategies we are discussing, however there is risk involved. Surrounding a problem with committees may be received as a sign of weakness, especially damaging if the problem concerns a challenge to your leadership.

3. **Destroy Heat at the Center.** An important tactical strategy used by the forest service is to bomb with an explosive in the center of the fire. This may deprive the fire of its oxygen or its heat source and quickly bring it under control. Red Adair and other oil-field fire fighters often use this approach (see Figure 17-4).

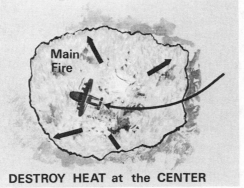

DESTROY HEAT at the CENTER

FIGURE 17-4

Managers can destroy the heat at the center of a crisis or a problem in two ways. If the problem is the work of an individual (or group of individuals), you can destroy the center by discrediting the leader or by bringing the leader into the overall effort to solve the problem. Destroying the problem leader is a very risky strategy, to be used *only* under extremely serious conditions. Discrediting that person's honesty, or motives, or ability may remove the immediate difficulty but may also leave a lingering atmosphere of distrust for you. This could backfire later.

Bringing the source of the trouble into the search for a solution is called *co-optation*. It is a wiser, more positive strategy, although it too has disadvantages. The most serious disadvantage is that you as a manager are giving up some of your authority, at least in the eyes of your subordinates. This would be no problem if you use a fairly democratic leadership style. However, if your leadership style is somewhat authoritarian, co-optation could be viewed as a sign of weakness and may encourage resistance to your efforts to overcome the problems and move on.

If there is no person involved in causing or encouraging the problem, the center of the problem can be defused by direct and fairly prompt action. Moving quickly to find the cause of the problems and dealing directly with the best possible solution can take much of the emotion out of the problem. What's left can then be resolved later, once the crisis has past. This won't work as well on problems that have been building for some time, as the cause (or cure) will be neither as obvious nor as simple. Taking steps to pull the plug on the center of the problem is, however, a major step in dealing with crisis.

4. *Build Fire Lines.* This is a more subtle strategy. It involves containing the fire by removing fuel from the edges of the fire and then waiting for the

fire to use up its remaining fuel and die a natural death. This is a risky strategy, because the wind could shift and the fire could go in several directions. To use this strategy successfully, one needs good information about the fire and the conditions promoting the fire. This, in turn, means good lines of communication between the supervisor and those directly involved with the fire (see Figure 17-5).

Letting a management problem "burn itself out" is full of danger. Your attempt to build defense lines and sit back to wait for the problem to go away might be viewed as a sign of weakness, or indecision, or inability to effectively deal with change. Be sure of the quality and correctness of your information before using this approach. Building fire lines is a fine solution. The real difficulty with this approach is in the waiting while the problem "blows over." Waiting too long, while conditions change, can be fatal to your management efforts.

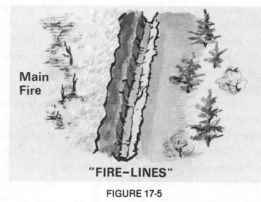

"FIRE-LINES"

FIGURE 17-5

5. *Building a "Back-Fire."* This is a more dynamic version of the fire-line strategy. It involves building a fire line by burning out a defense line directly in the path of the main fire. Although it is more "action oriented," it is extremely dangerous, because the back-fire can quickly get out of your control and become another major crisis (see Figure 17-6).

In a managerial sense, building a back-fire involves starting or encouraging a new crisis, to take attention of the employees off the major problem. While the employees' attention and energy is diverted, you can quickly attack the main problems with methods that might not be possible with everyone watching.

One manager using this strategy started a rumor in his department that the department would be shortly dissolved, with some employees transferred and some laid off. The attention of the employees quickly shifted to concerns for their own future. While they were diverted, the manager was able to deal with the real problem by firing one employee and transferring two others.

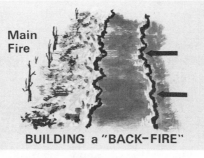

BUILDING a "BACK-FIRE"

FIGURE 17-6

This would probably not have been possible if the attention of the department's employees had been fixed directly on the main problem.

This approach can back fire (no puns intended) too, however. Regardless of whether or not you are successful in dealing with the main problem, the diversionary problem may flare up into a serious crisis. Our supervisor could have found himself in a position of loosing some valued employees who believed the rumors and found other jobs.

6. *Deny Fuel.* Occasionally, it is possible to direct a fire to an area in which there is no fuel (such as mountains or water). Without combustibles, the fire will quickly die. This strategy, of course, assumes that it will be possible to direct the fire *and* that an area suitably free of combustible material is available (see Figure 17-7).

It is possible to deal with a confrontation problem by giving the appearance of support for an opposing proposal or viewpoint. By going along, you have at least the possibility of directing the attention of the leadership to areas where the energy or interest of the conflicting group will burn out. By diffusing the energy (or credability) of a conflicting group, it is possible to overcome its appeal to others in the department.

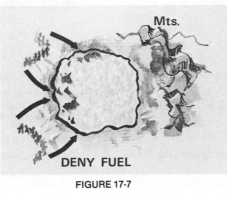

DENY FUEL

FIGURE 17-7

269

If the opposition (or the source of the conflict) is clearly wrong, it is usually an easy matter to pull the fuel away from the opposition by pointing out the obviously incorrect basis for its position. However, few managerial situations are clearly a case of "right" versus "wrong." In fact, we've already established the position that few things in life are "totally right" or "absolutely wrong" for all persons. Rather, there are shadings of opinion, with no one individual or group necessarily privy to *all* the *correct* information. When this happens, denying fuel to those in opposition is more difficult. It requires much more creativity.

Fuel can be denied by making the opposition's information obsolete. As a manager, you probably have information not generally available to others, including those persons in opposition to your point of view or that of the organization. By releasing this updated information at the right time, you can counterbalance the information in the hands of the opposition and deflate its importance.

Fuel for the opposition can also be denied by directly attacking the credability of the opposition leaders. However, as with many strategies for dealing with conflict, direct personal attack should be used *only* as a last resort. You may succeed in winning a conflict, but you can loose more in the long run. Bitterness and damaged interpersonal relations can be a natural outgrowth of such an approach.

The production coordinator for the Boulder Canyon Music Company found herself locked into a direct conflict with one of the semiautonomous production staff groups. The issue was over the scheduling of certain production phases, and each side had its own "facts" and "expert" opinions. In some ways, the split was a traditional line/staff conflict, yet the supervisor felt that her future ability to act independently would be seriously hampered if the opposing side was successful in having its views prevail.

She overcame the conflict by bringing out some long-buried (but still important) production problems and indirectly having these problems assigned to the production staff group for study and recommendation. By moving the attention of her opposition away from the main "battle," she was able to bring her facts to the surface without serious opposition and thus prevail in the crisis.

7. *Protect Key Installations.* When an important installation (such as a recreational center, group of homes or businesses, or a forest service post) is directly in the path of a fire, defensive measures are taken to ensure that these facilities are not damaged by the fire (see Figure 17-8).

Important projects, persons, or prerogatives can and should be protected from any harm during a crisis. If, for example, your department has a section working on an important matter, it is vitally important that they be protected or insulated from the effects of the crisis. For example, a manager in a conflict

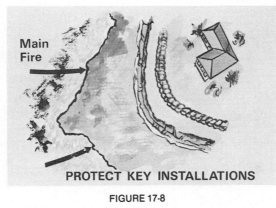

PROTECT KEY INSTALLATIONS

FIGURE 17-8

with another section over the selection of the department to be assigned new production equipment may want to protect the morale and working relationships that now exist within the department. If the department loses the new equipment, morale could suffer unless the morale is properly prepared (or protected). The manager can do this by giving full and complete information to all persons in the department about exactly what is happening during the conflict. By making the personnel a part of the conflict in an advisory way, their morale can be maintained without as much threat should the worst happen.

The ship's captain in the battle (Chapter 14) used the same communication strategy to earn the continued cooperation of the boiler-room crew. The captain installed loudspeakers in the boiler area and had a member of the ship's company with sports casting experience do a play by play of the entire battle. Using good, direct lines of communication, the captain was able to get maximum effort from the boiler crew while protecting them from the natural fears of being 20 feet below the water line while everything was coming unglued above.

8. *Selective Abandonment.* Forest fires often split off into several different directions. While the main fire is burning in one area, spin-off or new fires may be burning in other areas. If insufficient personnel or equipment is available, the fire boss may elect to abandon certain small fires and concentrate instead on the main fire or the one that has the greatest potential for harm (see Figure 17-9). The great risk in such a strategy is that a small, ignored fire can grow into a large mennace and quickly become a major concern. Ideally, the fire boss would like to work simultaneously on all the fires, because each has a great potential for damage. Realistically, however, this is often not possible. An executive decision must be made in light of all the facts and information currently available. Selective abandonment is a high-risk strategy,

271

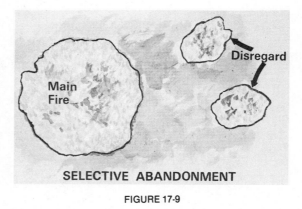

SELECTIVE ABANDONMENT

FIGURE 17-9

usually used when severe resource limitations (including time limitations) are a factor. Because there is always some "price" to be paid for abandoning some fires, the overall price for doing so must be balanced against the costs of the main fire itself.

Management is seldom faced with one problem at a time. Instead, problems (like birds?) seem to arrive in flocks. Even to attempt to solve all the problems at once is foolish and could be costly. Spread too thin, all resources (including human resources) suffer losses of efficiency and effectiveness. Experience and good communication links with your staff will help you identify these problems and concerns requiring your immediate attention and those matters that can be selectively abandoned or delegated to others. This, in turn, leads to another important strategy for fighting forest fires and dealing effectively with management problems — delegation.

9. *Conserve the "A" Team.* When a fire is under control or when it's judged to be less serious than a full-blown emergency, fire bosses will delegate full responsibility for working the fire (see Figure 17-10). Often, inexperienced personnel are used for these nonessential missions, for two good reasons.

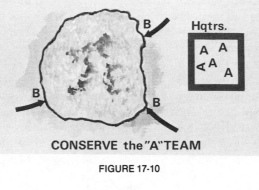

CONSERVE the "A" TEAM

FIGURE 17-10

272

Obviously, experience is a valuable tool in fighting a fire, yet it is often difficult to give personnel actual command experience during a major fire. By using smaller, less serious fires as training opportunities, inexperienced personnel can test and sharpen their skills in an atmosphere that is more forgiving of errors. A second reason for letting inexperienced personnel handle less serious problems is that doing so conserves the energy of the experienced personel. When a major fire breaks out, the fire boss needs the most experienced personnel available — and at their peak form. Tiring out the "A" team on minor problems can measurably reduce a manager's ability to mobilize maximum resources when a major problem arises.

If a problem or crisis can help you provide your staff with valuable experience, the credit they earn from their success will be reflected in the increased loyalty to their manager who had faith in them to do a good job. Such delegation thus has immediate benefits (conserving the experienced personnel's and your own managerial time) and long-term benefits (greater depth of experience and loyalty to the supervisor).

10. *Build Access Roads.* Our final strategy should perhaps be first, as it is preventive rather than defensive. In times of crisis, the forest service needs both information about the nature of a fire and a way to get into the fire area and put it out.

To make their job easier and safer when a fire does break out, the forest service spends time and effort building access roads throughout the forests. These roads are maintained and used for other purposes (such as fact finding, natural resource inventories, and recreation), but their main function is to be available when needed.

Managers, too, should build access roads, when they have the time and presence of mind to do so. The executive's access roads are the lines of com-

BUILD ACCESS ROADS

munication throughout the department and the organization. They are the friendships and supportive relationships between themselves and their co-workers, employees, suppliers, and staffs. When a problem erupts, little can be done to build a communication link if the groundwork hasn't been firmly set.

Building access roads through the organization is an extension of the supervisor's basic responsibilities to plan and communicate effectively. You can't expect people to support your actions in times of stress or crisis if you've made no attempt to do so under normal conditions. Attempts to draw information out of people with no prior communication lines built leads to suspicion and distrust. People will feel they are being "used" and will resent being put in such a position.

Like the access roads built by the forest service, the lines of communication need not be used solely in times of crisis. In fact, communicating in a personal way only in times of difficulty can be very unproductive. Good communication can be recreational. Enjoying the company of co-workers and employees, aside from the benefits of maintaining good "access roads," can make work and the work environment more rewarding. It can contribute measurably to developing an atmosphere in which good communication and motivation can flourish.

Farewell Smokey Bear

The forest service and its strategies for fighting forest fires is not the perfect analogy for organizational problem solving or crises. Some management situations don't neatly fit into our "fire" model. But by thinking about problems in your department in a creative way, you should be able to develop some unique and very useful methods for dealing with change, uncertainty or crisis.

Ways to Improve Your Communication Skills

1. Change is a constant state of life. Those who resist change, for whatever reason, usually end up making their jobs more difficult. This does not mean that, to be effective as a communicator, you must welcome every proposed change with open arms. It does mean, however, that managers who make a conscious effort to adapt to change and help their employees to do the same are more likely to avoid problems in an increasingly changing world.

2. Whenever possible, cut corners and ask questions. Don't take the "we've always done it this way before" answer to probing questions. This sort of answer from you, your colleagues, or your subordinates may be a signal that you'll be unprepared to adapt when change threatens.

3. Check your paperwork. Often, organizations with too much paperwork being completed signals an organization that has lost some of its sense of direction. Obviously, there is a need for some paperwork, but too much can slow down an organization or a department and make it sluggish. This can be a serious threat in times of rapid and unexpected change.

4. Develop a habit of planting seeds with your employees. The ideas they develop can be very creative, and they'll carry the added bonus of increased commitment when they're put into operation. Employees are far more likely to be committed to ideas they had a hand in developing.

5. Don't overplan or oversell your ideas for change, and don't fall in love with an excellent idea just because you thought of it. Your perspective on a self-generated idea isn't exactly unbiased. Treat your innovations and ideas with the same analytical skepticism you use on the ideas from your people. The outcome will be better decisions.

6. Communicate reassurance to your employees, especially in the face of threatening change. They look to their manager for guidance whenever something new threatens to upset the routines and arrangements they've come to understand.

7. Take care with threats of external enemies or pressures. Like the boy who shouted "wolf" too often, you may dull their ability to respond to real threats. At the same time, remember some of the strategies the forest service uses to combat forest fires. When change or threat poses problems for you or your department, plan your attack in a coordinated way and don't leave anything to chance.

V

SUMMING UP

18

Cases in Communication

"A case or incident shows neither right or wrong. It provides a basis for analysis, comparison, adaptation and study. The amazing thing is how often one case will trigger many other similar situations in a reader's mind."

Ellis M. Koontz

CASE 1: THE FOUR-HOUR JOB

Twas the day before Christmas at Coastal Motor Company in Monterrey. In the service garage, mechanics and technicians were planning to spend a leisurely afternoon completing work on customer cars and finishing necessary paperwork. At 2:15 P.M., Assistant Service Manager Vance Ellsworth approached mechanic Dudley White with a proposition. On the surface, it was an offer Dudley couldn't refuse.

"Dud, I've got a four-hour job here, no standard rate involved. Customer wants the car tonight, and I'll okay the time for you. Do you want it?"

Thinking about the already mounting Christmas bills, Dudley didn't have to consider very long replying "Sure" and getting to work on the car.

As in many new car dealer service operations, employees are paid an hourly wage rate for all work covered by new car factory warranties. However, on work being paid by the customer, mechanics are given 65 percent of the amount customers pay for direct labor on their cars. Thus, the four-hour Christmas eve rush job meant a substantial bonus to Dudley.

As the best mechanic in Coastal's garage, Dudley knew he could finish the job well within the four hours the standard shop rate manual indicated. However, he encountered some snags in the job and, at 7:00 P.M., was just finishing when the assistant manager came up with a long face.

"Dud, bad news. The lady who owns the car talked to Steve (the service manager) and convinced him that the job is covered by warranty. I'm sorry there's nothing I can do. Merry Christmas."

"Some Merry Christmas," thought Dudley as he slammed shut his tool boxes. "Five hours on the stupid car, for four hours standard pay and no bonus. Some outfit."

1. As an example of formal organizational communication, who is to blame for what happened to Dudley?
2. If you were Dudley's boss, how could you work things out with Dudley? What are your options?
3. Dudley feels betrayed and let down. Assuming that there is nothing either the assistant service manager or the service manager can do in this situation, how would you motivate Dudley the next time a similar rush job comes along?
4. What organizational procedures or communication channels should be established at Coastal to prevent other similar miscommunications from occuring?

CASE 2: THE BOSS[1]

Bill Smith, plant manager, walked into Don Ackles department and told Don (the head man) to immediately take two of his people off their machines to set up another machine to run some "hot" parts. Don knew that this change would severely affect his production schedule for the day and force him into overtime to catch up on stocking parts for the assembly line. Don said, "Mr. Smith, if I take those people off their machines now, my work will back up on me and my supervisor, Jim Ryan, will be all over me about the overtime I'll have to run." Smith replied, "Don't argue with me Ackles. Your job is to do what I tell you to do. Now, either you get this job done, or I'll find someone else who will."

1. Did Smith properly present a change to his subordinate?
2. Was Smith correct in giving orders directly to Ackles without consulting the supervisor first?
3. If you were Ackles, what would you have done?
4. If you were Jim Ryan, what would you do when you discovered what Smith did?

CASE 3: THE "WORKER'S DEMOCRACY"

"I believe in freedom for all people and in the democratic principles, but this is a factory, not a country! We've got work to be done, and, if I'm deprived of my rights as a supervisor, how can they possibly make me responsible for getting out the production they demand?"

Bryant Godfrey was mad. Last week, his company announced a trial program involving some of the principles of "job enrichment" combined with what has loosely been labeled "worker democracy." Under the plan, which was in the early stages and was only to affect this one plant (the company had eight in various parts of the country), the plant would be run with a minimum of supervision. Many of the functions that would normally be the province of management (such as assigning of work, rotation of employees through various operations on the line, and discipline and monitoring of employee performance) would now be done by committees of workers. The employee teams would make job assignments, schedule coffee and rest breaks, interview prospective new employees, and even have a hand in deciding the pay they were to receive for their work.

The system has been very successful experimentally in such diverse companies as Motorola (making remote paging devices), Sullair Corporation (making air compressors) and General Foods (making dog food). There was a mixed success, however, in getting supervisors to accept the new system and making it work. Workers seem to enjoy such a system, and it was widely viewed as a "model for the future."

"It's the screwiest thing I've ever seen," continued Godfrey. "Those crazy people upstairs (the top management) have even proposed changing what supervisors are called. It's not good enough to be a supervisor. Now, we're supposed to be the coach or some such nonsense. When I got to be a supervisor, it was a big deal. You got a private parking space in the management lot —even though it is still a long walk to the management entrance—and you got some recognition and some status. Now, they're going to take all that away. Last week in the supervisor's meeting, Ed Billa (Godfrey's boss) told us that we'd be in much better shape—easier job, less hassle, more challenge to perform. I can't see why we have to change. I've got 25 years experience in this industry, 15 with this company, and now there's not going to be a dime's worth of difference between me and my experience and those wet-behind-the-ears kids they're going to have running the plant and making all the decisions. If I wasn't five years from retirement, I'd quit. I'll tell you one thing, though ... this outfit has seen the last of Godfrey the dedicated supervisor. From now on, it's going to be lay back in the weeds and watch 'em mess it up."

1. Why do you think Godfrey is resisting the change in management methods?

2. Was there anything wrong with the way the new changes were communicated to Godfrey and the other supervisors?
3. If you were in Ed Billa's place, how would you overcome the resistance that your employees feel to such a change in their jobs and their work environment?
4. Comment on the changes taking place in Godfrey's company. Would you feel comfortable or uncomfortable in such an arrangement? Why? Do you have any experience in a so-called "worker's democracy?"

CASE 4: JAWS BEACH, R.I.

"It seems that every summer we have the same problems," according to Paul Kelly at his weekly meeting with the director of public safety and other department heads for the resort community of Jaws Beach, R.I. Paul had been captain of the beach patrol for the past six years and was considered a top professional in the water safety business. The director of public safety, Neal Rinker was having the weekly staff meeting at which each department head reported problems and progress in the previous week.

Kelly continued,

"The seasonal nature of the beach patrol is that 98 percent of the staff is nonpermanent. Each fall they head south and each spring they return. Don't get me wrong, they may be in a gypsy business, but each man and woman is a trained professional. They take their jobs seriously. Yet, when it comes to understanding formal organizations with their rules and procedures, they don't always fit the normal pattern."

Neal interrupted,

"Are the beaches safe, that is the big question! The whole summer economy of this town depends on whether or not the visitors feel the beaches are safe."

"You will be pleased that the incident last week revolved around just such an issue. As you know, I have four lieutenants who report directly to me and 53 lifeguards who are assigned to the beaches. To improve coordination and ensure that someone would be available to make decisions in my absence, last Monday I issued a directive that Mike Nelson would be acting captain in my absense. Thursday, while I was down at Rock Haven (a nearby city) Mike approached one of the other lieutenants and the following conversation took place.

Mike Nelson: "Hey Dale (Lt. Dale Rogers), when you have a few minutes I would like to talk with you".

Dale Rogers: "What for?"

Mike Nelson: "It concerns the relief set-up in your zone today."

Dale Rogers: "Why, what's the problem (in an arrogant and hostile tone of voice)?"

Mike Nelson: "I think you should have considered some pertinent facts about the staff assigned to your zone. As I see it (interrupted),"

Dale Rogers: "What are you trying to say?"

Mike Nelson: "I think you used poor judgment."

Dale Rogers: "I don't have to stand here and listen to this bunk. I was handling these beach assignments when you were in short pants (storming out the door)."

Mike Nelson: "You had better listen, I'm acting captain".

The next day when I returned from my trip Mike was waiting for me and told me about the confrontation with Dale Rogers. Mike insisted that Dale be given a written reprimand over the incident. "If you don't back me in this," Mike insisted, "you'll only show that the title of acting captain carried no authority" Mike concluded his report by saying, "If it had been you she talked to that way she would not even be here today."

After Mike left, I called Dale at the North Beach Station and asked her to meet me for lunch at the concession stand by the pier.

As Dale approached, she put her hand in the air as to surrender.

Dale Rogers: "I know what you've come for and I am as guilty as hell."

Paul Kelly: "What do you mean?"

Dale Rogers: "I jumped all over that new boy Nelson yesterday when he was out playing captain. I was wrong and I apologize. It was one of those mornings, and the last thing I needed was someone telling me that I did not have good judgment."

1. If you were Capt. Paul Kelly what would you have done differently?
2. How would Mike Nelson have reacted to your decision?
3. How would Dale Rogers have reacted to your decision?
4. How would you go about getting more facts on the incident?

CASE 5: THE INTRODUCTION TO THE JOB

Five new employees were brought in a group to the assembly line by a personnel clerk who took them over to the new supervisor who was sitting at his desk drinking a cup of coffee and smoking a cigarette.

Clerk: "Good Morning Mr. Jones, these are your new workers starting with you today."

As the personnel clerk leaves, Jones, glaring at the new people, puts his cigarette out slowly, takes one last swig of his coffee, and gets up from his desk.

Jones: "O.K. Did personnel give you people a list of the safety rules, policy rules, and a time clock badge? O.K. First, I will show you one time and one time only how to clock in and out. This badge is your paycheck, and, if you don't clock in or out you will not get paid and I couldn't care less."

"You people have one week to learn this job and I'll be watching you closely."

"I'm the boss and we do things my way. I okay overtime, I assign duties, I recommend promotions, and I can make your life here good or bad. I have been known to overlook a long coffee or lunch break and give a day off with pay once in a while. You make my day easy for me, with no kickback from upstairs or grief from the line, and we'll get along real fine. Louse me up, and it will take an act of God to save your skin."

1. Supervisor Jones clearly has the formal authority in his department. However, did he do a proper job of communicating his authority to his new employees?
2. Are these new employees likely to be productive? Creative?
3. How would you communicate to new employees?

CASE 6: PRIZE BULL[2]

The manager appeared to have no feelings and had tangled with the government and unions many times. Besides running his operation, he had a fine pure-bred stock dairy farm that had been in his family for years.

A long-time worker who had not received a raise in quite a while decided to ask for one as his bills began to mount up at home. After hearing of the situation, the manager said he would like to help out, but "things are rough." That evening the local newspaper ran a front page picture of the boss with a prize bull he had just purchased for $5,000.

The next day, the worker came in with the newspaper picture pinned to the front of his shirt. He sought out the boss and in mock sympathy shook his hand and said he now understood how bad things were and why he couldn't be given a raise. The shop manager saw the picture, asked the employee if he could have it because he was saving them, took it off the worker's shirt, turned on his heel and walked away with it.

1. What messages was the manager giving the employee when he was confronted with the picture of the prize bull?
2. Are the two situations (the prize bull and the turndown of the raise request) really related? Are they related in the employee's mind?
3. If you'd been in the boss' position, how would you have responded to the employee when he brought in the picture?

CASE 7: KIMBERLY NATIONAL BANK

"We're tired of being treated like children."

"They make us feel that our jobs and our feelings are meaningless."

"We demand to have a say in the decision making of this organization and to be told what's going on."

Considering the relatively tranquil and harmonious reputation of personnel relations at the Kimberly National Bank, employee statements and attitudes like these were something of a shock to Donald Pettit. As president and chief executive officer of the bank, he was facing a volatile and potentially dangerous crisis. Many of the people in the company, including some professional and support personnel, were in an uproar, demanding control over what had been viewed as managerial prerogatives. Communications at Kimberly had always been open, with a "family" atmosphere throughout the organization. Visitors frequently commented on the way the employees, including staff and support personnel and managers, worked together. The benefits of such an atmosphere were also quite obvious, because the lack of interpersonal tension left each member of the Kimberly National Bank "team" free to deal with important problems. It was only in the last year or so that the atmosphere in the company began to change, and Pettit was becoming increasingly concerned that the change in attitude was related to his own arrival at the bank.

The bank was founded in Lincoln City 40 years before by a dynamic young man, Amos Becker. It began as a small farm-oriented firm. Amos worked long hours running the new bank, and he personally supervised all the bank's operations. Using improved technology developed during World War II, the firm was able to branch out into several innovative service lines and to expand in the postwar years. As the bank grew, Becker was able to keep his close personal relationship with each and every employee intact. It was not unusual to see him in an animated conversation with anyone on the staff, at any hour of the day. He knew most of the personnel on a first-name basis and insisted on maintaining this relationship with new employees as well. Although his personal rapport with the staff was excellent, there was never any doubt about who was in charge. Becker made most of the decisions, although, in the last few years before his death, he was successful in decentralizing and having lower management make many of the decisions.

Personnel were promoted from within, going outside for administrative and supervisory talent only when local people could not be found for the jobs. The bank was owned totally by Amos Becker.

Donald Pettit's association with the Kimberly National Bank also went back many years. Orphaned at an early age, he was taken in by Amos Becker and raised as a son. From the time he was old enough, Donald worked in the bank. During the summer vacations and after school, he was at the bank, doing every job available, from the menial jobs to helping prepare the budget. At one time, he had hoped to become a doctor, but found that his skills were better suited to administration. At 18, he left Lincoln City for the university to study business administration. It was during his final year in his master's degree program that Amos Becker died, and he returned to take charge.

On his first day back at the Kimberly National Bank as the new president, Donald Pettit called all of the senior supervisors into his office. For two hours, they met behind closed doors. When they returned to their work stations and offices, their people asked what happened in the meeting. The reply was, "Nothing happened, nothing at all."

From then on, the Monday morning meetings continued. After each meeting, the personnel asked their supervisors what was happening, and the answer was always "Nothing."

It was during this period that the employees became restless and openly critical of the new administrative routine. They felt that they were not being told the full story behind the changes that were taking place all around them. They saw new people being hired, assignments changed and new activities being started. Their confusion with the changes was coupled with their fears that in the Monday meeting their entire future was being decided and they were being told nothing about it. It should be noted that similar changes had occured with Amos, when he was making or supervising most of the decisions.

Jane Latham was a senior staff supervisor at Kimberly National Bank. She joined Amos Becker in the early years of the firm and became one of his trusted lieutenants and close friends. On many occasions, Amos encouraged her to assume more managerial responsibility. Latham had great respect for the abilities of Pettit and was an early supporter of his selection as the president. She was also well aware that the feelings of the employees in the bank were changing, and she too was puzzled.

At a recent cocktail party, Jane Latham was discussing the situation at the bank with close friends from the university.

FIGURE 18-1

"After all, Don Pettit is like my own son. He worked in this bank as far back as any of us senior people can remember. All the employees like him a lot, and he, in turn, has a genuine feeling for the organization and for the staff that Amos put together over all those years. Everyone in the bank, from top to bottom, was delighted when Don returned to pick up where Amos left off. Don's also very realistic. Why, on his first day here, he called all of the senior people into Amos', I mean, his office for a meeting. Naturally, we were somewhat nervous, but he quickly put us all at ease. He said simply, 'You people are my family. Amos trusted and relied on you to help him make decisions. I want that to continue, and I want everyone in the bank to take a larger and more active role in decision making. No one can replace Amos, and I certainly recognize my limitations. I want to learn from you and I want you to assume more individual responsibility!' After that, the meeting became a sort of family reunion. We talked about where Don might build a new house in Lincoln City, now that he was married. In other meetings each week, we never talked business. One time, we even got into a discussion about where the best bass fishing was—we discussed golf, politics, and so on. Frankly, I don't see why the change in attitude of the employees. If anything, they'll be in a better position, with more responsibility, now that Don is in charge."

1. What happened at the Kimberly National Bank?
2. What should Pettit have done when he first returned?
3. What can be done now to resolve the situation before it degenerates further?

CASE 8: THE THOUSAND OAKS HOTEL AND CLUB

The Thousand Oaks Hotel and Club (the Club) is an old luxury resort hotel in the island country of Southwest Florida. It was founded to attract wealthy winter guests to Florida at the turn of the century and to bring needed midwinter business to the Coast's only railroad. In recent years, the original hotel and country club has become a year round operation, with a major convention center, a 20-story high-rise hotel tower addition, a beach-front cabana club and restaurant, a tennis complex, and a shopping mall. The complex has seven restaurants, all noted as both a volume food operation and a center for gourmet-style cooking. The main dining room in the original hotel building—The Seawatch—has a five-star rating from the Mobile Travel Guide and is the winner of several *Holiday* magazine awards for excellence of cuisine and service.

The Club's entire restaurant operation is managed by Chef Armand Chevalier. Trained in Paris, Chevalier is reputed to be one of the finest chef's in

North America and is given single-handed credit for the excellent reputation of all the Club's food facilities, even though he personally supervises only the food preparation in the Seawatch.

The Club is managed by Jack Cooney, and Chevalier reports directly to him. Under Chevalier are six deputy chefs, seven maitres d'hotel, and five assistant maitres d'. In theory, Chevalier supervises both food preparation and food service operations. In practice, Chevalier has permitted the maitres d' to supervise the administration of the individual restaurants. Chevalier personally buys all vegetables and meats and is content to maintain personal control in the kitchens, where he is an acknowledged master.

As the Club's operations have grown, responsibilities for various parts of the food service have been assigned to various individuals, with little regard for standard organizational lines of authority. For example, if an assistant maitre d' is good at scheduling but weak in record keeping, the responsibility for records will simply be given to someone else. Combined with growth, this has led to a potentially dangerous situation. In the past year, guests have been criticizing the food service. The quality of the food continues to receive high praise, but the quality of the service has been slipping. Waiters and other servers appear to be surly with guests, and all the kitchens seem to have more than the usual conflicts and hassles. In a well-run operation, dealing with such a problem would not be easy, but at least there would be a chain of command to use in attacking the problem. With the Oaks Club, there is so much confusion about whose authority is predominant that the situation is a bit like trying to contain seven frisky puppies with one arm tied behind your back.

There are several other symptoms of potential problems that may be related to the employees' morale. Often, there is insufficient silverware or serving trays to handle large convention groups. This means that silver must be taken from vacated tables and quickly washed and reset on other tables. The situation is symbolized by the advice that one assistant maitre d' gave employees who complained about a shortage of silver cocktail trays. "When you get one," he advised, "hang on to it. Hide it, take it home with you, but hang on to it." The Club actually has more than enough silverware and other service equipment. The only trouble is that it's stored and hidden all over the property. There has been no accounting for materials, and no attempt has been made to either locate materials or to assign new materials to a given restaurant. Thus, silver is shifted from one restaurant to another, often with the planning secrecy of a military skirmish. What's worse, room service appears to be a major culprit. It operates out of the three largest restaurants but actually picks up orders from wherever it is convenient. Room service is supervised by the maitre d' of the Tower restaurant, even though little of the room service food actually comes from the Tower.

Despite the problems, all the Club's management—from Jack Cooney to the assistant maitres d'—profess to "see no problems." Their reluctance to rock the boat or point fingers is tied directly to their admiration and respect for Armand Chevalier. All agree that Chevalier's departure could be a major —even fatal—blow to the Club's reputation and solid clientele. They further seem to agree that the wrong approach to the problem might be perceived by Chevalier as a personal attack on *him*, even though he is aware of his general weakness in the administrative area.

Assume that you have been hired as a consultant to make recommendations to possibly relieve this situation. Remember, you are constrained in your recommendations by these concerns:

1. Chevalier must be kept *at any cost*. He is a creative, artistic, sensitive, and a valuable asset to the Club.
2. Employee morale must be improved to the extent that better morale means better client satisfaction with the Club's food service.
3. The Club is a profitable company and has the money to spend on any reasonable recommendations that will produce the desired results.

With these factors in mind, discuss and develop a comprehensive consultant's recommendation. Include

1. A list of potential problems
2. A list of possible solutions, and the advantages and disadvantages of each
3. Your overall recommendation for the Club, and an assessment of possible repercussions that *might* result if your plan is put into effect

Ways to Improve Your Communication Skills

Cases don't show the "right" or the "wrong" way to communicate. They simply show how others get themselves into difficulties and provide us with an opportunity to apply some of our knowledge and experience to finding solutions. If you've taken a close look at the cases in this chapter, you've found that they have only one factor in common; they all deal with communication and miscommunication. Look at your own managerial behavior and see if someone could make a case out of your performance. If you've got some "cases" of your own, can you objectively look at them the way you've looked at the cases in this chapter? Your answer will tell a lot about your ability to solve problems with better communication and management.

19

The Bottom Line: How Do You Rate as a Communicator?

"What we have here is a failure to communicate!"

The Warden *in* Cool Hand Luke

Because it's such a common activity in all organizations, communication is often taken for granted. It is usually ignored until something goes wrong. Then, it becomes a convenient excuse.

"It's a communication problem ... you know how *they* are!"
"If we could only communicate better, we could ..."

Simply labeling a problem as a communication failure doesn't make it go away. It doesn't help when the real problem is lack of leadership or a failure to simply relate to people as people. Because productive behavior is essential in every credit union, let's look at some important ideas for managing people —ideas that relate not only to communication but also to basic human relations.[1]

USE TIRE CHAINS

A strange topic for managers? Not really. Chains help keep cars from slipping on ice. They hold the tires to prevent them from going out of control. Controls help an organization operate properly, on target, meeting its goals.

Applied figuratively to your tongue, tire chains can have the same beneficial effect. It's usually best to say less than you're thinking, or less than you could say—about anything. There's an old saying that one who remains silent risks being thought a fool. One who opens his mouth confirms he's a fool. We've already established that, whenever communication occurs, distortion is likely to crop up. Fewer words won't cure distortion, but carefully chosen words can help. Remember, too, that what you say is only part of interpersonal communication. How you say it is also important. Cultivate a controlled, persuasive voice. A perfume commercial on television suggests, "If you want to get someone's attention, whisper." Good advice. Once you've raised your voice to it's limit, you have lost a powerful tool. With a controlled voice and manner, you are better able to get and have at your command a much wider range of managerial options.

KEEP YOUR WORD

The art of management isn't practiced with contracts and formal agreements. It depends almost exclusively on trust and mutual respect between people. Your word, your agreement, or your clearly stated position will be used by others without question only as long as you demonstrate the value of your word. Break your word, even once, and you face an uphill battle to regain lost trust. For most managers, the cost of loss of trust is too high to risk.

Be careful, too, of the danger of others' assuming you've broken your word, even though they're only looking at part of the broken promises. Although it is unrealistic to assume that a manager can keep total control over all messages surrounding him or her, allowing misunderstandings to go unnoticed or unchecked is dangerous.

GIVE PRAISE AND RECOGNITION

As a manager, you must maintain control over the work of many other persons. This often means reprimanding, scolding, and occasionally even firing. It is possible that a manager's innocent comments to an employee can be viewed by that employee or others as a reprimand. As with so many communications, simple misunderstandings often cannot be avoided. Yet, there is a simple but often overlooked solution. Don't become only a "bearer of gloomy tidings." Give praise whenever possible and with at least the same enthusiasm and sincerity you use for reprimands and criticism. Nicolo Machiavelli, the sixteenth century master of political intrigue, contended that a good leader should be swift and ruthless in dispensing punishment, but spare and stingy with praise.

Such a philosophy may have been suitable for a medieval prince, but it's not terribly realistic for today's manager. People who work in our organizations are not all motivated solely by money, despite their frequent protests to the contrary (such as around raise, performance appraisal or contract negotiation time). Each of us is motivated by the kind of treatment we're given and by the opportunity to exercise some influence or control over our personal work environment. Honest praise can help maintain an open line of communication between the executive and his or her employees. It can also help employes feel their own importance in the organization.

Criticism, too, can contribute to positive communication *if* it's given in a helpful (rather than a spiteful) way. We all make errors and appreciate others who point out our errors without implying we're stupid or ignorant. The same consideration toward employees is a major element in good human relations and good communication.

BE INTERESTED IN OTHERS

Each of us feels some measure of personal worth or value. Yet, too often, we forget to make the personal side of our employees' lives an integral part of our relationship with them. Establish open two-way communication with others by asking about their families, friends, hobbies, interests, disappointments, and sorrows. Equally important, show a genuine interest in what these other persons say in response. A mumbled "How's it going?" as you hurry past hardly qualifies as an honest expression of interest. Take the time to learn more about your employees, *as individuals*.

KEEP AN OPEN MIND

This is always profitable, especially when there is some controversy surrounding a particular point at issue. Even if you are 100 percent absolutely sure about the answer, give others a chance to express their views openly, and without fear of your "putdown" when they finish. We can't always enjoy the luxury of absolute certainty. By remaining open minded to the ideas and inputs of others, we stand a better chance of getting help and support when we really need it.

BE MINDFUL OF INADVERTANT MESSAGES

Jokes, stories, and humor are always enjoyable—unless one is made the butt of the joke. No one (not even the manager) has a past completely free of embarrassing errors. Yet, too many times, we permit ourselves or others to enjoy humor at another's expense. Racial, ethnic, cultural, or physical jokes are simply in bad taste. They are rarely worth the effort, and they can needlessly (and perhaps unknowingly) hurt others.

A male manager in a Florida credit union made a habit of opening his staff meetings by saying "Gentlemen, let's begin." He did this despite the fact that 30 percent of his employees were female. He followed his "introduction statement" by apologizing to the "girls" and making a remark about "women's lib." Although a slip of this sort when women first joined the department might have been understandable, this "humorous" scene has been repeated monthly for about four years. The women in the group take the predictable "humor" with better grace than many men would in similar circumstances. The manager, whether meaning to or not, has clearly expressed his opinion and attitude toward his female employees. His communications (and his attitudes) need rebuilding — fast.

USE A "YOU" VIEWPOINT

In management, we've become increasingly aware of the benefits of participation. Usually, we tend to think of participation as the process of getting employees to get together and make decisions about work-related matters. However, we can also expand participation to include both manager *and* employee jointly. It's been observed that bosses say "I," whereas leaders say "we." The "you" viewpoint and the "we" orientation are two complementary ideas that reflect a basic attitude toward other people, an attitude that provides a useful starting point for successful communication. You should examine the statements that you make to colleagues and employees. Too many "I"s may suggest a "superior to them" attitude and may interfere with effective communication and effective management.

SET THE EXAMPLE

Wise managers set an example of what they expect in the behavior of others. It's difficult to get employees to work productively when they see their boss apparently loafing. Of course, what may appear as loafing to the employees can actually be a "deep thought" session or the "self-time" recommended in many discussions of time management. Nevertheless, remember that what others perceive about you is true — to them. Cultivate actions that give positive examples and sharpen your awareness of the negative examples that are often out of our awareness.

LOOK FORWARD, NOT BACK

We all err in dwelling excessively in the past instead of looking forward into the future. Mistakes or past conflicts, if not put aside, can impede any progress in any organization. Anyone can, and should, admit errors freely and learn from them. However, by constantly bringing up the past, a manager creates the impression that an employee is too stupid to remember his or her past errors.

Consider, instead, the benefit of a future-looking attitude. Anticipation of results and performance is one of the most powerful motivators. Remember your willingness as a child to work (or behave, or study) before Christmas or Hanukkah or your birthday. Notice how your energy levels rise as you prepare for a vacation trip or a new job challenge. Often, the anticipation of an event is more enjoyable than the actual attainment of a particular goal.

Looking to the future means setting realistic personal and professional goals and encouraging your employees to do the same. All employees, young and old, can develop an optimism for their futures if their supervisors give them support. Be realistic, however, in setting goals. If they are too far in the future, or if the standards are too high, the benefits of looking toward the future can turn to frustration and anxiety. Don't lose sight of the past and the valuable lessons we can derive from it. Treat it for what it is—a lesson that cannot be changed no matter how hard we try. The only thing that we can really influence is our future. The thought that "today is the first day of the rest of your life" can be more than just a slogan. It can establish a positive and forward-looking perspective for all your communications.

With your future orientation, remember there are two futures—a short-run future and a long-run future. Many times, a decision that's right for the short run can have very bad effects in the long run (or vice versa). The simplest solution to an immediate problem may be to work your employees harder. Go to overtime, cut down on breaks, demand and enforce closer controls over employee behavior on the job. If the employees are willing to go along (and sometimes even if they're not), this strategy can produce short-term results. However, in reaching your short-term goals, you may have seriously threatened a department's basic work relationships and may, in turn, have reduced your ability to meet longer-range goals. The histories of business, government, and educational and financial organizations are filled with examples of managers' "burning out" their productive capacity to reach immediately pressing goals, only to find that their ability to deal with longer-run demands had vanished.

Wise managers recognize that, in crisis situations, most people are willing to put forth an extra effort. But continued use of "crisis management" methods can seriously harm a group's long-run productive capacity.

When planning, setting goals, or communicating with employees, consider carefully both the short-run and long-run effects before taking action.

294

LOOK BEHIND THE TEARS

Crying is seldom a real problem. It's usually a symptom that something more basic is troubling the individual. Managers often fall into the error of trying to resolve a symptom without really finding or treating the real cause of the problem. Thus, we put bandages over the symptoms and assume away the root problem. Of course, it's not all that simple.

Employee gripes about money, the "quality of their supervision," or their personal aches and pains may not be aimed directly at what's bothering them. We've assumed that anything affecting the productivity of a department is the logical concern of the employee's immediate supervisor or the firm's top management.

To discover what's really at issue, managers must sharpen and use their listening skills. As we've seen, labeling a problem or treating its symptoms won't solve anything for very long. A problem papered over with a bandaid will sooner or later break out somewhere else. Many state legislatures, after years of trying to solve problems by patching more and more laws and amendments onto their state constitutions have discovered that the real cause of the problems was the inadequacy or obsolesence of the basic constitution. Years of solving symptoms gave way to attacking the basic problem, by writing a completely new state constitution. In the same way, managers who manage symptoms instead of coming to grips with the real problem are just spinning their wheels.

Look and listen for what people are really trying to say. Doing so has two benefits. You get valuable clues to the real problems facing you. You also develop a reputation as a concerned and interested supervisor who is willing to relate to employees as individuals rather than simply as cogs in a large, impersonal machine.

DON'T PASS THE BUCK

Harry Truman was fond of saying that in the office of the President the "buck stops here." It should be as obvious to employees as it is to their bosses that managers can't and don't make all the decisions in an organization. Many plans, ideas, suggestions, and problems must be referred elsewhere for action. Employees are usually aware of the range of responsibility of their boss. If he or she constantly blames the "people upstairs," or the "union," or the computer department, some of buck passing may be legitimate. Some buck passing, however, may be nothing more than an unwillingness to exercise authority or accept responsibility. When this happens, a manager's basic ability to supervise begins to erode. Pass the buck only when necessary, or when you honestly have little or no control over the outcome of a situation. On the other hand, be willing to accept responsibility for your actions, good or bad, as a natural part of your job.

TRY TO UNDERSTAND YOUR EMPLOYEES
AND MAKE YOURSELF UNDERSTOOD BY THEM

Choose your words, examples, and communication opportunities carefully. Whenever possible, try to put yourself in your employee's place and critically evaluate the clarity and power of all your messages. A major part of all communication is an effort to reduce distortion (or noise) in communication. Let's summarize briefly some of the ways managers can reduce the distortion in their communications.

1. Reduce the number of people through whom a message must travel. However, beware of bypassing, because this may cause friction with various departments in your organization.
2. Minimize distortion by reducing differences between you and the other person. Things like clothes and furniture arrangements can interrupt the smooth flow of messages between you and your staff.
3. Orient your message to a specific receiver if at all possible. Use your knowledge of the receiver to your advantage, to get the idea across.
4. Limit the amount of information in your message. Remember, the average person only receives five to nine bits of information at any one time.
5. Incorporate redundancy in your messages. Do this by using additional media (pictures, etc.) or with examples.
6. If there is a great deal of information in a message, incorporate this material into some form of "permanent" communication, like notes, handouts, memos, etc.
7. Increase opportunities for feedback.
8. Wait for a response. Do not feel that you have to fill in the silences. Be calm and confident.
9. Preview and review the material in your message—the rule of three!! ("Tell 'em what you're going to tell 'em, tell 'em, then tell 'em what you told 'em.")
10. Simplify your messages—distinguish between important and unimportant information.
11. Report details in order—use some form of consistent organization such as chronological, spatial, or cause-effect sequencing.
12. Place important material at the beginning or the end of a message, *not* in the middle.
13. Highlight the important material—use phrases such as "the crux of the issue appears to be …".
14. When presenting material orally, SLOW DOWN!!!
15. Remember clever Hans. Give approving signals and show your genuine interest in the persons involved in a transaction. Be especially mindful of the unintended, nonverbal putdown that sometimes comes from the pressure of time. Watch the tone of your voice. Be pleasant, friendly, and interested.[2]

REVIEW: THE COMMUNICATION QUIZ

In Chapter 1, we asked you to answer ten questions on various aspects of managerial communication. Each statement was followed by a question, "Do you agree or disagree?" For some questions, you likely found that the answer depended on some of your assumptions and on the interpretation of the statement. However, some general guidelines make the "agree" or "disagree" answers the better ones for a particular statement. Let's see how you did.

Statement 1 was "Happy employees are always productive employees." In general, it's better to have happy employees than to have unhappy employees. However, just because your employees are happy does not mean that they will be productive, and, in fact, it's possible that the fact they're happy also means that they'll be unproductive. They may spend so much time enjoying themselves on the job that they don't have much time left over for productive work. Real productivity comes not from smiles and friendly relationships, but from having a meaningful and challenging job to do. Real motivation comes from recognition and a sense of personal satisfaction with one's work. As a manager, you can contribute to that satisfaction by giving encouraging messages of reassurance and recognition. In doing so, you'll be creating those "fire lines" that we've suggested are so important to developing and maintaining an atmosphere of open communications with your employees.

Statement 2 was "The greatest danger to good communication is the illusion of it." This is an "agree." Often, we are so confident that we've communicated clearly that we fail to check to be sure our listeners have heard what we said in the way we meant.

Statement 3 was "Managers should spend most of their time listening." This is a tough one to answer, because a manager who spends all his or her time listening won't have any time for giving instructions and getting the work done. However, if the question is interpreted to mean that the effective manager should spend a *large portion of his or her time* listening to employees and others, then the answer would be a hearty "agree."

Statement 4 was "In getting employees to listen, how you listen, how you send a message is far more important than what you say." This is another "agree." The relationship level in communication and the manner in which a message is transmitted are almost always more important than the message itself. Of course, if you're in that burning building, and the janitor comes out screaming obscenities and shouting that the "_____, _____ building's on fire!," you'd probably not pay much attention to the way he sent his message. Clearly, content is important, but the "out-of-awareness" parts of communication are usually the ones that control.

Statement 5 was "Supervisors short on time may have problems with delegation and communication." Again, "agree." Too little time may mean that you're spending too much time trying to do work that others should be doing for you.

Statement 6 was "The best way to get feedback from employees is to ask, 'Do you have any questions?'" "Disagree." Asking for questions puts the employee in the position of having to admit that he or she didn't understand. This, in turn, can mean either that the employee feels that he or she isn't too bright or that the boss (you) is not an effective communicator. This can lead to the "phony feedback" of "No, boss, I understand completely." Instead of asking for questions, ask, "How do you feel about this assignment?" Or, "Where do you feel we'll have problems getting this into action?" Even better, you can get feedback by watching for nonverbal signals, such as furrowed eyebrows or rapid eye movement. These signals and the actions that the employees take after you've given them your instructions are the best form of feedback, and conscientious managers make a habit of watching for these signals.

Statement 7 was "The use of a large vocabulary can hurt your communication effectiveness." Again, a two-sided issue. The answer is "agree" if you feel that people with large vocabularies tend to use big words just to impress others with their intelligence and education. However, if people with large vocabularies use the many words they know as a way of finding the "right" word for each situation, they'll usually come across as better communicators.

Statement 8 was "If a message is written, it is almost certain to be more clear than if given orally." "Disagree." Written messages don't have the facial expressions, body language, and changes in voice tone to help make them clear. When a message is written, the receiver has many possible interpretations. Even with a very well-written message, there's always the possibility that someone can misinterpret and get the message wrong. When it's possible, the best combination for clear and effective communication is to deliver a message orally, followed by a written summary.

Statement 9 was "Groups of employees or managers will usually make decisions better than individual employees or managers." In general, "agree." The reason is that a group has access to many more points of view and to much more information than is available to one individual, even a very smart one. Further, when people make decisions in groups, they have a chance to react to each other, to use what one person says as a "springboard" to other creative thoughts. In this way, the decisions that emerge are usually better than would have been reached by individuals.

Statement 10 was "Groups of employees or managers tend to take more risks in decision making than do individual employees or managers." Here, the best answer is "agree." When people are in groups, it's easier for each individual to take risk, because the risk is being spread among all group members. However, when an individual makes a decision alone, he or she is completely responsible for the decision and will usually decide to be more conservative in choosing an option. Statements 9 and 10 show two very important sides to the issue of group decision making and participative management. Although there are clear benefits to a "group-centered" approach to managerial communication (such as better decisions), there are also costs (more "risky" decisions). As a manager, you must be able to balance these costs in making your own decisions on strategies and styles that work best for you in your managerial communications.

IN CONCLUSION, DOES COMMUNICATION *REALLY* MATTER?

A logical question: If you have carefully thought about the ideas we have developed in this chapter, you know the answer is a resounding "yes."

In a recent study of "typical" employees, those surveyed were asked to rate 20 key motivators that they felt had the greatest impact in their on-the-job performance. The study results confirmed the notion that self-esteem, recognition, and the nature of the employee's job itself are more important in producing performance than are money, status, the organization's image, or its administrative policies. High on the list of all those responding to the study was the importance of communication:[3]

the degree to which one is kept informed (by one's manager) about specific assignments, department and organizational goals, developments, and so forth, and is able to keep managers informed about one's views on these matters."

We're right back to the basics—communication is a two-way process. To be effective communicators and managers, we must send messages clearly, concisely, accurately, and with a minimum of distortion. We must also develop workable habits as message receivers. We must "tune in" to the nonverbal and out-of-awareness messages as well as to the more obvious oral and written messages.

Good Communicating.

Notes

Chapter 1

[1]This section was shared with the author by Joe Floyd, President, Aquatech Corporation, Atlanta, Georgia. The source and author are unknown.

Chapter 2

[1]This portion of the chapter and the visuals are from the author's article "The Many Dimensions of Managerial Communication," *Industrial Management,* Vol. 20, #6: 18-20 (November-December 1978). Copyright © 1978 by the Industrial Management Society. Used with permission.

Chapter 3

[1]This chapter is based in part on an article by the author, "Know Thyself: The Art of Self Appraisal," *Credit Union Management,* Vol. 1, #6:23-26 (November-December 1978). Copyright © by the Credit Union Executives Society. Used with permission.

[2]Rensis Likert, *New Patterns of Management,* (New York: McGraw-Hill, 1961), p. 103.

[3]Arthur Pell's "Leadership Quotient Test," *Association Management,* Vol. 25, #6: 54-56 (June 1973). Copyright © 1973 by the American Society of Association Executives. Used with permission.

Chapter 4

[1]This section is based on an article by Alfred B. LaGasse, "How to Keep Staff Morale High," *Association Management,* Vol. 25, #8: 44-47 (August 1973). Copyright © 1973 by the American Society of Association Executives. Used with permission.

300

Chapter 5

[1]Portions of this chapter are based on the author's article, "Listening Habits, Listening Skills," *The Deltasig*, Vol. 66, #1: 11-17 (November 1976). Copyright © 1976 by the International Fraternity of Delta Sigma Pi. Reprinted with the permission of the executive director, Delta Sigma Pi.

[2]Some material on the bad habits of listening is based on Ralph Nichols and Leonard Stevens, *Are You Listening?*, (New York: McGraw-Hill, 1957).

Chapter 6

[1]Antony Jay, "How to Run a Meeting," *Harvard Business Review*, Vol. 54, #2: 43-57 (March-April 1976).

[2]"Meeting Strategy," *Nation's Business* (November 1975), p. 46.

[3]Diane K. Shah, "Pro Football's Pete Rozell," *The National Observer*, (May 16, 1977) p. 18.

[4]Some of these same ideas were discussed in more detail in "Why Staff Meetings Fall Flat," *Nation's Business* (May 1973) pp. 52-54.

[5]Michael Korda, *Power*, (New York: Ballantine Books, 1975), p. 117.

Chapter 7

[1]Portions of this chapter are based on the author's article, "They've Asked You to Give a Speech," *The Deltasig* (January 1978), pp. 9-12; the illustration at the beginning of this chapter is also from the same issue. Both are Copyright © 1978 by the International Fraternity of Delta Sigma Pi, reprinted with the permission of the executive director, Delta Sigma Pi.

[2]Stephen Wallace, "A Cure for Toastmaster's Trembles," *MBA Magazine*, Vol. 13, #6:43 (June 1977).

[3]Rudolph F. Verderber, *Communicate!* (Belmont, Calif.: Wadsworth, 1975), p. 158.

[4]This section is based on an article by John Costello, "Jests Can Do Justice to Your Speeches," *Nation's Business*, Vol. 64: 37-44 (January 1978). Copyright © 1978. Reprinted with permission.

[5]Wallace, p. 45.

[6]This section is also from Costello, p. 44.

Chapter 8

[1]Caroline Meyer, "How to Think Through a Job Offer," *Money* (July 1973), pp. 60-63.

[2]Richard K. Irish, *Go Hire Yourself an Employer* (New York: Anchor, 1976).

[3]Portions of this section are from the author's article, "The Professional Resume," *The Deltasig* (June 1969). Copyright © 1969 by the International Fraternity of Delta Sigma Pi. Reprinted with the permission of the executive director, Delta Sigma Pi.

[4]Irish, cited above.

Chapter 9

[1]This section is adapted from the author's article, "Space: The Frontier of Interpersonal Communication," *The Executive*, Vol. 13, #1: 24-29 (Spring 1974). Copyright © 1973 by the Credit Union National Association, Inc., Madison, Wisconsin 53511. Reprinted with permission.

[2]This section is adapted from the author's article, "What Does Your Office Say About You?," *Supervisory Management,* Vol. 19: 28-37 (August 1974). Copyright © 1974 by AMACOM, a division of the American Management Associations. All rights reserved.

[3]C. Boutin, "What, No Desk?," *This Week* (January 26, 1969), p. 17.

[4]Michael Korda, *Power* (New York: Ballantine Books, 1975), p. 117.

Chapter 10

[1]Edward Hall, *The Silent Language* (New York: Doubleday, 1959), pp. 21-24.

[2]This selection is from Michael L. Johnson, "The Productive Manager," Part 2, *Industry Week* (April 12, 1976), p. 35. Copyright © 1976, Penton/IPC, Inc. Used with permission.

[3]This section is based on the author's article, "How to Make the Best Use of Your Time," *Association Management,* Vol. 28, #1: 26-29 (January 1976). Copyright © 1976 by the American Society of Association Executives. Used with permission.

[4]Tips 3 through 7 are based on suggestions in Marvin Rudin's book *Practical Time Management,* excerpted in *M. B. A. Magazine,* Vol. 13, #6: 9-10 (June 1977).

[5]"Principle No. 1," *The National Observer* (May 16, 1977), p. 11.

Chapter 11

[1]Portions of this quiz are based on material developed by Brian L. Hawkins. Used with permission.

[2]Jack McClintock, "She Talked Her Way onto TV," *TV Guide* (May 28, 1977), p. 16.

[3]Diane K. Shah, "Pro Football's Pete Rozell," *The National Observer* (May 16, 1977), p. 18.

[4]M. E. Day, "Eye Movement Phenomenon Relating to Attention, Thought, and Anxiety," *Perceptual and Motor Skills,* Vol. 19, #2: 444-46 (1964).

[5]Julius Fast, "How Well Do You Read Body Language?" *Sales Management* (December 15, 1970), pp. 27-29.

[6]R. Rosenthal and L. Jacobson, "Pygmalion in the Classroom," in *Communication Involvement: Personal Perspectives* (New York: Wiley, 1974), p. 383.

[7]Leonard Brickman, "Clothes Make the Person," *Psychology Today* (April, 1974), pp. 49-50.

[8]This section is from an article by Dale W. Sommer, "How Clothes Shape Your Future," *Industry Week* (October 10, 1977), pp. 23-30. Copyright © 1977 Penton/IPC, Inc. Used with permission.

Chapter 12

[1]This section is based on the author's article, "Use the Spoken Word to Put Across Your Message" *Association Management,* Vol. 30: 71-76 (Aug. 1978). Copyright © 1978 by the American Society of Association Executives. Used with permission.

[2]This section is based on an article by Michael A. Verespej, "Boss, I Have a Great Idea," *Industry Week* (February 2, 1976), pp. 22-25. Copyright © 1976 by Penton/IPC, Inc. Used with permission.

[3]This section is from an article by Don North, "Pushing for Power," *St. Petersburg Times* (August 14, 1977), pp. 17-18. Copyright © 1977 by the Times Publishing Company. Used with the permission of the editor and author.

Chapter 13

[1]This section is based on an article by John Hogan, "How to Say 'NO'," *Industry Week* (September 27, 1971), pp. 25-28. Copyright © 1971 by Penton/IPC, Inc. Reprinted with permission.

[2]This section is based on an article by John Hogan, "How to Fire an Executive," *Industry Week* (May 31, 1971), pp. 26-30. Copyright © 1971, Penton/IPC, Inc. Reprinted with permission.

Chapter 14

[1]"The Obstinate Employee," *Psychology Today,* Vol. 3: 52-60 (November 1969).

[2]Frederick Herzberg, *Work and the Nature of Man* (Cleveland: World, 1966).

[3]This summary of Mr. William Oncken's story is reprinted from William W. Parson, "Barriers to Communication," *Communication in Public Administration,* ed. Robert Highsaw and Don Bowen (University, Ala.: Bureau of Public Administration, 1965). Reprinted with the permission of the Bureau of Public Administration, University of Alabama.

[4]David C. McClelland, *The Achieving Society* (Princeton: Van Nostrand, 1961).

[5]Robert Presthus, *The Organizational Society* (New York: Knopf, 1962), pp. 164-286.

[6]Lawrence J. Peter, *The Peter Principle* (New York: Holt, Rinehart & Winston, 1968).

[7]Portions of this chapter, including the test at the end of the chapter, are reprinted from an article by Thomas M. Rohan, "Should a Worker's Personality Affect Your Managing?," *Industry Week* (May 5, 1975), pp. 28-38. Copyright © 1975, Penton/IPC, Inc. Reprinted with permission. Table 14-1 and the employee categories are based on research by V. Flowers and C. Hughes.

[8]Portions of this section are from an article by Donald B. Thompson, "Profit from the Wisdom in Your Shop," *Industry Week* (February 14, 1977), p. 57. Copyright © 1977, Penton/IPC, Inc. Reprinted with permission.

[9]Carlos A. Gonzales, "Eastern Airlines' Successful Marketing Effort in South Florida," Second Latin Market Seminar (Miami, Fla.: Florida International Univ., October, 1972).

Chapter 15

[1]This section is from an article by David Cook, "Discipline: Laying Down the Law —Productively," *Industry Week* (May 17, 1976), pp. 28-31. Copyright © 1976, Penton/IPC, Inc. Reprinted with permission.

[2]This section is from a publication of the Louisiana Power & Light Company, "How to Reprimand Constructively" (Baton Rouge: 1961). It is used here with the permission of the Louisiana Power & Light Company.

[3]This section is from Cook above, p. 30.

[4]This section is based on material developed by the Alcoa Aluminum Company (Pittsburgh: 1959). Used with permission.

[5]Excerpted by permission from Western Electric Company, "Complaints and Grievances: Supervisory Conference Material," issued by the training department of Western Electric's Hawthorn Works (Chicago: 1960).

[6]This "advice" is from *Industry Week,* cited above.

Chapter 16

[1]This section is based on an article by the author and Brian L. Hawkins, "Performance Appraisal: Evaluation and Communication," *Industrial Management,* Vol. 20, #1: 13–17 (January–February 1978). Copyright © 1978 by the Industrial Management Society. Used with permission.

[2]Douglas McGregor, "An Uneasy Look at Performance Appraisal," *Harvard Business Review,* Vol. 35: 90 (May–June 1957).

[3]Lawrence L. Steinmetz, *Managing the Marginal and Unsatisfactory Performer* (Boston: Addison-Wesley, 1969), p. 130.

[4]Lyman W. Porter, Edward E. Lawler, III, and Richard Hackman, *Behavior in Organizations* (New York: McGraw-Hill, 1975).

[5]Jack R. Bigg, "Defensive Communication," *The Journal of Communication,* Vol. 11, #3: 182–86 (September, 1961).

[6]H. H. Meyer, E. Kay, and J. R. P. French, Jr., "Split Roles in Performance Appraisal," *Harvard Business Review,* Vol. 43: 123–29 (January–February 1969).

[7]Meyer, Kay, and French, Jr., pp. 127–28.

[8]This section is from the author's article, "Selling Performance Appraisal to Line Managers," *Business & Economic Perspectives,* Vol. 2, #1: 27–32 (Fall 1976). Copyright © 1976, University of Tennessee, Martin. Used with permission.

Chapter 17

[1]Portions of this chapter are based on the author's article, "How to Adapt to Change and Put It to Work in Your Association," *Association Management,* Vol. 29, #12: 102–5 (December, 1977). Copyright © 1977 by the American Society of Association Executives. Used with permission.

Chapter 18

[1]Cases 2 and 5 were prepared for a supervisory training program developed by William D. Litzinger, William G. Mitchell, Gary C. Raffaele, and the author. All are principles in University Associates, a management consulting firm in San Antonio, Texas.

[2]Case 6 is adapted from an incident report in "Managers I Wish I Hadn't Met," *Industry Week* (February 16, 1976), p. 37. Copyright © 1976, Penton/IPC, Inc. Used with permission.

Chapter 19

[1]Portions of this chapter are based on the author's article, "The Bottom Line," *Credit Union Management,* Vol. 1, #1: 27–29, 42 (January–February 1978). Copyright © 1978 by the Credit Union Executives Society. Used with permission.

[2]Many of the suggestions for reducing distortion were originally developed by Brian L. Hawkins. Used with permission.

[3]H. J. DiMarco and C. R. Kuehl, "Winning Moves in Motivating Junior Staff." *S. A. M. Advanced Management Journal,* Vol. 17:42 (Summer 1975).

Index